PORNOGRAPHY

A Human Tragedy

TOM MINNERY, Editor

Christianity Today, Inc.
Tyndale House Publishers, Inc.
WHEATON, ILLINOIS

ACKNOWLEDGMENTS

Several people were especially important in the publication of this book. Harold Myra and Tim Stafford provided unerring editorial guidance at every step. Paul Robbins was able to convince several key individuals that contributions from them would be essential to the book. My advisor and best friend—my wife Deb—realized the project was important enough to require my long evenings away from our family. For her patience and understanding I am especially thankful. *Tom Minnery*

First printing, October 1986

Library of Congress Catalog Card Number 86-51139
ISBN 0-8423-4947-2
Copyright 1986 by Christianity Today, Inc.

CONTENTS

Why This Book?

I spent a year watching eleven people slog through a sewer. They were the members of the Attorney General's Commission on Pornography. Their assignment, not the most elegant in public life, was to determine whether current varieties of pornography had finally sunk beneath the depths of public tolerance, inviting more government regulation.

It seemed that every police expert and every social scientist who testified before the commission brought along his execrable video or slide show to illustrate new trends in degradation. Victims told tragic tales of broken marriages and scarred psyches, the result of mates forcing them to act out what the movies and magazines were portraying as fun.

It wasn't until close to the end of the whole dismal process, while sitting in a basement meeting room of the City Hall in Scottsdale, Arizona, that I grew deeply disappointed with the media's handling of the issue.

Before I joined the staff of *Christianity Today* magazine,

I was a Capitol Hill correspondent in Washington, D.C., for the country's largest newspaper chain. I entered Christian journalism in 1980, when moral issues began taking center stage in political debate. It was disappointing to see my former colleagues retreat time and again to cliche and caricature as they reported on these issues. Pornography is one on which the press has waffled badly. It simply can't decide whether to approach the issue seriously or not.

In March 1985, for example, *Newsweek* ran a hard-hitting cover story on pornography that concluded with this comment: "Airing the fear and pain of the victims of pornography is a useful exercise—and may help change the hearts, minds, and habits of a nation that sometimes seems to have lost its shame."

That's the very essence of what the Attorney General's Commission on Pornography said in its own hard-hitting report in 1986. But when that report was released, the press as a whole caricatured the issue as a fight between conservative religious zealots on one side, and the defenders of free speech, led by the American Civil Liberties Union, on the other side. This trend was epitomized by the *Time* magazine cover of July 21, 1986. It bore the headline "Sex Busters," and it showed three curmudgeons brandishing scissors, a rubber stamp that read "censored," and a Bible.

Here are three examples of press bias on this issue:

The first lesson every undergraduate journalism student learns is the definition of censorship. It is the prior restraint of publication—that is, the suppression of material *before* it is published. By that definition—its plain definition—no obscenity law in the country constitutes censorship. Anyone can publish any obscenity, no matter what it contains. Only *after* publication is the material subject to the scrutiny of law, whether libel law, or privacy law, or obscenity law.

This is an elementary distinction. Yet how often has the press allowed that sinister word "censorship" to be leveled at the antipornography movement without setting the record straight? Indeed, how often has the press leveled the charge itself in an editorial, a column, or on a *Time* cover?

Second, how often has the press allowed the pornography establishment—led by the American Civil Liberties Union—to assert that the publication of obscenity is a free speech issue? Constantly. This is done in spite of the fact that the U.S. Supreme Court not only has *never* said that obscenity is protected by the Constitution, it has said several times now that obscenity is expressly *not* protected by the Constitution. Yet the misinformation continues.

Third, the press has yet to note, let alone critically examine, the extremist view of the ACLU that all pornography—soft-core, hard-core, even the most brutal of child pornography—deserves First Amendment protection. This position is patently absurd, without any foundation in American law, but it goes unchallenged. (The press has also yet to report the close working relationship between the ACLU and *Playboy*. Burton Joseph, chairman of the Playboy Foundation, is on the Illinois ACLU board. Christie Hefner, the president of Playboy Enterprises, is also on that board and belongs as well to the national ACLU President's Committee. Joseph acknowledges that *Playboy* has contributed about $150,000 to the ACLU. No one is hiding this relationship, but it is never mentioned when ACLU is quoted in defense of *Playboy*.)

As a former newspaper reporter, it has been disappointing to see this bias. But the worst of it, somehow, is not the fact itself. It is the small, telltale signs that make the fact

unmistakably true. It is the reporter from the large West
Coast paper who arrives very late at a meeting of the pornography commission and, before filing his story, gets his
update from the ACLU representative in attendance, hardly
an unbiased source. It is the correspondent from the national
news magazine chortling with the pornography press in the
back of the room as one of the conservatives on the commission labors to make a point. It is the rolling eyes, the
snickers. I had seen enough of it by the Scottsdale meeting,
the second-to-last gathering of the commission, to realize
that even the pretense of fair play was gone. To me, as a
journalist, this was humiliating. That humiliation derives
from my deep love for news journalism, and my appreciation for the role it plays in maintaining this democracy.
When the press fails to report a significant issue fairly, it
diminishes itself as an institution, and loses the confidence
of those who do understand the issue.

This book is an attempt to look beneath the cliches, to recast into more realistic shapes the caricatures in the minds
of many people as they try to think through the issues surrounding pornography.

To those who hear that First Amendment rights are the
primary issue, let's clarify:

Antiporn activists are fully justified in demonstrating
peaceably against the sale of *Playboy*, in order to convince
stores to drop it voluntarily, if they believe its philosophy
degrades society. This is not a question of calling *Playboy*
legally obscene. Antiporn marchers have just as much constitutional right to march as Hugh Hefner has to publish.

At the same time, there is much legally obscene material at every hand. This is where most of the battle rages, even though the media attention has been on the convenience store issue, because this is where the antiporn movement has made its biggest gains. In regard to hard-core pornography, the leaders of the antiporn movement ask for enforcement of *existing* laws based on well-established Supreme Court principles. The obscenity laws are sufficient to eradicate the evils that all of us as citizens perceive, regardless of our religious beliefs. These evils are the rancid exploitation of child pornography, the victimization of adult actors in hard-core films, and the outrageous idea that women secretly desire to be raped or tortured. That these phenomena exist in a principled society should be intolerable to all. These wrongs can be righted by the prudent use of properly drawn laws, without threat to American freedoms. This is the argument presented here.

As for the rest of it, the milder forms of pornography which injure a Judeo-Christian understanding of life, the enlightened leaders of the antiporn movement recognize that law does not apply here. They know that religious morality cannot and must not be forced on the populace at large, and some forms of pornography will always be legally permissible. These leaders know that against this kind of pornography their task is limited to persuasion. They can demonstrate peaceably and debate publicly, trying to convince the consumers that they should not buy the material.

Distinctions such as these are subtle, but real. They are nearly always lost in the heat of battle. They are certainly missed by the media. The writers in these chapters draw important distinctions between the kinds of protests that can be aimed at soft-core pornography, and the kinds of campaigns that can and should be waged against hard-core (illegal) pornography.

This book assumes that the reader will have some basic orientation to Judeo-Christian moral principles, although there has been so much lopsided reporting that many Christians simply do not know what they should believe about the issue. For this reason, very little is taken for granted. Basic principles are explained thoroughly, but dispassionately. At the same time, we have purposefully included some very strong material. The statements of the victims are hardly dispassionate. James Dobson's experiences as a member of the pornography commission have rendered him exceedingly passionate, and his chapter reflects his particular perspective.

The material is organized as a handbook, with four distinct sections. The reader need not feel he must begin at page 1 and read straight through to learn something of value.

- The first section, "The Cause for Concern," addresses the problem from a moral orientation. The presence of the well-known writers in this section signifies that this matter is no longer a fringe issue. It is now squarely before the mainstream church.
- The second section deals with the most important social science research bearing on the issue of pornography and harm. The work of the major researchers has been explained carefully and clearly so that lay people may come to their own conclusions about one of the most critical questions in the debate: "Does pornography cause harm?"

- The third section, "How the Battle Is Being Won," illustrates quite simply that there are effective anti-obscenity laws on the books, and they can be made workable by the application of proper strategy and tactics. In this section, those principles come to life in three case studies. This is not so much a "how to do it" section as it is a "how they did it" commentary.
- The last section deals with two major reports issued from Washington in the summer of 1986: the report of the Attorney General's Pornography Commission, and the report of the surgeon general. Only the highlights of these reports appear here, and these are in digest form. The actual attorney general's report includes nearly a hundred specific recommendations, and since most of these are technical, aimed mainly at the law enforcement and judicial communities, they are not included here.

The strongest evidence against pornography is missing from this book. This evidence is the actual words and the pictures contained in hard-core pornography, circa 1986. The pages that follow contain only small samples and descriptions. The full scenes, the visual depictions, in their context, do not appear. Were they to be included here, this book would be, frankly, too repugnant for its audience. But anyone who wants to learn about this issue and has not seen X-rated material does not really know the issue.

The shock of hard-core pornography can be catastrophic for the uninitiated. And there are those who want to fight pornography who should remain uninitiated. Richard McLawhorn has more to say on this in chapter 13. But the truth is that many people now leading the antiporn campaign were able to ignore the issue altogether until they saw the material itself. Once that happened, they could no longer be true to themselves without acting.

In its 1985 cover story, *Newsweek* noted that the pornography industry has turned unbridled sex abuse into entertainment. And it is the pornography trade that is now beginning to pay the consequences, in better law enforcement and clearer understanding of the harm caused by pornography.

Tom Minnery
Bloomingdale, Illinois
September 1986

The good influence of godly citizens
causes a city to prosper,
but the moral decay of the wicked
drives it downhill.
PROVERBS 11:11, TLB

INTRODUCTION

Charles Colson

The traffic at the intersection of church and state is getting heavier.

Seventy years ago, religious leaders and public authorities dueled over education, temperance, and the social gospel. The middle decades introduced new controversies—pacifism, civil rights, conservative politics, and constitutional confrontations. Now virtually all public issues—from nuclear deterrence to agricultural policy—resound in the church sanctuary. And most church issues—from the authority of Catholic bishops to the definition of "evangelical"—echo in the halls of secular power.

The years have brought increasing polarization. Some on the religious side talk about "Christian America," suggesting that they want to create a theocracy in the United States. Some secular theorists and opinion-molders would like to shut up the church people permanently; all public expression of religious values, they say, gravely threatens the common good.

But the intensifying debate also highlights the most important issues. As we approach the end of a century of turmoil, we finally see the basic issues in the conflict between church and secular culture. Two stand out. They are the ground we battle over, the crucial questions we will ask for the rest of the century and beyond.

1. Will the sanctity and dignity of human life be preserved in our society or will it continue to be eroded?
2. Will our society recognize and protect fundamental religious liberties?

The Dignity of People

There is no more telling measure of a society's values than its view of the sanctity and dignity of the individual. In *Cancer Ward,* Alexander Solzhenitsyn exposes the totalitarian society's view. When a patient in a Soviet hospital is diagnosed as terminally ill, he is quickly discharged, left to fend for himself, and abandoned to die alone. And why not? If there is no Creator-God, an individual is simply the result of a chance collision of atoms, and is easily disposable—particularly when he is useless and hospital beds are scarce.

The Christian view is in stark contrast, as Mother Teresa illustrates. Every day her Sisters of Charity walk the squalid streets of Calcutta, rescuing from alleys and gutters those who are dying. Beggars with only days to live are brought to her shelter, cleaned up and loved. They die with dignity denied them all their lives—because Mother Teresa believes a loving God created every person in his image, with the innate need to be treated with respect, even to die with dignity.

What is the attitude toward human life and dignity in America today? Collectively, are we more like Mother Teresa or the Soviet Union?

We who are Christians cannot help but point to the holocaust begun in 1973 for our answer. Since abortion became a constitutional right, the disposal of 16 million unborn babies has been legal. The right to choose death for those who are helpless has become part of the American way of life. It seems logical to project similar trends for future years. Surgeon General C. Everett Koop calls abortion, infanticide, and euthanasia ''the three dominoes.'' They have already begun to fall.

Other dominoes fall as well. The spread of pornography is evidence that society has lost its sacred respect for human life. For the Christian, who has a high view of individual dignity, pornography is not only disgusting, it is debasing, a many-fingered beast that rakes dignity from both those it exploits and those it titillates. It corrupts the very root of life—the sexual union ordained and blessed by God.

''Like all the sins,'' writes British author Henry Fairlie, ''lust is . . . solitary. It is self-abdication at the very core of one's own being, a surrender of our need and ability to give and receive. Lust does not come with open hands, certainly not with an open heart. It comes only with open legs.''

It has long been said that pornography makes women into objects, pieces of meat on public display; it increasingly makes children into pieces of meat as well. But the people who make and appear in pornography are human beings, the Creator's greatest creations, beloved of God. Of mankind, the psalmist wrote with praise and wonder: ''Thou has made him little less than God, and dost crown him with glory and honor.'' Pornography reduces these glorious creatures to trash. As it does so, it jeers at the God who has conferred human dignity.

Believing this, we should not allow ourselves to be portrayed as censors when we seek to halt this corruption. Christians, of all people, value the protections of the First Amendment—free expression, free press, and freedom of religion.

But, though it may be unpopular to say this nowadays, the First Amendment is not a blank check. As Justice Homes wrote, the right to free speech does not extend to shouting "fire" in a crowded theater. Nor, I submit, does it extend to unrestricted license to pump raw sewage into the minds of a culture.

No one accuses us of censorship, of impinging on people's rights to self-expression, when we support efforts to clean our streets of crime. Yet obscenity is as much a psychological menace to society as crime is a physical threat.

This, then, is the first great issue pornography confronts us with: Are we as a nation still committed, as we were in our beginnings, to the preservation of individual liberty and human dignity?

The Christian opposes pornography not just because it offends public sensibilities, but because it is such a blatant violation of a person's God-given dignity. That is a religious issue, which raises the second great issue confronting our church and culture: Do religious values have any place in public discourse today?

Religion in the Marketplace

Certainly we have cause to worry about our religious liberties. Our society is coalescing around the proposition that religion means trouble and people who speak publicly from religious convictions should be silenced.

Examples abound. The ACLU argues in court that the Hyde Amendment barring federal funds for abortion should be overturned because its sponsor, Representative Henry Hyde, is a devout Catholic. The Los Angeles school board orders that prayers—even general ones—cannot be uttered from the podium at any high school commencement. The Roman Catholic cardinal in New York is condemned for discussing his church's teaching on abortion during a presidential campaign. (Here, as is often the case, human life and religious freedom are linked.)

Recent political campaigns have sharpened the focus. The plethora of Christian political organizations have done much to organize political campaigns for the restoration of traditional religious values in American life. Much of this has been healthy. Some, however, suggest an effort to Christianize America by imposing Christian values on government. Such excesses tend to link the cross and the flag, merging Christian values and a conservative Republican agenda.

Understandably, such over-zealousness has sparked countermovements—People for the American Way, the ACLU, and the like—that see Christians as bigots who want to cram their values down everyone else's throat and in the process destroy religious pluralism. Some argue that the arena of public debate should be free of all religious values and influences.

While these critics are enraged by the Religious Right, they are much less threatened by Christians sharing the view of the presidential candidate who assured the public that his faith was "intensely personal," and thus presumably had nothing to do with public policy.

New York Governor Mario Cuomo has espoused this view as well, eloquently arguing that an official who professes to be a sincere Christian can advocate positions contrary to his church's teaching. As a practicing Catholic, he subscribed to his church's teachings on abortion—but as an office-holder in a secular society, he argued, he could not impose his views on anyone else. So far, so good.

But Governor Cuomo went on to say that he was under no obligation to advocate his views or to work for a public consensus based on those views, until such a course is justified by what he calls a "prudential judgment." So God's truth is binding only when ratified by a majority vote? That may be good politics, but it is disastrous theology. It reduces Christianity to a religion of personal tastes that has no place in the political arena.

Neither Cuomo's privatized religion nor the theocracy espoused by some on the right is very likely to impose a long-lasting impact in government, however. In both cases there is no spiritual substance to impose. Both positions deny what was the first baptismal confession of the earliest Christians: "Jesus is Lord."

I believe the great danger today is that, with the church polarized and weakened, those who seek to expunge all religious influence from society will have an open field. Separation of church and state is one thing: the amputation of religion from the body politic is altogether different.

After all, our nation was explicitly founded on the assumption that Christian values would provide the moral foundation upon which society would function. Religion was not to be a prop of the state, but, as John Adams wrote in 1798, "We have no government armed in power capable of contending in human passions unbridled by morality in religion. Our Constitution was made only for a moral and religious people, it is wholly inadequate for the government of any other.''

For nearly two centuries, this remained general public wisdom; accordingly, for two centuries Christians have actively pursued biblical justice and righteousness in society. Consider the abolitionist movement and the establishment of public education, public hospitals, prison reform, and in the twentieth century, prohibition, women's suffrage, child labor laws, and civil rights.

Religiously founded values have long functioned as the cutting edge in shaping our national character. Until recent years, no one has shrieked that the Christian religion was becoming the official state religion or that such morality was being imposed upon an unwilling people.

But today the battle lines are clearly drawn. In one camp is the view of secular America that religious influence is to be studiously scrubbed from public life. This view erroneously supposes that separation of church and state means there should be no religious influence in the formation of public values. In the other camp is a church raggedly divided between those who escape into the hollow comfort of privatized faith and those who do battle for the sake of an unholy hybrid of politicized religion.

Will We Act on What We Believe?

The social ill of widespread pornography offers us an opportunity to make a Christian consensus known. If Christians are faithful to our biblical calling, if we believe passionately in the dignity of human life, then we must be involved in making these values felt in American culture today. So what do we do?

Most of us immediately think of that ten-letter magic word: government. And indeed, there are political issues that must be dealt with in the pornography debate. As the commission appointed by Attorney General Meese in 1985 demonstrated, government has a legitimate interest. Laws are necessary to restrain evil; these laws must be enforced. Local governing bodies and aggressive prosecutors *can* make business difficult, even impossible, for pornographers.

But we must not delude ourselves that laws alone have the legal bite to stop smut. As Barry Lynn of the American Civil Liberties Union has boasted, "there are enough constitutional questions here to litigate for the next twenty years."

So while we fight it out in court, let us also concentrate as well on the power of ordinary citizens doing their jobs in a free society. The story of what happened when one man was converted to Christ illustrates how effective this can be.

Jack Eckerd, founder of the Eckerd drugstore chain, became a Christian in 1983. Shortly afterward, he walked through one of his drugstores and saw with new eyes the pornographic magazines for sale there.

Jack called his company president. "Take the magazines out," he ordered. The executive was stunned. The magazines in question, *Playboy* and *Penthouse*, brought in several million dollars of profit a year. Eckerd insisted—and prevailed. The magazines were cleared from the bookshelves of the 1,700 Eckerd drugstores.

I called Jack and asked if he had pitched the pornography

because of his conversion to Christ. "Of course," he replied. "Why else would I throw a few million dollars out the window? But," he continued, "as I thought about it, the Lord wouldn't let me off the hook." He was simply yielding to the lordship of Christ.

That was only the beginning. Jack quietly resolved to do something about the shocking fact that drug chains and convenience stores were the largest single outlet for pornography in the nation. Glossy-paged corruption was available as easily as milk, eggs, and a loaf of bread. Jack first wrote to the executives of the major drug chains, describing what he had done, testifying that it hadn't killed him, and nudging them in the same direction. No one answered his letters: after all, pornography is a profitable business.

But Jack continued lobbying his friends, including the president of 7-Eleven, who happened to serve on his board of directors. At the same time public campaigns began to build. National antipornography organizations continued their pressure, boycotting and picketing chain stores. The stores felt the pressure where it hurt most—in the pocketbook.

Soon a small convenience store chain in Florida announced it was discontinuing porn magazines. Then came High's chain in Washington, D.C., followed by Peoples, then Revco, the largest drug chain in America. Finally, 7-Eleven, the largest convenience chain, capitulated as well. The reasons, I suspect, were more economic than moral. These giant retailers became convinced that pornography was not good business. While it might make money, it was incurring public hostility.

And so the lesson here is clear. *Playboy* and *Penthouse*

were cleared off the shelves of some 10,000 neighborhood stores by the voluntary actions of committed people, not by the laws of a government.

The Power of Living Faith

The lesson is encouraging. While we should continue to press government in the fight against pornography, results aren't always dependent on the passage of laws. The most crucial action may come from how you and I live, from the individual decisions of faithful Christians who act in obedience to their Lord.

Most of us don't have the lobbying influence of a Jack Eckerd. But his pressure was coupled with the actions of thousands of Christians—people who were willing to make a statement by boycotting stores selling trash for human consumption. And that's how we can make a difference.

Edmund Burke understood this well. He wrote that it was not big government, but actually the "little platoons," groups of people working in their particular areas for positive social reform, that changed culture. Long before Edmund Burke, God wrote about the little platoons as well. But he called them salt, yeast, and light—his instruments for righteousness and holiness in a given nation.

As you read this book, I hope you will become not only convicted of the horrors of pornography, but that you will see it as an issue reflecting the heart of our culture's values. Mirrored in the pornography epidemic are disturbing indicators measuring how much we as a society believe in a relativistic, hedonistic, utilitarian view of life, and how much we believe that man is created in the image of God and is thus entitled to God-given dignity.

I hope, too, that you will accept your biblical responsibilities and take your post in the great battle for the soul of our culture. For as you read, you may get mad—but don't just sit back and say it's time Washington or Richmond or Austin or Albany did something about it. Remember that Jesus commanded you to be salt. In biblical times, salt was used not only as a flavoring, but as a preservative. Meat exposed to the elements would spoil—unless salt was rubbed into its fibers.

So when we look around us and see a culture corrupted by pornography, whom do we blame? A sinful, fallen people? No, the unredeemed culture, like the meat to which Christ alluded, will inevitably rot. Stopping that process isn't just a question of political action, but of individual faithfulness. Moral decay, after all, and the pornography that springs from it, are the results of too little salt—and salt is exactly what you and I are called to be.

PART ONE

The Cause for Concern

Religious people confronting pornography must be clear about what their faith requires them to do, and what their citizenship permits them to do. Sometimes violations of moral law can be redressed by civil law, but not always. It is important to know the difference.

The present moral outrage stems from the Judeo-Christian view of sex that is violated by pornography. What is the biblical standard, and what is contained in pornography? This section deals with these issues. The writers are

James Dobson, founder and president of Focus on the Family.

Jerry Kirk, president of the National Coalition Against Pornography and co-pastor of the College Hill Presbyterian Church in Cincinnati, Ohio.

Stephen V. Monsma, former professor of political science, Calvin College, and currently deputy director, Michigan Department of Social Services.

David Leigh, free-lance writer (with assistance provided by Paul McGeady, director of the National Obscenity Law Center, and by staff attorneys of Citizens for Decency through Law).

C. Everett Koop, surgeon general of the United States.

CHAPTER ONE
Enough Is Enough

James C. Dobson

The chapter you are about to read may shock you. That has not been my purpose in writing, but I do hope it makes you angry. Irritation interferes with sleep, and we desperately need to experience a moral awakening in this country. While we were slumbering these past three decades, an $8 billion pornography industry was assembled by members of organized crime, operating virtually tax free and with governmental acquiescence. This empire now pervades our lives and contributes to the destruction of countless families each year. Something must be done to deal with the plague that infects our beloved land.

It was this moral concern that led President Reagan to authorize a second commission to study the affects of pornography on individuals, on families, and on society at large. I happened to be at the White House that day as he made this proposal, not knowing that I would be asked to participate in the effort. One year later, Attorney General Edwin Meese responded to the president's mandate by appointing an eleven-member commission. My name was on the list. Shortly after my appointment, a congressman offered this personal advice from his heart: "If I were you, I would call members of my local church and ask for prayer every day for the next twelve months."

"Why?" I asked.

"Because," he said, "you're about to experience one of the most difficult years of your life. You'll be exposed to material that is terrible beyond description. But also, you will soon draw the fire of the pornography industry. They will try in every way possible to embarrass you, intimidate you, and discredit your name. You're going to need all the support you can get from your Christian friends!"

The congressman was right on all counts. During my term of service, I have been ridiculed consistently in men's magazines and in newspaper editorials. Unauthorized recordings of my voice have been included in an X-rated movie. My fellow commissioners and I have been sued for $30 million in damages by *Playboy, Penthouse,* et al., and we are personally liable if we should lose in court. During the commission hearings, photographers were sent to take my picture for six or eight hours at a time. They apparently hoped to catch me asleep or in an embarrassing pose, or to intimidate me during subsequent deliberations. Nevertheless, I coped with these tactics rather well. The greater struggle came in response to the materials we were asked to evaluate.

Having been a faculty member at a large medical school and having served on the attending staff at a major children's hospital for seventeen years, I thought I had seen and heard about everything. I have stood in an operating room while a team of surgeons massaged a woman's heart for hours after her husband blasted her at point-blank range with a shotgun. She never regained consciousness. I've

seen children with pitiful deformities that tore at my heart.
I've witnessed cancer in its final stages and all of the tragedies that arrive in hospital emergency facilities on busy
weekends. Even under such circumstances, I have learned
to control my emotions and have continued to function.
Nevertheless, nothing in my training or experience fully
prepared me for the confrontation with pornography that
was to come. Purchasers of this material, like vultures, prefer their meat rancid and raw.

From Bad to Worse

I knew that the world of X-rated movies and obscene magazines had steadily deteriorated since 1970, but I was
unaware of the depth of that plunge. Most American citizens are even more uninformed. They think pornography
consists largely of airbrushed nudity in *Playboy* magazines.
Such images are pornographic, of course, but they are not
even in the same league with mainstream hard-core material sold in sex shops today. The world of hard-core
obscenity has become unbelievably sordid and perverse. Its
dimensions are wretched beyond description.

Let me explain how we got into the mess we face today.
One of the characteristics of human nature is the natural
progression that occurs in sexual experimentation. For
example, a boy and a girl may find it exciting to hold hands
on the first date, but more physical contact is likely to occur
on the second encounter. Unless they make an early effort
to slow that progression, they will move systematically
down the road toward sexual intercourse. That is just the
way we are made. Now obviously, pornographers understand that principle. They know that their products must
constantly change in order to avoid boredom, and that

change must always be in the direction of more explicit materials. Thus, the public has been taken from peek-a-boo glimpses of nudity in the mid-fifties to the infinitely more graphic publications offered today.

That progression from soft-core to hard-core pornography got an enormous boost in 1970 when the First Presidential Commission on Pornography issued its report. They said, in effect, that sexually explicit materials were a good thing and should not be inhibited in any way. Not only did they tell us that smut was not harmful; they perceived it to be advantageous to society, reducing sexual tensions and promising to lower the incidences of rape and child abuse. The pornography industry was delighted! Barriers that had stood for 200 years began to tumble as photographs were published of consummate sexual acts between men and women. *Heaven help us,* we thought. *They have shown it all!*

Well, not quite. It seems that this mad dash toward explicitness presented the pornographers with a minor challenge. What could they do for an encore? What could they offer to customers who had become bored with photographs of normal, heterosexual activity? Something new and exciting was needed, and indeed, they found it in the presentation of perversions. Thus, the course was set for a journey into the incredibly debased hard-core pornography available in massive quantities today.

The Shock of Hard-core Pornography
How can I describe that world to my readers without being obscene myself? I don't know. I struggle at this moment as I weigh the terribleness of this subject against the need for Christians to understand their enemy. In order to fight this plague with the passion of a crusader, it is necessary to

comprehend the virus that is rotting us from within. Forgive me, then, for the explicitness with which I am about to write. I urge you to skip the next two paragraphs if you really don't want to know. But someone must have the courage to describe the pornographic scene in sufficient detail to stir us into action, and someone else must have the courage to read it.

X-rated movies and magazines today feature oral, anal, and genital sex between women and donkeys, pigs, horses, dogs, and dozens of other animals. In a single sex shop in New York City, there were forty-six films and videos available which featured bestiality of every type. Other offerings focused on so-called "bathroom sports" including urination (golden showers), defecation, eating feces and spreading them on the face and body, mutilation of every type (including voluntary amputation, fishhooks through genitalia, fists in rectums, mousetraps on breasts), oral and anal sex between groups of men and women, and (forgive me) the drinking of ejaculate in champagne glasses. Simulated child pornography depicts females who are actually eighteen years of age or older but appear to be fourteen or fifteen. They are shown with shaved genitalia, with ribbons in their hair and surrounded by teddy bears. Their "fathers" are often pictured with them in consummate incestuous settings. The magazines in sex shops are organized on shelves according to topic, such as Gay Violence, Vomiting, Rape, Enemas, and topics that I cannot describe even in a frank discussion of this nature.

The ACLU and Child Porn

By far the most distressing experience for me personally during the twelve-month assignment was the child pornography to which we were exposed. Though categorically illegal since 1983, a thriving cottage industry still exists in this country. Fathers, stepfathers, uncles, teachers, and neighbors find ways to secure photographs of children in their care. Then they sell or trade the pictures to fellow pedophiles. I will never forget a particular set of photographs shown to us at our first hearings in Washington, D.C. It focused on a cute, nine-year-old boy who had fallen into the hands of a molester. In the first picture, the blond-haired lad was fully clothed and smiling at the camera. But in the second, he was nude, dead, and had a butcher knife protruding from his chest. My knees buckled and tears came to my eyes as hundreds of other photographs of children were presented showing pitiful boys and girls with their rectums enlarged to accommodate adult males and their vaginas penetrated with pencils, toothbrushes, and guns. Perhaps the reader can understand my anger and disbelief when a representative for the American Civil Liberties Union testified a few minutes later. He advocated the free exchange of pornography, all pornography, in the marketplace. He was promptly asked about material depicting children such as those we had seen. This man said, with a straight face, that it is the ACLU's position that child pornography should not be produced, but once it is in existence, there should be no restriction on its sale or distribution. In other words, the photographic record of a child's molestation and abuse should be a legal source of profit for those who wish to reproduce, sell, print, and distribute it for the world to see. As the child grows up and becomes an adult, this visualization of his rape and molestation could continue to face him in the marketplace for the profit of pornographers. The victim would have no legal recourse against them. Likewise, the photographs of a woman's rape could be legally reproduced and sold despite her objections. And that, the ACLU representative said, was the intent of the First Amendment to the Constitution.

Despite the objections of the ACLU, the work of our commission continued in high gear. Lengthy hearings were held in six U.S. cities, during which testimony was taken from victims of pornography, police officers, FBI agents, social scientists, and even from the producers of hard-core materials. So many people wanted to testify that hearings sometimes lasted as long as twelve hours a day with minimal breaks. Hundreds of pounds of reports were sent for our consideration between meetings, leaving us exhausted and emotionally depleted. Finally, on July 8, 1986, the final report was released to Attorney General Edwin Meese and to the president.

The Bias of the Press

What occurred thereafter was an enlightening exercise in censorship by the press. Trying to get newspaper and television editors to tell the truth about the commission findings, I learned, was like trying to inflate a tire bearing an eight-inch gash. For example, there was not a single secular publisher in America who would print the report. Nor would network television present the facts. CBS sent Bob Schieffer to my office to videotape a forty-five-minute interview for use during Dan Rather's evening news program. When edited, I was seen for exactly six seconds of irrelevancy between two full statements of objection by Hugh Hefner. Similar interviews with *Time* magazine, *The Washington Post* and *USA Today* went unpublished. *People* magazine also requested an interview. The reporter and I spoke for an hour after she gave me assurances that my time would not be wasted. The following week, *People* carried a lengthy cover story on the subject of pornography, and guess what? Not a single comment of mine was included! Why? Because what I had to say was in direct contradiction to the distorted portrayal conveyed by the press. Their conscious effort has been to make the American people think that our commission damaged the First Amendment by attacking soft-core publications like *Playboy* and *Penthouse*. In truth, all of our recommendations dealt with material that is clearly illegal. The press perpetuates the belief that pornography is limited to relatively mild material in men's magazines—surrounded by good literature and fashion features. Waving the banner of censorship and accusing the commission of sexual repression, they have withheld the truth from the American people. Thus, I'm grateful for this opportunity to set the record straight. And that is why I have been so explicit in this statement.

The final report of our commission does no violence to the First Amendment to the Constitution. The *Miller* standard, by which the Supreme Court clearly reaffirmed the illegality of obscene matter in 1973, was not assaulted during any of our deliberations. No suggestion was made that the Court had been too lenient, or that a Constitutional Amendment should lower the threshold of obscenity, or that the Justices should reconsider their position. No, the *Miller* standard was accepted and even defended as the law of the land. What *was* recommended, to the consternation of pornographers, was that government should begin enforcing the obscenity laws that are already on the books, criminal laws that have stood constitutional muster! Considering the unwillingness of our elected representatives to deal with this issue, that would be novel, indeed.

The Harm of Pornography

But why *should* these laws be enforced? Why is it the business of government to object if some people want to amuse themselves with explicit materials? Is obscenity really a threat to society and to the individuals within it? The answers to those questions are linked to the findings that emerged from commission hearings. Many specific sources of harm associated with pornography became evident from professional testimony and from the wrenching stories told by victims of pornography. A few of those harms are described as follows:

1. Depictions of violence against women are related to violence against women in real life. Our commission was unanimous in recognizing that fact. Among the totality of evidence that supported this linkage was a study by Malamuth and Feshback[1] at the University of California at Los Angeles, who found that 51 percent of male students exposed to violent pornography indicated a likelihood of raping a woman if they could get away with it. Violent pornography also contributes to the so-called "rape myth," leading men to believe that women really want to be abused even when they vigorously deny it. Thus, it was the conclusion of the commission that there is no place in this culture for material deemed legally obscene by the courts which depicts the dismemberment, burning, whipping, hanging, torturing or raping of women. The time has come to eradicate such materials and prosecute those who produce it. There was no disagreement on that point.

2. Pornography is degrading and humiliating to women. They are shown nude, bound, and hanging from trees, being penetrated by broom handles, covered with blood, and kneeling submissively in the act of fellatio. These depictions assault female modesty and represent an affront to an entire gender. I would take that case to any jury in the land. Remember that *men* are the purchasers of pornography. Many witnesses testified that women are typically repulsed by visual depictions of the type herein described. It is provided primarily for the lustful pleasure of men and boys who use it to gratify themselves. And it is my belief, as stated above, that a small but dangerous minority will then choose to act aggressively against the nearest available females. Pornography is the theory; rape is the practice.

3. For a certain percentage of men, the use of pornography is progressive and addictive in nature. Like the addiction to drugs, alcohol, or food, those who get hooked on sexually explicit materials become obsessed by their need. In time it encompasses their entire world. These images can also interfere with normal sexual relationships between husbands and wives, since nothing in reality can possibly compete with airbrushed fantasies. Thus, even the casual use of pornography in a marital context carries some risk.

For vulnerable men, such exposure will set off a lifelong passion for explicit materials, leading inexorably toward marital disinterest and conflict. Many victims of this process testified before our commission.

4. Organized crime controls more than 85 percent of all commercially produced pornography in America. The sale and distribution of these materials produces huge profits for the crime lords who also sell illegal drugs to our kids and engage in murder, fraud, bribery, and every vice known to man. Are we to conclude, as the libertarians would have us believe, that the industry that produces millions of tax-free dollars for the Mafia each year is not harmful to society? Is malignant melanoma destructive to the human body?

(Incidentally, the Mafia tolerates no competition in the production and distribution of pornography. Those who attempt to grab a piece of the action are usually mutilated or killed. One ambitious man who insisted on barging into this business was tied against a brick wall and a truck was driven into his knees. He got the message.)

5. *Pedophiles, who abuse an average of 366 boys and girls in a lifetime, typically use pornography to soften children's defenses against sexual exploitation.* They show them nude pictures of adults, for example, and say, "See. This is what mommies and daddies do." They are then stripped of innocence and subjected to brutalities that will be remembered for a lifetime. And incredibly, this horror often leads to the sexually transmitted diseases (STD's) that are rampant among children today. More boys and girls are infected by STD's per year than were stricken with polio during the entire epidemic of 1942-1953.

6. *Outlets for obscenity are magnets for sex-related crimes.* When a thriving adult bookstore moves into a neighborhood, an array of "support-services" typically develops around it. Prostitution, narcotics, and street crime proliferate. From this perspective, it is interesting that law enforcement officials often claim they do not investigate or attempt to control the flow of obscenity because they lack the resources to combat it. In reality, their resources will extend farther if they first enforce the laws relating to por-

nography. The consequent reduction in crime makes this a cost-effective use of taxpayers' funds. In Cincinnati, Ohio, for example, the city demonstrated how a community can rid itself of obscenity without inordinate expenditures of personnel and money.

7. *So-called adult bookstores are often centers of disease and homosexual activity.* Again, the average citizen is not aware that the primary source of revenue in adult bookstores is derived from video and film booths. Patrons enter these three-by-three-foot cubicles and deposit a coin in the slot. They are then treated to about ninety seconds of a pornographic movie. If they want to see more, they must continue to pump coins (usually quarters) into the machine. The booths I witnessed on New York's Times Square were even more graphic. Upon depositing the coin, a screen was raised, revealing two or more women and men who performed live sex acts upon one another on a small stage. Everything that is possible for heterosexuals, homosexuals, or lesbians to do was demonstrated a few feet from the viewers. The booths from which these videos or live performers are viewed become filthy beyond description as the day progresses. The stench is unbearable and the floor becomes sticky with semen, urine, and saliva.

Holes in the walls between the booths are often provided to permit anonymous sexual encounters between adult males, etc. Given the current concern over sexually transmitted diseases and especially Acquired Immune Deficiency Syndrome (AIDS), it is incredible that local health departments have not attempted to regulate such businesses. States that will not allow restaurant owners, hairdressers, counselors, or acupuncturists to operate without licenses have permitted these wretched cesspools to escape governmental scrutiny. To every public health officer in this country I would ask: "Why?"

8. *I want to give special emphasis to the harm associated with pornography that falls into the hands of children and adolescents.* It would be extremely naive for us to assume that the river of obscenity that has inundated the American landscape has not invaded the world of children. There are more stores selling pornographic videos than there are McDonald hamburger restaurants. Latchkey kids by the millions are watching porn on cable and reading their parents' adult magazines. For fifty cents, they can purchase their own pornographic newspapers from vending machines on the street. At an age when elementary children should be reading Tom Sawyer and viewing traditional entertainment in the spirit of Walt Disney, they are learning perverted facts which neither their minds nor bodies are equipped to handle.

Adolescents are even more commonly exposed to explicit pornography. The Canadian study by Check,[2] reviewed by our commission, indicated that children between twelve and seventeen had the greatest interest in pornographic matter and were prime purchasers of it. Also, a study by Zillman and Bryant[3] surveyed 100 males and 100 females from each of three age categories: junior high, high school, and adult 19-39.

They found:

1. 91 percent of males and 82 percent of females had seen a magazine which depicted couples or groups in explicit sexual acts.
2. The average age of first exposure was 13.5 years.

3. A larger percentage of high school students had seen X-rated films than any other age group, including adults.
4. 84 percent reported exposure to such films.
5. 46 percent of junior high school students had seen one or more X-rated movies, and the average age of first exposure for these students was 14 years, 8 months.

Selling Obscenity to Kids

What a tragedy! If the explicit descriptions I've offered in this chapter have been disturbing to you, the mature reader, imagine how much more destructive the actual visualizations are to children and adolescents. Teenagers especially are prone to imitate what they see and hear. One year ago, the American Broadcasting Company featured a prime-time television program on teen suicide. In the drama, two attractive adolescents took their lives by piping carbon monoxide from their automobile exhaust to the passenger compartment. Immediately after the program aired, teenagers began imitating what they had seen on the screen. In the days that followed, reports of similar tragedies came from despairing parents around the country. Everyone who works with teenagers is familiar with this ''herd'' behavior. Modeling, good and bad, directly shapes the thoughts and actions of the next generation. It is a measurable phenomenon.

Why would it not be true, then, that the behavior of an entire generation of teenagers is adversely affected by the current emphasis on premarital sexuality and eroticism seen in adult materials and even in the movies? It is not surprising that the incidence of unwed pregnancy and abortions has skyrocketed since 1970. Teens are merely doing what they've been taught—that they should get into bed together, early and often.

Even more disturbing to me is the current effort by pornographers to market their product directly to our children and teenagers. Two examples of this outrage are worthy of specific concern. The first focuses on pornography in rock music. I invite you to turn to the appendix of this book and read excerpts from a verbal report submitted to the commission by Kandy Stroud on June 19, 1985. Of course, by the time this chapter is printed and distributed, the songs and even the musicians cited by Mrs. Stroud may have passed from the scene. But one thing is certain: if something is not done to police the rock music industry, these examples will be succeeded by even more wretched songs and singers.

Dial-a-Porn

The second example of pornography that is being peddled directly to our children often involves even younger boys and girls.

It has been difficult enough to shield our sons and daughters from explicit adult sexuality on television, rock videos, and immoral movies. But now, a new plague has appeared on the horizon, this one invading our homes via the telephone. It's known as ''dial-a-porn,'' and it delivers the most obscene and profane messages imaginable to anyone choosing to call—anyone. Predictably, the word has spread rapidly among school-aged children, and thousands of boys and girls now tune in to the pornographic recordings (or live conversations) every day. Some are younger than eight years of age. One mother wrote a letter of protest after discovering that her children had been phoning a dial-a-porn. She said:

I am angry and upset. I received a telephone bill with approximately $25 worth of calls made to dial-a-porn numbers. All of the calls were made by my children, none of whom is over eighteen. I am appalled that there are no restrictions placed on these businesses that prohibit them from being able to sell their product to children. It seems incredible to me that I must pay $25 to a company that may have done emotional damage to one or all of my children. I called one of the numbers listed on my bill to see what my children had heard. The recording was fashioned in a child's voice and invited sexual contact! I shuddered when I hung up the phone and wondered how many sex offenders may have made a call like this, and then went out and attacked an innocent victim.

Another mother, Judith Trevillian, gave testimony before the Attorney General's Commission on Pornography during the Los Angeles hearing. The following is a portion of her written remarks:

I discovered the dial-a-porn number on my February 1984 telephone bill. I called the phone company, asking the location and content of the calls, and was told they could not give me that information. I decided to dial a number myself before confronting my children, anticipating hearing dial-a-sport or dial-a-joke or dial-a-horoscope. What I heard was horror of another kind! The chilling horror I felt in my kitchen after my first encounter with dial-a-porn lingers with me today. After my initial reaction of disbelief subsided, I was overcome with grief. I cried uncontrollably for myself, my son, and my country. I, like many other average Americans, had no idea our society's standards had been so badly infected by pornography's spew. Then, my grief turned to anger and the anger turned to action. The shocked numbness of all audiences for whom I've played these tapes the past year and a half also convinces me that something must be done.

Mrs. Trevillian now heads an organization called Citizens Against Pornography in Michigan. She is still fighting to stop dial-a-porn in her state.

Also testifying at the Commission of Pornography hearings was Brent Ward, United States attorney in the Utah District. His important report contained this observation about children:

Indeed, the most alarming aspect of the dial-a-porn problem is the exposure of large numbers of children across the country to these vivid dramatizations of sexual conduct. We know of many cases involving children as young as eight years old. Children are being exposed to this material at a time in their lives when they are especially vulnerable and impressionable and lack the experience, perspective and judgment to recognize and avoid sexually oriented material that may be harmful to them. For some children, the very first explicit information they receive about the sex act comes from these recordings. We know from our work that these recordings conjure up images in the minds of young people which become powerfully anchored in the memory and which have a powerful, addictive effect. They are like morphine to some children. These listening experiences become vivid memories which the mind continually "replays," stimulating the child again and again and suggesting the need for even further stimulation by making more calls. Some children make hundreds of calls. They gain such a hold that some parents, teachers and counselors have found themselves powerless to do anything about it. This is especially true of "latchkey" children whose parents are gone from the home until after their children return.

How did it happen? How did this pipeline to pornography come to exist? It started in 1983 when *High Society* Magazine, Inc., obtained a "dial it" number in a lottery conducted by the New York Telephone System. This service was intended for use by organizations which offered information to the public (sports, weather, finance, etc.). But *High Society* had other intentions. It used the "dial it" number to provide audio messages depicting actual or simulated sexual behavior. State law provided no controls over the content of recordings, and pornographers suddenly discovered a new vehicle for selling their uncensored messages to the public at large. It's a sad commentary on Western civilization that this "service" became an overnight success. Sources estimate that *High Society* now receives up to 500,000 calls every twenty-four hours from people across the country. That's lucrative business for the entrepreneur who reportedly earns $10,000 daily; it's even more profitable for New York Telephone which collects as much as $35,000 each day. It is not surprising that similar "services" are springing up in other locations across North America. Now is the time, as Judith Trevillian says, to do something about this exploitation of children. Indeed, a few irate mothers and fathers have been protesting to their congressmen and to the Federal Communications Commission in recent months.

Attempting to respond, the FCC adopted regulations in 1985 that required these pornographic services to operate only between 9:00 P.M. and 8:00 A.M. But the U.S. Second Circuit Court of Appeals in New York overturned the ruling, stating that the FCC had violated First Amendment rights and had not demonstrated sufficient research on this issue. Strike another blow against the family!

Since the FCC anticipates that the debate over this issue will undoubtedly be extended, it is eager for public input. You can be assured that the pornographers have mobilized their forces to oppose these proposals. In fact, the FCC has already received scores of letters from dial-a-porn customers who want no limits placed on their access to the service. In effect, the pornography industry and telephone companies are sitting on a gold mine and they want no restrictions that will limit their profits. If children are among their customers, then so be it. Unfortunately, there has been minimal response from parents or citizens who oppose this assault on our children. I do not understand the deafening silence!

The Response from Washington

Raising healthy children is the primary occupation of families, and anything that invades the childhoods and twists the minds of boys and girls must be seen as abhorrent to the mothers and fathers who gave them birth. Furthermore, what is at stake here is the future of the family itself. We are sexual creatures, and the physical attraction between males and females provides the basis for every dimension of marriage and parenthood. Thus, *anything* that interjects itself into that relationship must be embraced with great caution. Until we *know* that pornography is not addictive and progressive, until we are *certain* that the passion of fantasy does not destroy the passion of reality, until we are *sure* that obsessive use of obscene materials will not lead to perversions and conflict between husbands and wives, then we dare not adorn them with the crown of respectability. Society has an absolute obligation to protect itself from material which crosses the line established objectively by its legislators and court system. That is not sexual repression. That is self-preservation.

Presumably, members of Congress were cognizant of the dangers when they drafted legislation to control sexually explicit material. The president and his predecessors would not have signed those bills into criminal laws if they had not agreed. The Supreme Court must have shared the same concerns when it ruled that obscenity is not protected by the First Amendment.

How can it be, then, that these carefully crafted laws are not being enforced? The refusal of federal and local officials to check the rising tide of obscenity is a disgrace and an outrage! It is said that the production and distribution of pornography is the only unregulated industry remaining in America today. Indeed, the salient finding emerging from twelve months of testimony before our commission reflected this utter paralysis of government in response to the pornographic plague. As citizens of a democratic society, we have surrendered our right to protect ourselves in return for protection by the state. Thus, our governmental representatives have a constitutional mandate to shield us from harm and criminal activity, including that associated with obscenity. It is time our leaders were held accountable for their obvious malfeasance.

Attorney General Edwin Meese, who has courageously supported other unpopular causes, has been reluctant to tackle this one. Now that he has the report of the commission, we will see whether he mobilizes the Department of Justice. But his predecessors have no such excuse for their dismal record. Under Attorney General William French Smith, there was not a single indictment brought against the producers of adult pornography in 1983. There were only six in 1982, but four of those were advanced by one motivated prosecutor. In 1981 there were two. Of the ninety-three U.S. attorneys, only seven have devoted any effort to the prosecution of obscenity. Obviously, the multi-billion-dollar porn industry is under no serious pressure from federal prosecutors.

Considering this apathy, perhaps it is not surprising that the Department of Justice greeted our commission with something less than rampant enthusiasm. For example, the first presidential commission received $2 million (in 1967 money) and was granted two years to complete their assignment. Our commission was allocated only $500,000 (in 1985 money) and was given one year in which to study an industry which had expanded exponentially.

Repeated requests for adequate time and funding were summarily denied. Considering the presidential mandate to establish the commission, the Department of Justice had no choice but to execute the order. But it did very little to guarantee its success or assist with the enormous workload. Quite frankly, failure would have been inevitable were it not for the dedication of eleven determined commissioners who worked under extreme pressure and without compensation to finish the task. We were also blessed with a marvelous staff and executive director who were committed to the challenge.

Who's at Fault?
Other branches of government must also be held accountable for their unwillingness to enforce the criminal laws. The U.S. Post Office Department makes virtually no effort to prosecute those who send obscene material through the mail. Attorney Paul McGeady testified that there are conservatively 100,000 violations of postal regulations every day of the year. Likewise, the Federal Trade Commission and Interstate Commerce Commission do not attempt to

regulate the interstate transportation of obscene material. Eighty percent of all pornography is produced in Los Angeles County and then shipped to the rest of the country. It would not be difficult to identify and prosecute those who transport it across state lines.

The Federal Communications Commission does not regulate obscenity on cable or satellite television. The Customs Service makes no effort to prevent adult pornography from entering this country, and catches only 5 percent of child porn sent from abroad. The Internal Revenue Service permits organized crime to avoid taxes on the majority of its retail sales, especially the video booth market. The Federal Bureau of Investigation assigns only 2 of 8,700 special agents to obscenity investigation, even though organized crime controls the industry. And on and on it goes.

Local law enforcement agencies are equally unconcerned about obscenity. The city of Miami has assigned only 2 of 1,500 policemen to this area, neither of whom is given a car. Chicago allocates 2 of 12,000 officers to obscenity control. Los Angeles assigns 8 out of 6,700, even though L.A. is the porn capital of the country. Not one indictment has been brought against a pornographer in Los Angeles County in more than ten years, despite the glut of materials produced there.

Another serious concern is also directed at the court system and the judges who have winked at pornography. Even when rare convictions have been obtained, the penalties assessed have been pitiful. Producers of illegal materials may earn millions in profit each year, and yet if convicted, serve no time in prison and pay fines of perhaps $100. One powerful entrepreneur in Miami was found guilty on obscenity charges for the sixty-first time, yet received a fine of only $1,600. The judge in another case refused to even look at child pornography which the defendant had supposedly produced. He said it would prejudice him to examine the material. That judge had never sentenced a single pornographer to a day in prison.

In another striking example, the producer of the movie *Deep Throat* invested $25,000 and earned more than $50 million in profits. He was subsequently charged with obscenity, requiring three years of litigation to obtain a conviction. He was finally sentenced to two years in prison, but was permitted instead to work nights in the Salvation Army headquarters. Is there any wonder why America is inundated with sexually explicit material today?

Conclusion

So we come to the bottom line. We've looked at the conditions that have led to the present situation. Now we must consider the mid-course maneuvers that will correct it. I believe that the recommendations offered in the commission's final report will provide an effective guide toward that end. We not only attempted to assess the problem; we have offered a proposed resolution. The testimonies on which it is based make it clear that we are engaged in a winnable war! According to a recent Gallop Poll, 73 percent of the American people are opposed to hard-core pornography; with this support, we can rid ourselves of obscenity in eighteen months if the recommendations offered in the report are implemented. We have provided a roadmap for fine-tuning federal and state legislation and for the mobilization of law enforcement efforts around the country.

Unfortunately, I can tell you with certainty that aggressive action against pornographers *will not occur* unless our citizens demand the response of government. Our leaders have ignored the violations in the past and they will continue their malfeasance unless we besiege them from every corner of the land. Our commission report will either become another expensive dust collector on bureaucratic shelves or it will serve as the basis for a new public policy. The difference will be determined by the outcry that accompanies its release or the deafening silence of an unconcerned populous.

If you wish to add your voice to those who demand immediate action, may I ask you to make four specific contacts with government? Write and call President Reagan, and write and call Attorney General Meese. Insist that Mr. Meese establish a strike force to oversee implementation of the commission recommendations, and that he supervise it personally. If he delegates the assignment to the do-nothing bureaucrats who failed us in the past, their same apathy will recur.

It is this kind of public response that the pornographers fear most. They can slither past our public officials, our judges and our police chiefs. But they can't override the great democratic system when it cranks into action. If that outcry does not occur, then we have labored in vain.

During the hearings in Chicago, we met on the twenty-fourth floor of a government building which overshadowed a smaller structure in the process of demolition. I stood at the window and watched the wrecking ball do its destructive work. I thought to myself as it crashed into the remaining walls on the roof, *That is what the pornographers are doing to my country. They are hammering down the sup-*

porting columns and blasting away the foundations. We must stop the devastation before the entire superstructure crashes to the earth! With the diligent prayers and personal involvement of God-fearing people, we can save the great edifice called America. But there is not a minute to lose. "But each one is tempted when he is carried away and enticed by his own lust. Then when lust has conceived, it gives birth to sin; and when sin is accomplished, it brings forth death" (James 1:14-16, NASB).

Notes

1. N. M. Malamuth, M. Heim and S. Feshback, "Sexual Responsiveness of College Students to Rape Depictions: Inhibitory and Disinhibitory Effects," *Journal of Personality and Social Psychology* 84, 1980. See also N. M. Malamuth, F. Haber, and S. Feshback, "Testing Hypotheses Regarding Rape: Exposure to Sexual Violence, Sex Differences and the 'Normality' of Rapists," *Journal of Research on Personality* 14, 1980.
2. J. V. P. Check, "A Survey of Canadian Attitudes Regarding Sexual Content in the Media," *Report to the Lamarsh Research Program on Violence and Conflict Resolution and the Canadian Broadcasting Corporation* in Toronto, Canada, 1985.
3. Unpublished testimony of D. Zillman and J. Bryant before the U.S. Attorney General's Commission on Pornography in Houston, Texas, on 13 September 1985.

CHAPTER TWO
Christianity and Good Sex

Jerry Kirk

Something very odd has been happening.

The Bible says that in the beginning God created everything and declared it to be very good—man, woman, bodies, sexuality. Furthermore, he commanded us to be fruitful
and multiply.

The odd thing then is that Christians—people to whom
this declaration should mean the most—have gotten themselves characterized as prudes, as people who disdain sex.

Are Christians really prudes? We certainly seem to be
when we see ourselves portrayed on television and in the
popular press. People who go to church are assumed to be
ignorant or disgusted with sex. Moreover, television and
film often present clergy as corrupt or incompetent,
shocked by the slightest allusion to body functions. How
accurate is the media image? What is the biblical teaching
on sex that Christians actually should embrace?

It's hard to know how to write for Christians on this subject. Many Christian couples hold fast to these biblical prin-

ciples and have found in them a deep wellspring of
contentment and joy. But other Christians have been
clamped hard by the world's view of casual sex and tran-
sient relationships. Speaking to them on this subject is like
addressing non-Christian people who have only the vaguest
idea about what the Bible teaches. That is how far secular
culture has invaded some of our people. I do not know how
large this group is, but I fear it is large indeed. Therefore I
will assume very little understanding as I make my case.

The Scriptures teach that sex is marvelous, created by
God. Sex, marriage, and family life were his ideas in the
beginning: "So God created man in his own image . . .
male and female he created them" (Gen. 1:27, NIV). Sex
was the physical bond of Adam and Eve's human love in
the Garden of Eden—not the cause of their fall, not something they discovered after leaving Paradise. Sexual intercourse is intended by God to be doubly re-creational: for
re-creating children (Gen. 1:28), and for re-creational nur-
ture, pleasure, and fun between wife and husband ("This is
now bone of my bones and flesh of my flesh; . . . and they
will become one flesh." [Gen. 2:23, NIV]).

Proverbs 5:15-21 is an excellent example of the biblical
approach to sexuality. The context is that of marital love
with a call to faithfulness, and to the ecstasy of sexual love.
Through oriental imagery, the wife is described as a fountain, and sexual enjoyment as the drinking of water.
"Drink water from your own cistern, running water from
your own well" (v. 15, NIV). Husband and wife are actually commanded to be infatuated with one another and with
sexual pleasure, to delight in one another, all under the
beneficent eye of God.

May your fountain be blessed,
and may you rejoice in the wife of your youth.
A loving doe, a graceful deer—
may her breasts satisfy you always,
may you ever be captivated by her love (v. 18, 19, NIV).

Does that sound like one who tolerates this sexuality reluctantly and with begrudging acceptance?

Then we have the Song of Solomon, a magnificent song of praise extolling the erotic beauty that the king finds in his bride and that his bride finds in him! They rejoice in one another and in the gift of physical beauty and of sexual union.

As Christians, we should not wish to ban all romantic sexual literature. The Song of Solomon is certainly erotica. We need to, however, discriminate between beautiful, positive sexuality, and pornography—material that exists only to cause sexual arousal, degrade women, and lower human sexuality to the level of prurient interest.

In the New Testament, 1 Corinthians 7 includes many principles about marriage. It says that the husband should give to his wife her conjugal rights, and likewise the wife to her husband. ''The wife does not have authority over her own body, but the husband does; and likewise also the husband does not have authority over his own body, but the wife does'' (NASB). This is self-giving love. The fundamental principle of Christian relationship is giving up one's own desire and pleasure for the good of another. The same principle is the basis for Christian marriage and for sexual fulfillment within marriage—seeking the pleasure and well-being of the partner. God's way is right. Losing ourselves in loving our spouse leads to greater personal sexual blessings. This is the secret pleasure of self-sacrifice that the hedonist can never know.

A woman is most able to give herself sexually if she feels loved and cared for through deep communication. When we fail one another and face up to that failure, we are forgiven. When we are spiritually and relationally healed, sex is so much better. It is better because it grows naturally out of harmony, out of intimacy of thought and sharing and appreciation. Our sexual love is based on lasting relationships, deep communication, and trust.

Sex: The Church Versus the Bible

With all the power and beauty of the biblical teaching about sex, how did Christians get such a reputation for prudery? Do we deserve it? Some of it, yes. I readily admit that both Protestant and Catholic traditions have repressed sexuality at various periods in history.

Sexual repression in the first centuries of the Church rose out of the Greek idea that the spirit is good and the flesh is bad. It gradually grew into a stress on virginity. Eventually, the church required celibacy for the priesthood in the fourth century. But that decision was far from unanimous. Many scholars argued that marriage was also a blessed state, pointing to Peter who was married and to Paul's teaching that a bishop or deacon is to be husband of one wife. The orthodox position on sexual activities within marriage swung back and forth through the centuries from "a blessing of God" to "a necessary evil." In the Roman Catholic Church, the debate over the celibate priesthood continues to the present.[1]

The Protestant Reformers rejected the idea of a celibate

clergy, and insisted that married sex was part of God's good creation. Luther, Zwingli, and Calvin all took wives and affirmed sex as a part of that good creation.

How ironic that today the term "Puritan" is a synonym for prudery. Actually, Puritans were blasted by the Catholic Church for promoting lechery—that is, for declaring that sexual desire was created by God and therefore good. Paradoxically, the Puritans who bear the stigma of prudery today were pioneers in the struggle to vindicate the goodness and blessing of sex.

Calvin wrote, "Conjugal intercourse is a thing that is pure, honorable and holy, because it is a pure institution of God." The Catholic Church condemned William Tyndale's Puritan theology as indulgent to the point of license, charging Protestants with "sensual and licentious living."[2]

Tyndale's "radical" teaching is illustrated in one of his expositions of Scripture: "For God hath blessed thy wife, and made her without sin to thee, which ought to seem a beautiful fairness. And all that ye suffer [experience] together, the one with the other, is blessed also, and made the very cross of Christ, and pleasant in the sight of God."[3]

In the nineteenth century, a curious reversal of positions occurred. Certain forerunners of liberal Protestantism agreed with the American medical community that sexual activity was harmful and should be avoided to conserve bodily strength. Victorian intellectuals distanced themselves from sex as part of a comprehensive ideal of spiritual, intellectual, and physical health, believing that Enlightened Man could usher in the kingdom of God on earth by evolving into greater spirituality.

During this same period in American history, waves of immigrants from Roman Catholic Ireland, Germany, and

Italy entered the country. Prejudice and fear influenced the popular press. There were accusations of priestly lust, seduction, and lechery. Alarmed Victorians reacted by drawing their laces tighter and buttoning their collars higher to emphasize their opposition to the imagined "loose living" of the immigrants.

What does the hedonist, or playboy, believe in contrast to Victorianism? Claiming the Marquis de Sade as their philosophical mentor, hedonists insist that individual pleasure is the highest good, and that each man (very rarely "woman") has the right to pursue that pleasure to the furthest extent his means allow. Some, like de Sade, go so far as to declare that man may seek his pleasure without regard for whatever harm may thereby be inflicted on others. Most, though, limit the pursuit of pleasure to "consenting adults." This "Playboy Philosophy" includes any imaginable sexual activity, conspicuous consumerism, and all aspects of "the good life," including fashion, sports, art and music, and gourmet dining.

Who Is Missing the Fun?

The secular media—particularly movies and television—strongly suggest that those who are faithful in marriage are missing out on all the fun. But who is actually missing out on the really good times?

In order to have "good sex," a relationship must be built on the traditional values of commitment and sacrificial love. Psychological studies confirm biblical principles. Good sex does not suddenly happen on a one-night stand, nor does it appear magically on the wedding night. Sexual intimacy must be learned like any other skill. And because it is a cooperative act between two persons, it takes time, practice, and the commitment of both partners to learn and perfect that skill together. This requires love, not just a desire for an orgasmic experience.

In marriage, a husband can take the time necessary to learn how to please his spouse. He is able to learn her intimate desires, and meet them, and she can teach him how to please her. The same is true for the wife; she develops a continually growing understanding of how to please her husband. When egos are hurt, there is time for healing and reconciliation.

But when persons fall for "recreational sex," there is none of this. If a playmate fails to please her partner one night, or if the playboy is clumsy, the partner hustles away to find someone more exciting or more compatible. There is always the need to perform and the struggle of constant comparisons. Promiscuity diminishes the sexual experience by taking what is meant to be precious and making it casual.

In the properly functioning Christian marriage the emphasis is not a one-night performance. Times of sexual difficulty can be corrected when there is the commitment to work together. In a lifetime together, the strength and security of mutual faithfulness and self-discipline allow a couple the necessary freedom to grow into greater self-appreciation, mutual understanding, and deeper intimacy. (The tragedy is that many Christian couples who should know better succumb to worldly ideas of sex.)

William Banowsky says it well: "Sex is not essentially something man does, but something he is; sex does not designate a simple function, it relates to the totality of existence. The biological side of sex cannot be isolated and viewed as autonomous because it is but one aspect of the whole, indivisible man. Sexual intercourse is not merely one physical act among many; it is, instead, an act that engages and expresses the entire personality in such a way as to provide insight into the nature of man."[4]

A husband and wife are secure in knowing that when youth ripens into age and firm flesh softens or sags, the lover will continue to love. As bodies mature and change over the years, partners who are committed to each other may change their habits of lovemaking to continue to meet one another's changing needs. It is a relationship one can count on and it protects one from the momentary distractions that lead to self-hatred and self-destruction. Based on a lifetime of commitment, God allows each partner to learn how to bless and meet each other's deepest needs. The sacrament of human love is custom-designed for one partner and one partner only. It is personalized. One-of-a-kind. Just for her. Just for him.[5]

The challenge of such love is greater. The enjoyment is deeper. The agony is minimized and the ecstasy is multiplied. How tragic that many are incapable of such intimacy and sustained closeness! The playboy longs and searches for such intimacy, but refuses to take the risk necessary to achieve it.

Supporting Evidence
It has been shown that commitment and Christian devotion result in better sex. The 1975 *Redbook* survey found that 72 percent of women who described themselves as "very religious" also said that they were "almost always orgasmic" compared to 62 percent of women who described themselves as "non-religious."[6]

More recently, *Parade* magazine reported a 1984 study of sexual styles. It revealed that in a category of respondents described as "satisfied sensualists," 74 percent said they were "very devout." Two "erotic" categories, including "unsatisfied erotic," and "lonely erotic," had majorities describing themselves as less religious. Clearly there is something about religious commitment that also makes a sexual relationship better.[7]

Why is this so? Professor Thomas C. Oden writes, "Intimates are aware that their most significant exchanges are not merely body transactions, but as persons in encounter, or the meeting of spirit with spirit. What really happens in intimacy has to do with spirit-spirit communion or interpersonal communion, two persons experiencing their beings poignantly united."[8]

Dangers of the Playground

"Well," some may say, "maybe the religious fanatics can have good sex. But that's no evidence that recreational sex is wrong." Ah, but there is plenty of evidence, and from secular as well as religious authorities. Promiscuous sex is not only wrong, but dangerous. And the chorus of voices is growing rapidly.

Karl Menninger states in *Love Against Hate*: "It is an axiom in psychiatry that a plurality of direct sexual outlets indicates the very opposite of what it is popularly assumed to indicate. Dividing the sexual interest into several objectives diminishes the total sexual gratification, and men whose need for love drives them to the risks and efforts necessary to maintain sexual relationships with more than one woman show a deficiency rather than an excess in their masculine capacities."[9]

And as Thomas Oden quips, ''Sex without interpersonal intimacy is like a diploma without an education.''[10]

Games That Hurt

In transactional analysis, intimacy is defined as ''a game-free exchange of emotional expression without exploitation.'' Promiscuity, multiple sex partners, and short and superficial relationships are factors that identify ''loser life scripts'' rather than the ''good life'' the pornographers portray. The labels ''playboy'' and ''playmate'' are appropriate when compared with ''power plays'' as Claude M. Steiner used the term, where each individual attempts to control and use another for individual gratification. Sexual individualism and competition underlie the promiscuous life-style, and as such are destructive elements that make intimate, long-term relationships impossible. ''If one has no close ties to anyone, one hardly notices how individualism and competitiveness are destructive forces.'' It is also revealing to see that in Steiner's description of the ''power play,'' women are invariably forced into a ''one-down position to men.'' The men have power and the women must manipulate or submit in order to survive in the pathological system. Nothing could better describe the content and message of pornography. It is simply pathological.[11]

From sex therapists we learn that there are no dysfunctional individuals, but rather, dysfunctional couples. Sex is an activity learned with a partner—and sex therapy is effective when the couple is committed to working through difficulties on a long-term basis, each partner willing to sacrifice immediate gratification for the other's well-being. That is the key—putting the other person first and having that person believe it.

The most common dysfunction seen by therapists in men is impotence caused by a dread of losing power. Therapists understand that women who experience frigidity dread being "cold" or lacking in affection. In both male and female, the major difficulty is inability to achieve orgasm with the chosen partner when desired. In very simple terms, the function of a sex therapist is to dispel misinformation about sex and to give permission to the couple to enjoy one another—allowing them both to relax and accept themselves in the reality of their physical bodies.

But please notice that therapy can be effective only in committed relationships. There must first be a foundation of trust and responsibility toward one another *before* therapy can begin its healing work. Generalizing from these observations, it is obvious that commitment to the partner must come before building a sexual relationship.[12]

"An intimate relationship is ordinarily sustained over a period of time with a shared interpersonal memory, yet it may intensify in ecstatic moments. . . . Some confuse the two (the sustained intimate relationship and the ecstatic intimate moment), assuming that when one experiences a brief moment of intense closeness with another, there exists consequently an intimate relationship. . . . There is no instant intimacy, even though the encounter culture appears to be trying to facilitate it on a brief basis. It succeeds to some extent, but the short-term relationships often yearn for sustenance in time, and thus for the conditions of true intimacy."[13]

Intimacy, in the authentic use of the term, requires a relationship that is sustained in time, developing a profound, mutual understanding. The Hebrew use of the verb "to know" for the sexual act implies this intimacy. Ecstatic moments, such as mutual orgasmic experiences, enhance intimacy, but do not constitute intimacy.

Psychologists observe that promiscuity among both men and women stems from childhood emotional wounds, deep personality deficiencies, or lack of personal self-worth. For example, a 1982 report by the American Medical Association's Council on Scientific Affairs stated that "Any person, of whatever sexual preference, who shows a dominant pattern of frequent sexual activity with many partners who are and will remain strangers, presents evidence of shallow, narcissistic, impersonal, often compulsively driven genital-rather than person-oriented sex and is almost always regarded as pathological."[14]

Healthy, mature individuals seek out and are successful in maintaining mutually satisfying long-term sexual relationships. Extremes in sexual activity reflect an "acting out" of emotional and relational distress.

"The Playboy Philosophy promotes and perpetuates the synthetic view of man, in which sex is reduced to his genital parts."[15] The error of this view is that it minimizes sex because it separates the physical act from the family, from the home—from all that enhances sex, and all that ought to be enriched by sex.

"The post-Freudian period has rightly taught us that sexual closeness is an important aspect of human fulfillment, but wrongly and excessively told us that our human fulfillment depends almost frantically and unilaterally on sexual fulfillment, so much so in fact that many are engaged in a desperate search for sexual gratification. . . . It is precisely the urgent and demanding character of this sexual quest that reduces actual and potential intimacy."[16] The irony is that the quest defeats its goal of true intimacy by manipulating others for one's own gratification.

Ignoring the Warnings

We haven't yet mentioned the physical dangers of promiscuity. There isn't space here to describe it completely, but certainly we have to look at those consequences that the pornographers never mention: unwanted pregnancy, sexually transmitted diseases, and personal stress.

The birthrate among unwed teenagers in the United States, which is one in every five live births, is two to seven times higher than in any other developed country. In 1984 there were 90,000 new cases of syphilis reported, 500,000 new cases of incurable herpes, and an estimated 2 million cases of gonorrhea, with increasing numbers of penicillin-resistant strains. New cases of venereal warts and chlamydia are reaching epidemic proportions, involving over 4 million people. In 1985 alone, more babies were affected by sexually transmitted diseases than were affected by polio during the entire epidemic of the 1950s.

Only a handful of AIDS cases were found in 1979. By 1984 there were 14,000 victims and 7,157 deaths. At the time of this writing, those figures were doubling every six months.[17] If no cure is found and measures are not implemented to stop its spread, by 1996 nearly one-half of the population will be infected.[18] Recent studies also indicate that unlike many common viruses, the AIDS virus is prone to mutation. This means that if a vaccine is developed it may quickly be rendered ineffective against new, mutated forms of the virus.[19]

Where is the public health campaign to protect people from sexually transmitted diseases? We require warnings on cigarette packaging, and ban tobacco advertising in various media—yet the plague of sexually transmitted diseases endangers more people than cigarette smoke. Where is the

public health campaign to proclaim that promiscuous, recreational sex is hazardous to your health? As medical
advisor for ABC news, Dr. Timothy Johnson states: "Face
it. Monogamous marriage is the greatest safety net in
America."

On top of all this, there is the constant stress of competition, the continual effort to find a sex partner while avoiding the pain of rejection. The pages of the sex magazines
imply that beautiful, talented partners are available every-
where you look—but of course that is not true. How great a
cost is paid by the "swinging single" in loneliness, frustra-
tion, rejection, and loss of self-esteem?

A pathetic example is the testimony of a person involved
in the "swinging" life-style, also known as "wife-swap-
ping." As a staff member of *Connection* magazine, Dibri
L. Beavers worked to promote the image of "unlimited,
uninhibited sexual opportunity, unquestioned sexual acceptance, and a free healthy atmosphere wherein the most for-
bidden fantasies could be exercised without fear. . . ."
But the reality was far different. In a statement filed with
the Attorney General's Commission on Pornography, this
journalist said:

"However idyllic swinging may have sounded, the fact
was that it was practiced by less than ideal people. . . .
Discrimination and segregation were widespread as those
who were overweight, black, old, handicapped, unattractive, or considered too "kinky" found themselves
unwanted. . . . Rejection was commonplace and health
risks a threat despite the obsessive interest swingers seemed
to have about being "clean" . . . it is very exploitative of
women who are often the "bait" for men who want to
make swinging contacts. Because the life-style promotes a

pornographic view of sex and because the women involved place an inordinate amount of concern on the male's pleasure instead of their own, I found many women who had allowed themselves to be coerced into attending these conventions simply to please their partners. In addition, women most specifically found themselves forced into bisex. . . ."[20]

Can you imagine such rejection? Most of us feel rejected at times in our youth, in the dating and courtship experience, and also in our adult life as single persons or in difficult times with our mates. But to offer oneself for "free sex" experiences and to be rejected? It must be devastating.

One of my greatest joys is knowing that the one I loved, the one I admired and idolized and dreamed of—the one I chose—also chose me. With all my frailties and faults, all the wrinkles and bony joints and bulges, I am secure in the confidence that I am loved. And I love her, after she has borne five children and is now a grandmother. Does the swinger have that kind of confidence? Does the playboy?

Finally, the use of pornography itself is destructive to a healthy sexuality. Victor Cline of the University of Utah, a specialist in the treatment of sexual deviances, states without reservation that exposure to pornographic materials has a distinct pattern. The user experiences sexual stimulation from the materials that quickly replaces normal sexual activity . . . leading to addiction. Then tolerance develops, and progressively stronger materials are needed to achieve the same "kick." Gradually, the user becomes desensitized so that he no longer feels distaste for sexual deviances or compassion for the victim of rape or beating. Finally, fantasizing often will become overt behavior, in acts of seduction, rape, and violence.[21] (More about this in chapter 6.)

"With each overindulgence, the level of physical and emotional expectation gradually rises so that an increasingly greater thrill is required to satisfy the urge. Eventually, the thrill begins to diminish but the hunger for stimulation is ever present, now stronger than ever. . . . One begins by seeking pleasure to fill his boredom and ends by being bored with his pleasures."[22]

The great proportion of pornography that mixes sex with violence requires still greater concern. Researchers Edward Donnerstein and Neil Malamuth have done numerous studies regarding violent sexual material, and find that users are not only aroused sexually, but experience increases in both aggressive attitudes and behavior. Men who are regularly exposed to these materials admit to having more aggressive rape fantasies, and are more willing to believe rape myths (such as "women ask for it," or "they really like it"). There is increased callousness and less sensitivity about rape, and the process actually leads to men's admitting an increased possibility of raping someone themselves—particularly if there is reason to believe they will not be caught. (See chapter 6 for more information on these studies.)

Conclusion

In God's plan, sex is all about children and families. Faithfulness creates families—promiscuity destroys families. Children who grow up in a home where the mother and father obviously respect and enjoy one another will learn to seek that kind of relationship in their own marriages. In a home where there is modesty as well as honesty and respect for one another's bodies, children will learn that there is a holy mystery to sex. Children see and absorb their parents' concern for each other, their pleasure at being home again after separate work days, and their excitement when coming together after a business trip. They see their parents sharing problems and sorrows together, and they learn the trust, security, and joy of the Christian home.

Beyond even this, the act of Christian marriage is a symbol of Christ and the Church. Sex is a mystery of love: husband to wife and wife to husband, comforting, caring, giving oneself to the other. It is a concrete image of the love Christ has for his earthly body, the Church, his bride. There is no other aspect of humanity that is so perfect an illustration of the depth of passion with which God desires his people. Wholistic sexuality is a cornerstone in the Christian life.

Notes

1. For further reading see O. G. Oliver, Jr., "Celibacy," in *Evangelical Dictionary of Theology*, ed. Walter A. Elwell (Grand Rapids: Baker Book House, 1984), 202, 203; Henry Charles Lea, *The History of Sacerdotal Celibacy in the Christian Church*, 4th ed. (New Hyde Park, New York: University Books, 1966); George H. Frein, ed., *Celibacy: The Necessary Option* (New York: Herder & Herder, 1968).
2. Leland Ryken, "Were the Puritans Right About Sex?" *Christianity Today*, 7 April 1978, 13-18.
3. From G. E. Duffield, ed., *The Work of William Tyndale* (Philadelphia: Fortess Press, 1965). Also see Ewald M. Plass, comp., *What Luther Says: An Anthology* (St. Louis: Concordia Publishing House, 1959), 884-908; Hans J. Hillerbrand, *The World of the Reformation* (New York: Charles Scribner's Sons, 1973), 193-196.
4. William S. Banowsky, *It's a Playboy World* (Old Tappan, N.J.: Fleming H. Revell Co., 1969), 78.
5. Thomas C. Oden, *Game Free: A Guide to the Meaning of Intimacy* (New York: Harper & Row, 1974), 24, 25. "Intimacy is an intensely personal relationship of sustained closeness in which the intimate sphere of each partner is affectionately known and beheld by the other through congruent, empathic understanding, mutual accountability, and contextual negotiability, durable in time, subject to ecstatic intensification, emotively warm and conflict-capable, self-disclosing and distance-respecting, subject to death and yet in the form of hope reaching beyond death. . . ."

6. C. Travis and S. Sadd, *The Redbook Report on Female Sexuality* (New York: Delacorte Press, 1975), 97-100.
7. Criteria defining the "erotic" life-style as opposed to "sensualist" included questions about oral-genital sex, pornography, sex fantasizing, and masturbation. Devout persons scored low on these questions, while less religious respondents tended to score much higher. Earl Ubell, "Sex in America Today," *Parade*, 28 October 1984, 11-13.
8. Oden, 23.
9. Karl A. Menninger, *Love Against Hate* (New York: Harcourt, Brace & Co., 1942), 72, 73.
10. Oden, 33.
11. Claude M. Steiner, "The Good Life, Cooperation," in *Scripts People Live,* (New York: Bantam, 1974), 353; Eric Berne, *What Do You Say After You Say Hello* (New York: Bantam, 1972), 207 ("Sex and Scripts"), 443 (definition of *intimacy*). Also see Eric Berne, "Rape and the Stocking Game" (as resembling the games played in pornography), in *Games People Play* (New York: Ballantine, 1964), 126-130.
12. For further reading see J. R. Heiman, L. LoPiccolo, and F. LoPiccolo, "The Treatment of Sexual Dysfunction," in *Handbook of Family Therapy*, eds. Alan S. Gurman and David P. Kniskern (New York: Brunner/Mazel, 1981), 592-627; Frederick G. Humphrey, *Marital Therapy* (Englewood Cliffs, N.J.:Prentice-Hall, 1983); Gerd Arentewicz and Gunter Schmidt, eds., *The Treatment of Sexual Disorders: Concepts and Techniques of Couple Therapy* (New York: Basic Books, 1983).
13. Oden, 11, 12.
14. Cited by Patrick J. Buchanan and J. Gordon Muir, "Gay Times and Diseases," *The American Spectator*, August 1984, 15-18.
15. Banowsky, 79.
16. Oden, 31, 32.
17. Michael S. Serrill, "A Scourge Spreads Panic," *Time*, 28 October 1985, 50.
18. Jean Seligmann, "A Scourge Spreads Panic," *Newsweek*, 4 February 1985, 72, 73.
19. Matt Clark with Mariana Gosnell, and Deborah Witherspoon in New York, Mary Hager in Washington, and Vincent Coppola in Atlanta, "AIDS," *Newsweek*, 12 August 1985, 27.
20. Excerpts from written testimony of Dibri L. Beavers, "Swinging within the Realm of Pornography," presented to the U.S. Attorney General's Commission on Pornography in Los Angeles, California, on 17 October 1985.
21. Victor B. Cline, "Aggression Against Women: the Facilitating Effects of Media Violence and Erotica" (Paper delivered at a meeting of the Associated Students of the University of Utah, Salt Lake City, 8 April 1983), 23.
22. Banowsky, 50.

CHAPTER THREE
Should Christians Push Their Views on Others?

Stephen Monsma

"You can't legislate morality." Some believe that to be an axiom in a pluralistic society. But don't we do it all the time? We have laws that punish burglars, restrict the drinking age, and prohibit child abuse. All of these laws have very real moral meaning.

Yet very few would support laws requiring church attendance or punish adults engaging in premarital sex. Such laws would also have moral meaning. Why would most people support the former and oppose the latter?

When we answer this question, we can decide whether laws against pornography ought to be enacted, and how strenuous they should be. Then we can address another important question. To what extent should Christians try to eliminate the milder forms of pornography that the laws don't prohibit, by using the economic pressures of consumer boycotts and picketing?

The Issue

The pornographers, and the attorneys who defend them in court, usually make the following argument. They say we live in a pluralistic society. Our religious faiths and our personal life-styles differ greatly. What is acceptable behavior to one, shocks another. What is a deeply held belief to one, is foolishness to another. Nowhere, so the argument goes, is this more true than in pornography. One person's pornography is another person's healthy lack of inhibition. The only way everyone's freedom is protected is if all are free to take part in, produce, or purchase what some—maybe even most—would consider pornographic and obscene, just so no one is forced to do so. All persons must be free to pursue their own standards of right or wrong without another defining those standards for them. The American Civil Liberties Union articulated this position in a policy statement put out in 1963, when the modern pornography debate was just starting:

What may strike one man as pornographic may be a matter of complete indifference to another. What may be offensive to one person may be great art to another person. And frequently such individual judgments condemn most severely only controversial expression—the very kind of speech for whose protection the First Amendment was written. . . .

We do not say that every book or publication carries ideas of importance to the community, but we do believe that very act of deciding what should be barred carries with it danger to the community. Because of the special need in a free society to guard against the stifling effect of censorship, no ban should be placed on allegedly obscene material, even though much material may be intensely disliked by many persons.[1]

This approach to questions of law and morality can be traced back to the influential thinker John Stuart Mill

(1806-1873), who said there are only two conditions under which freedoms could be limited:

The only purpose for which power can be rightfully exercised over any members of a civilized community, against his will, is to prevent harm to others. His own good, either physical or moral, is not a sufficient warrant. . . . We are not speaking of children or of young persons below the age which the law may fix as that of manhood or womanhood. Those who are still in a state to require being taken care of by others, must be protected against their own actions as well as against external injury.[2]

Freedom—including the freedom to produce or indulge in pornography—should only be limited in order to prevent harm to others or, in the case of minors, to prevent harm to themselves.

We better not dismiss this argument too quickly. Freedom of expression also includes the freedom to worship God as we choose, to witness freely to our faith, and to challenge the wrongs we see in our society. The long, sad history of religious persecutions and the stifling of dissent (still seen in many countries today) is so great that no one must, without careful thought, argue that government should prevent pornographers from expressing their views.

Government and a Just Order

Two points are crucial in considering the role of government in society. First, God has instituted government, or the state, and given it rule or authority in society. The rulers and kings of ancient Israel are clearly presented in the Old Testament as ''the Lord's anointed.'' (See, for example, Exodus 18:25, 26, 1 Samuel 24:6, and 2 Kings 9:3.) When Jesus stood before the Roman governor, Pontius

Pilate, he was asked, "Do you refuse to speak to me? . . . Don't you realize I have power either to free you or to crucify you?" Jesus replied, "You would have no power over me if it were not given to you from above" (John 19:10, 11, NIV). Romans 13:1 states, "There is no authority except that which God has established" (NIV). Thus the state is acting in keeping with God's will when it exercises rule in society, when it prescribes some actions and encourages others.

The more difficult question is this: How much authority does the state have, and what are the standards for exercising it? Clearly there is an appropriate and an inappropriate use of political authority. How does one tell the difference?

The promotion of a just order is the purpose for which God has instituted the state. Moses, in speaking to the Israelites before they took possession of Canaan, made this clear when he gave the following instructions to the judges who were to rule in the towns the Israelites were about to possess: "They shall judge the people fairly. Do not pervert justice or show partiality. Do not accept a bribe, for a bribe blinds the eyes of the wise and twists the words of the righteous. Follow justice and justice alone . . ." (Deut. 16:18-20, NIV). Throughout the Bible there are many references to civil government promoting justice, order, and righteousness, and opposing injustice, oppression, and wrong-doing. (See, for example, Psalm 72:1-4, Isaiah 10:1-2, Amos 5:12, Romans 13:3-4, and 1 Peter 2:14.)

But what does this mean today in a Western democracy such as the United States? These biblical references could be interpreted so as to lead to a government which stresses order and righteousness to the point that it becomes an ever-present religious busybody, such as some Muslim states. Or the references could be interpreted so as to lead to a government which makes freedom absolute, thus turning it into license which eats away at the very bonds that hold society together.

The classical definition of justice, stretching back to St. Augustine in the fifth century, is giving all persons their due. Or, as political scientist Bernard Zylstra has put it, "Justice requires a social order in which people can express themselves as God's imagers."[3] The idea here is that, as God's image-bearers, human beings have certain rights which are their due: the right to life, to physical security, to freedom of religion, and more. Government's God-given role of creating a just order thereby means working toward a society in which persons have the freedom, opportunity, and environment in which they can be (without being forced to be) all that God intends them to be as his image-bearers.

This is different than saying government should impose Christian morality onto all persons in a society. Just because a Christian believes it is against God's will to engage in the production, dissemination, and reading or viewing of pornography, that is not enough *in and by itself* to advocate the use of government's authority to ban pornography. If this were so, then governmental authority should also be used to require church attendance, daily prayer, tithing, and other acts of morality; and it should be used to put persons in jail for premarital sex, gossiping, and a host of other sins. I know of no Christian who advocates writing all of God's moral law into our civil and criminal codes. The case for outlawing or restricting pornography must rest upon the position that pornography tends to break down a just order in society—not simply because it runs counter to Christian morality.

Pornography and a Just Order

Pornography is a commercial activity involving many people: the actors, the producers, the distributors, and the consumers. It is much more than a personal act, confined to the privacy of home.

In contrast, think for a moment of sexual practices engaged in by an individual, or by two or three or more persons at home. These may be inappropriate by Christian moral standards—and perhaps even grossly objectionable and corrupt. But if they are essentially private, not flaunted in public, even those most deeply concerned about pornography do not usually attack them.

Although pornography is social in that it involves a network of people, its effect on society is negative. In that sense it is profoundly antisocial. It tears away at the bonds that hold a society together. Societies are clearly made healthy by a sense of trust and respect, which recognizes a shared worth or value in all persons. We can live together and engage in mutually beneficial commercial, artistic, recreational, political, and other activities because we respect each other's rights. A sense of civility enables us to work, play, and live together in families, neighborhoods, and nations, instead of living in a jungle where everyone preys upon everyone else, brute force is the only law, and narrow self-interest the only guide for conduct. Mutual respect can rest upon non-Christian beliefs, but surely Christians recognize that their belief in human beings created as God's image-bearers translates into mutual respect and a recognizing of other persons' rights.

Yet pornography rejects any concept of respect for others. Human beings are to be manipulated for one's own pleasure, no matter how degrading it may be to them. Human relationships of trust and respect are replaced by relationships of exploitation.

This fact can be especially seen in the strong antiwoman nature of most pornography and in the willingness of the pornography industry to exploit children. At best, women are pictured as sexual objects existing for the pleasure of men and at worst as objects of male sexual violence.[4] Much pornography, especially that which has been labeled hardcore, centers around themes of women enslaved and chained, subjected to violence and sexual brutality—all the while enjoying it. Children who are coerced or pressured into abusive sexual practices for the pornographer's camera are deeply harmed, and those who purchase and enjoy the material have a potential for seeking to live out their fantasies to the severe injury of other children. If all human relationships were marked by these types of exploitation, society and human civilization would cease to exist.

What is true of pornography in relationship to women and children applies more generally in regard to its treatment of people and human relationships. It does not rest upon trust and mutual help, delight, and respect. This makes pornography strongly antifamily. The husband-wife and the parent-child relationships are both made possible by love, respect, and a seeking of each other's welfare. Pornography is a cruel and violent caricature of human sexuality and families. Exploitation and dehumanization replace love and respect. The evidence is mounting, even from secular researchers, that stable families are crucial for a healthy society. Yet pornography is based on a wholly different, antifamily sense of values.

In short, the values and relationships on which pornography rest are profoundly antisocial. They tend to break down society and the social order.

My argument is now nearly complete. Pornography is (1) a social activity involving human relationships, and (2) as such, it is an antisocial force that destroys the human relationships on which society rests. Thus it works against a just order in society. As we saw earlier, justice is a matter of giving all persons their due, of recognizing that all persons have certain rights as image-bearers of God and then respecting those rights so that persons can be all that God intends for them to be. We also saw earlier that God has instituted governmental authorities in order to promote a just order in society and to oppose those forces in society which would destroy a just order. The conclusion is clear: Government has the right—even the duty—to protect a just order by suppressing pornography. In so doing it protects that just order as fully as it does when it outlaws racial discrimination in housing, fights crime, forbids false and misleading advertising, enforces legally binding contracts, and more.

Nonsense Damned by God

But this does not yet answer all questions or silence all objections. We must specify more clearly what is meant by "suppressing pornography."

One objection frequently raised is that pornography has no proven effect on human behavior. This position says, in effect, that producing or selling pornography, when it is made a crime, is a "victimless" crime. There is no victim, since there is no causal link between pornography and such crimes as rape, murder, spouse abuse, or child molestation and incest.[5] Thus, suppressing pornography does not "prevent harm to others" (in the words of John Stuart Mill), and there is then no legitimate basis on which to suppress it in a free society.

Part of my response to this objection is that there is mounting evidence, as documented elsewhere in this book, that there is indeed a link between heavy involvement with pornography and specific crimes with victims who are all too real. But even if such direct links could not be demonstrated, I would still argue that society itself is the victim. To argue that persons can take part in the degrading, sordid, exploitative business of posing for, producing, and selling pornography, or can avidly fill their minds with descriptions and scenes of fellow human beings as nothing more than objects of lust or hate and torture, and not be affected is damned nonsense. I use the word "damn"—as C. S. Lewis once did in his writings—thoughtfully and with a sense of awe. Such a belief is both nonsense and damned in the sight of a holy, pure God. One who says pornography has no effect on persons in spite of repeated involvements would, if they are to be consistent, have to argue that good literature and ennobling art also have no effect. In fact, to make the argument that pornography has no effect is to deny any environmental influence on human beings. No reputable psychologist or sociologist—Christian or otherwise—has argued that people's environments have *no* influence on their beliefs, fears, hopes, behavior, or personalities. To argue otherwise is nonsense—it flies in the face of common sense and scholarly research alike. And to argue that in general environmental influences on persons are real, but that there is one exception—pornography—is nonsense damned in the sight of almighty God.

To What Lengths Shall We Go?

What then should be the limits of governmental suppression of pornography? Is outright banning by all available legal means the only form of suppression government should engage in? Is *Playboy*, with its displays of bare breasts and pubic hair, to be treated the same as the chains, whips, and mutilated genitalia of hard-core pornography? Is child pornography to be treated the same as pornography involving only adults? Clearly there are distinctions in pornography. In addition, governmental actions can vary from total and complete banning to limiting and discouraging access. Besides that, Christians can use economic pressures and unfavorable publicity to eliminate or suppress pornography through such actions as picketing or organizing consumer boycotts of stores that sell pornography. One ought not to ignore these latter steps, since most of the nation's major newspapers have stopped running graphic ads for X-rated movies, some stores have stopped selling so-called "adult" magazines, and X-rated movie theaters have been kept out of neighborhoods by a variety of public pressures without recourse to legal, political authority.

There are no easy, absolute answers to these questions. Government should not use the full legal force of law to totally ban the publication, sale, or possession of *Playboy*. Nor is a little polite picketing an adequate response to the opening of a movie house featuring sadism, child pornography, rape, and sodomy. It is important to note that there is a range of pornography, and a range of reactions to it. One should be made to fit the other. Even among equally sincere and concerned Christians there will sometimes be honest differences of opinion as to what is the proper response. There is no easy formula. But let me suggest three points.

First, all pornography—including so-called soft-porn—is an evil and can appropriately be opposed by Christians. Let no Christian be intimidated by the claim that we have no right to impose our morality onto all of society. Our opposition rests fundamentally in the antisocial nature of pornography. These antisocial tendencies may be less severe in soft-porn, but they are still there. In these cases persons are advised to limit themselves to organized boycotts or other such means of opposition, instead of turning to legally enforced prohibition. But I underscore the fact that action is certainly appropriate.

Second, in cases of blatant hard-core pornography, especially that of a violent nature or that involving children, Christians should seek to use the full force of law to stop it. Our Lord instituted government precisely to suppress destructive social evils, and we should not shirk from using that which God has given us.

Third, in cases that fall between soft-porn and the violent or degrading hard-core porn, Christians should make use of a variety of tools aimed at a variety of objectives, all tailored to specific situations they face. No absolute rules can be set down. Prayerful consideration and a learning from one another will help show the way our Lord would have us go.

It is as we do so that, by God's grace and in his strength, the Christian community will have both the wisdom and the courage to oppose the social evil of pornography in ways that are appropriate and effective. It is as we do so that we strengthen the just order of the society in which he has placed us and are a witness to the truth he has entrusted to us. We need to move carefully and thoughtfully—but also persistently and boldly. In so doing we will be seeking justice, encouraging the oppressed, defending the cause of the fatherless, pleading the cause of the widow (Isa.1:17).

Notes

1. From Franklin S. Haiman, ed., *Freedom of Speech: Issues and Cases* (New York: Random House, 1965), 134.
2. John Stuart Mill, *On Liberty,* Currin V. Shields, ed. (Indianapolis, Bobbs-Merrill, 1965), 13.
3. Bernard Zylstra, "The Bible, Justice, and the State," in James W. Skillen, ed., *Confessing Christ and Doing Politics* (Washington, D.C.: Association for Public Justice Education Fund, 1982), 42.
4. See Kathleen Barry, *Female Sexual Slavery* (New York: Avon, 1981); Gloria Steinem, "Erotica and Pornography," *Ms.*, 7 (November 1978), 53, 54, 75-78; and John H. Court, *Pornography,* (Downers Grove, Ill: Inter-Varsity, 1980), 65-67.
5. See, for example, the argument made along these lines in the majority report of the 1970 Commission on Obscenity and Pornography, *Report of the Commission on Obscenity and Pornography* (New York: Bantam Books, 1970), 169-309.

CHAPTER FOUR
The View from the Supreme Court

David R. Leigh

Like many publishers of sleazy books and magazines in the 1950s, Samuel Roth's mail-order business had earned him, besides a lot of money, a few run-ins with the police. But when a New York City federal court convicted Roth on four counts of mailing obscene advertising and an obscene book, Roth decided he'd had enough. He appealed, on grounds that his right of free speech had been violated. He didn't know at the time that his appeal would make him a household name in the annals of constitutional law.

About the same time Roth was peddling porn in New York, David S. Alberts was busy running his own pornography operation a continent away in Los Angeles. Whereas most of Roth's materials were rather mild by today's standards, Alberts was into much rougher stuff—explicit, deviant sex. It wasn't long before he was hauled before a Beverly Hills city court judge, who found Alberts guilty of a misdemeanor—a minor crime. Like Roth, Alberts appealed, citing the First Amendment's guarantee of free speech.

By 1957 both cases had wound their way up through the appeals process until they reached the United States Supreme Court. There, the justices found serious questions of free speech and free press at stake. As they frequently do when similar cases confront them, the justices bound these cases together, and they called them both *Roth v. United States*. In one of the most important statements of constitutional principles ever to come from the high court, the justices, voting 5 to 4, upheld the convictions of Roth and Alberts.

The Non-Issue of Censorship

Writing the opinion for the Court's majority, Justice William Brennan said, "Although this is the first time the question has been squarely presented to the Court . . . expressions found in numerous opinions indicate that *this Court has always assumed that obscenity is not protected by the freedoms of speech and press*" (emphasis added).[1] Brennan noted that all fourteen of the states that ratified the Bill of Rights had laws making either blasphemy or profanity, or both, statutory crimes. Ten had laws restricting other types of speech. Tracing legal developments from colonial times up to his own, Brennan demonstrated that obscenity has never been considered a constitutional right.

But history was not the Court's only rationale. Brennan stated: "All ideas having even the slightest redeeming social importance—unorthodox ideas, controversial ideas, even ideas hateful to the prevailing climate of opinion— have the full protection of the [Constitutional] guarantees, unless excludable because they encroach upon the limited area of more important interests.'' Obscenity falls *outside* this category, the Court decided. It is not part of any exposition of ideas and is of such slight social value as a step to truth that it is clearly outweighed by the interest in order and morality. Therefore it is not protected by the Constitution.

On this basis then, the U.S. Supreme Court affirmed the convictions of Roth and Alberts. To this day, the Court's fundamental stance has not changed. Obscenity is not a constitutional right; therefore it is not a protected form of expression. There are many interests that want to see all restrictions against obscenity dropped—from the American Civil Liberties Union, to *Playboy* magazine, to the adult bookstore owner. But none of them have been able to respond to this central fact: Obscenity is not protected by the Constitution. That is why prosecutors who enforce properly drawn obscenity laws win convictions against pornographers.

About all the pornography trade can do against this clear constitutional principle is to invoke that particularly un-American word ''censorship.'' It has done this so long and so loud (and the cry has been picked up by a misinformed but sympathetic press), that many people actually believe that when government places limits on pornography, it is guilty of censorship.

Censorship means the suppressing of material *before* it is published. This is illegal and unconstitutional. Government does not censor even legally obscene material. It is allowed to be published, and *then* it is liable for punishment under the law. The censorship argument is a red herring.

What the Court Meant by "Obscene"

Although the Court's policy was established by *Roth*, questions about the definition of obscenity began to grow.
Unless the Court could agree on what it meant by obscenity, there would be no way to enforce obscenity laws. In the *Roth* case, Brennan tried to solve the problem. He defined a work as obscene when, to the average person applying contemporary standards, the dominant theme of the material taken as a whole appeals to prurient (lustful or lascivious) interest. The Court stated that *because* something was obscene, it *therefore* had no redeeming social importance and that is why it is not a protected freedom.

In a 1966 decision, *Memoirs v. Massachusetts*, the Court changed the order of things and caused confusion. In that decision, no redeeming social value became a *precondition* for finding something obscene. This was a complete reversal of Brennan's reasoning in *Roth*. Before, obscenity was banned because it had no social value. Now, social value became a criterion of obscenity. The social value criterion was one part of a three-part test for obscenity established by the *Memoirs* decision. The other two parts were these:

—The dominant theme of the material taken as a whole must appeal to prurient interest in sex. Prurient appeal was to be determined by its impact upon the average man or woman, not upon a child or extremely sensitive person. And it had to be the dominant theme which did this, not just a few pages or a section.
—The Court must find the material patently offensive according to contemporary community standards. Something is patently offensive if it is clearly indecent. The standards were to be those current in the community. Unfortunately, the Court did not define what it meant by "community." This would not be clarified until 1973.

New Questions for the Court

The "social value" issue as stipulated by the *Memoirs* decision caused the biggest stir. Between 1957 and 1973 obscenity trials became clogged with expert witnesses who purported to know whether the particular pornography in question had social value. Because of the uncertainty about what constituted social value, more and more pornographers were being acquitted. By 1973 the Supreme Court, its dockets filled with appeals over obscenity cases, found itself with what Justice John Marshall Harlan called an "intractable obscenity problem." Another important ruling by the high court was needed to clarify things, and it was not long in coming.

The *Miller* Test

Marvin Miller had intended to make his fortune by republishing out-of-print legal textbooks. But with profits flat, he began publishing pornography instead. He obtained a selection while on a trip to Paris, and he reprinted it without the authors' permission.

Success was soon singing in his ear, but before long, Miller found himself in court on charges filed by the Paris publisher from whom he had pirated. He went to court again on obscenity charges. He was convicted, but wasn't out of business. In fact, he grew innovative. He decided to introduce his pornography to Orange County by a mass mailing campaign. In five brochures, he advertised four books and a film. The book titles were *Intercourse, Man-Woman, Sex Orgies Illustrated,* and *An Illustrated History of Pornography.* The film was entitled *Marital Intercourse.*

The five pictorial brochures left little doubt about the explicit contents of the merchandise.

Imagine the surprise of a Newport Beach, California, restaurant manager and his mother when they opened their mail one morning and found Miller's brochures in an envelope, unsolicited. The couple complained to the police, charges were brought, and a jury found Miller guilty. Miller appealed, and his case began working its way up through the court system. By 1972 it was one of those jamming the dockets of the Supreme Court.

The Court agreed to rule on the Miller case and several others that posed similar First Amendment questions. On June 21, 1973, the Court handed down a stunning series of five-to-four rulings which reaffirmed the principle of *Roth:* obscenity is not protected by the Constitution. By far, the most important of these cases was that of *Miller v. California.*

Once again, as in *Roth-Memoirs,* the Supreme Court posed a three-part test for determining whether an utterance, or a depiction, is obscene. For a finding of obscenity, every part of the test must be passed.

First, the average person, applying contemporary community standards, must find that the work taken as a whole appeals to prurient interest. In a critical departure from *Roth,* the Court now explicity rejected a national standard of morality. Actually, in *Roth,* the Court had never subscribed to a national standard, but many persons believed only a national standard could make obscenity laws work. For instance, how could Hollywood make a movie for distribution across the nation if each community had a different standard of obscenity? Conversely, opponents asked, "Why should people in Maine be bound by the mores of people in Hollywood?'' The court settled the matter: Hollywood has the problem, but individual communities do not, if they choose to set their standards higher. They can determine for themselves what is acceptable. A movie, or a publication that violates those standards, is liable for a finding of obscenity.

(The following year, the Court's decision in a case entitled *Hamling v. United States* further clarified the meaning of community standards. In it, Justice William Rehnquist wrote that jurors are entitled to rely on their own knowledge to determine community standards. Each juror must judge ''neither on the basis of each juror's personal opinion nor by [the material's] effect on a particularly sensitive or insensitive person or group.''[3] Instead, each juror must draw on his knowledge of the standards of the *average* person in that community.)

The second part of the *Miller* test says that a court must find that the material depicts or describes in a patently offensive way sexual conduct specifically defined by the applicable state law. In other words, this part of the test limits obscenity laws to materials depicting explicit sexual conduct and sexual conduct that is *patently offensive*. This usually refers to what is commonly called ''hard-core'' pornography. In its decision, the Court gave some examples of what it meant:

''Patently offensive representations or descriptions of ultimate sexual acts, normal or perverted, actual or simulated. Patently offensive representations of or descriptions of masturbation, excretory functions, and lewd exhibition of the genitals.''

(Those who defend pornography often say that once *anything* is allowed to be censored, there will be no stopping

THE CAUSE FOR CONCERN

the censor. It will only be a matter of time before truly literary works will be banned as obscene. This argument is untrue. First of all, obscenity laws do not permit the censorship of *anything,* as we stated earlier. Secondly, any published matter which does not fit the above description is legal and *cannot* by law be found obscene. The Court has drawn very tight borders around the definition of obscenity.)

The third part of the *Miller* test says that the work, taken as a whole, must lack *serious literary, artistic, political, and scientific value.* If the work has any one of these, it is not obscene. Here the Court openly abandoned the criterion of social value that it declared in the *Roth-Memoirs* test, calling it "a burden virtually impossible to discharge under our criminal standards of proof." The Court believed this new standard was more concrete, and thus would be more effective.

The shift away from social value to serious literary, artistic, political, and scientific value, at first glance, would hardly seem to eliminate the need for "expert" testimony in obscenity trials. It would seem to broaden the category of experts who could testify about the worth of a publication. To some degree the attorneys for pornographers have done this. But the key word is "serious." It is far easier to show something has no *serious* value, than it is to show that something has *utterly* no social value at all, as *Roth-Memoirs* required. Furthermore, in two of the other cases handed down the same day as *Miller,* the Court clearly stated that no expert testimony is needed to show a work obscene, because this decision is strictly a community matter. In a footnote to one of those cases, *Paris Adult Theatre I v. Slayton,* Chief Justice Burger wrote: "This is not a subject that lends itself to the traditional use of expert testimony. Such testimony is usually admitted for the purpose of explaining to lay jurors what they otherwise could not understand. . . . No such assistance is needed by jurors in obscenity cases; indeed the 'expert witness' practices employed in these cases have often made a mockery out of the otherwise sound concept of expert testimony.''

Why then have ''experts'' continued to take the stand in many local obscenity cases? Because this decision does not *exclude* the possibility of presenting expert testimony. In the third of the cases handed down the same day as *Miller, Kaplan v. California*, Burger notes that while the Court rejects any constitutional need for expert testimony on behalf of the prosecution, even so, the defense should be free to introduce appropriate expert testimony. Nonetheless, a jury can find material obscene even if experts say it is not obscene and no experts say it is obscene.

While the *Miller* test was meant to make it easier to prosecute obscenity violations, it is not without its problems. Reactions to the ruling are still mixed, more than a decade after the decision. Because obscenity is also regulated by state laws, it is critical that states have laws that agree with the *Miller* guidelines. If they do not, local prosecutors will find it difficult to gain convictions and have them sustained on appeal.

Presently, forty-four states and the District of Columbia have laws complying with the *Miller* standards. (One of them is Oregon. A state court there held in 1986 that its law violates the state constitution. Some expect the state Supreme Court to reverse the decision and reinstate the law.)

Among those states that do not have state laws comporting with *Miller* are Maine, New Mexico, Vermont, and South Dakota. These states have laws protecting only minors from exposure to pornography, although several of them have local ordinances governing adult obscenity. Alaska has a child pornography statute. Wisconsin had a law that did not comport with *Miller,* but it was struck down in 1980 and not replaced, although there are efforts every year in the state legislature to pass a new law.

The 1986 Attorney General's Commission on Pornography concluded in its report that the *Miller* guidelines are enforceable at the local level. The problem is not with the law, the commission said; the problem is that local prosecutors must enforce it.

When state pornography laws are properly drawn and consistently enforced, great gains can be made. (Chapters 10 and 11 describe the success stories in Fort Wayne and Atlanta, the result of years of hard work by local prosecutors and citizens.)

While state laws can keep obscenity out of local communities, they can never stop it at its source. Federal law, which governs importing, interstate transportation, mailing, broadcasting and cablecasting, *can* stop the distribution of obscenity at its source. Retired FBI agent Homer Young, an expert in obscenity law violations, is among a number of people in the law enforcement community who believe that all obscenity could be eliminated soon if current federal laws simply were enforced. Alan Sears, a former assistant U.S. attorney who served as executive director of the attorney general's pornography commission, has reached the same conclusion (see chapter 15). The commission recommended that U.S. attorneys in the Justice Department start investigations without delay, because there have been relatively few.

The principles established in *Miller v. California* now stand as a settled question of constitutional law. But on that day in 1973, when the high court handed down that decision, it had much more to say on the matter of obscenity. Another important principle emerged in a case that had originated in an out-of-the-way pornographic outlet in Fulton County, Georgia, called the Paris Adult Theater.

The Question of Consenting Adults

The Paris Adult Theatres I and II shared a single, conventional, inoffensive entrance. The building front had no pictures, only signs advertising "Atlanta's Finest Mature Feature Films." A sign on the door said: "Adult Theatre— You must be 21 and able to prove it. If viewing a nude body offends you, Please Do Not Enter." There was no question that the owners did not want children or teenagers on the premises.

Inside, the films *Magic Mirror* and *It All Comes Out in the End,* with graphic scenes of group and oral sex, left little to the imagination, and in 1971 Fulton County Solicitor Hinson McAuliffe filed obscenity charges.

The trial judge acknowledged that obscenity was established by the prosecution, but he dismissed the case on grounds that adequate precaution had been made to protect minors. Therefore, he said the films were permissible under the Constitution. McAuliffe appealed the decision, and the case found its way to the U.S. Supreme Court.

Writing for the majority, Chief Justice Warren E. Burger established another critically important advance in the Court's thinking about obscenity. He said: "We categorically disapprove the theory . . . that obscene, pornographic films acquire constitutional immunity from state regulation simply because they are exhibited to consenting adults only.'' Burger went on to state: ''There are legitimate state interests at stake in stemming the tide of commercialized obscenity, even assuming it is feasible to enforce effective safeguards against exposure to juveniles and to passersby.'' Noting the Hill-Link Minority Report of the Commission on Obscenity and Pornography (1970), Burger asserted, ''There is at least an arguable correlation between obscene material and crime,'' and, ''although most pornography may be bought by elders, the heavy users and most highly exposed people to pornography are adolescents.''[4]

Burger said further that the obscenity question ''concerns the tone of society . . . the style and quality of life.'' A person has a right to read an obscene book in the privacy of his own home, or ''expose himself indecently there,'' and ''we should protect his privacy. But if he demands a right to obtain the book and pictures he wants in the market, and to foregather in public places—discreet, if you will, but accessible to all—with others who share his tastes, *then to grant him his right is to affect the world about the rest of us, and to impinge on other privacies*'' (emphasis Burger's). Burger declared the ''right of the nation and the states to maintain a decent society.''

Obscenity without Pictures

The third key decision handed down by the Supreme Court on that June day in 1973 originated four years earlier, on May 14, 1969, when Sergeant Donald D. Shaidell, a Los Angeles detective, entered the Peek-A-Boo Bookstore. Shaidell was responding to a complaint that the store sold obscenity. (There were some 250 pornographic outlets in Los Angeles at the time.) Inside the store, Shaidell found the walls lined with pornographic magazines and books. A glass counter displayed artificial sex devices.

After Shaidell perused several paperback books and magazines the store owner, Murray Kaplan, said, "This is not a library. Can I help you?"

Shaidell said, "Yeah. Do you have any good sexy books?" At this, Kaplan opened up a magazine for Shaidell, saying, "All our books are sexy." Kaplan continued to display magazines and books, even reading aloud from a paperback. At Kaplan's suggestion, Shaidell purchased it. It was titled *Suite 69*, and on the basis of this sale, a jury found Kaplan guilty of a California misdemeanor.

Suite 69 was a pictureless paperback book, made up entirely of what Chief Justice Burger would later call "repetitive descriptions of physical, sexual conduct, 'clinically' explicit and offensive to the point of being nauseous; there is only the most tenuous 'plot.' Almost every conceivable variety of sexual contact, homosexual and heterosexual, is described. Whether one samples every fifth, tenth, or twentieth page . . . the content is unvarying."[5]

At the trial, both sides presented expert testimony, but when the entire book was read to the Court, the jury found the defendant guilty. (Remember, the Supreme Court views the evidence itself as more compelling than any expert testimony.) The case was appealed, eventually to the Supreme Court. In ruling on *Kaplan v. California* the high court upheld the jury's decision and found *Suite 69* obscene, even though it contained no pictures. This was another important brick in the foundation of obscenity law.

In the opinion of the Court, Burger wrote: "When the court declared that obscenity is not a form of expression protected by the First Amendment, no distinction was made as to the medium of expression."

A book, Burger said, "seems to have a different and pre-ferred place in our hierarchy of values, and so it should be. But this generalization, like so many, is qualified by the book's content. As with pictures, films, paintings, draw-ings, and engravings, both oral utterance and the printed word have First Amendment protection until they collide with the long settled position of this court that obscenity is not protected by the Constitution."

Obscenity and the Court since 1973

In the years since the landmark rulings of 1973, the Supreme Court has continued to uphold and clarify the principles of those cases. It has consistently maintained that the determining factor in obscenity is, within the sharp boundaries of the *Miller* test, local community standards.[6]

In three notable cases since 1973, the Court permitted regulation of certain forms of expression even when its con-tent had not been found obscene.

The first of these cases was that of the *FCC v. Pacifica Foundation* (1978). When the Federal Communications Commission determined that a radio station violated federal law by broadcasting indecent language, the Supreme Court ruled that the FCC has the power to do so, even though the content is not technically obscene. The Court defined "indecent" as "nonconformance with accepted standards of morality."

The second case was *New York v. Ferber* (1982). In this case, the Supreme Court took a tough stance against child pornography, giving the states greater leeway in regulating pornographic depictions of children.

This case arose when Paul Ferber, the owner of a Man-hattan adult bookstore, sold to an undercover police officer two films devoted almost entirely to scenes of young boys masturbating. A jury found Ferber guilty on two counts of promoting a sexual performance by a child under sixteen years of age, a felony under New York law. While the maximum punishment for this is seven years, Ferber's sentence was only forty-five days. The New York statute did not require proof that the films were obscene, and at the trial itself the jury found Ferber innocent of charges that he promoted obscene sexual performance. On appeal, the Supreme Court said the states have a right to stricter regulation when child pornography is in question.

The Court ruled that not only can the states legislate against depictions of children engaged in sexual activity, regardless of whether the depictions are obscene, but that the states may also forbid "the distribution of material [of this nature] with serious literary, scientific, or educational value."

The Court, in *Ferber*, gave five reasons for its strong stance against child pornography:

1. The use of children as subjects of pornographic material is harmful to the physiological, emotional, and mental health of the child.

2. The *Miller* test is not a satisfactory solution when children are the subjects of pornography, because in these cases the issue is one of abuse and exploitation of the child actors as well as an issue of pornography.

3. Advertising and selling child pornography provides an economic incentive for more child pornography, and thus ensures more child abuse.

4. The value of this kind of pornography is "exceedingly modest, if not *de minimis*," and thus the chances of it having serious literary value are remote.

5. Because of its ill effects on the children engaged in

74141

the production of this material, this form of expression "heavily and pervasively" conflicts with their welfare. The Court declared: "The balance of competing interests is clearly struck" and child pornography is therefore "outside the protection of the First Amendment" and "outside the compass of the phrase 'freedom of speech.'"

The *Ferber* decision opened the way for easier prosecution of child pornography cases, because material no longer had to be found obscene before a conviction could be obtained. This important ruling has greatly diminished the flow of commerical child pornography in the United States, although some still enters by mail from foreign countries. Most child pornography now produced domestically is homemade material traded by child molesters for their own use.

The third notable decision handed down by the Supreme Court was that of *Renton v. Playtime Theatres, Inc.* (1986). Renton, Washington, has a city ordinance prohibiting adult motion picture theaters from locating within 1,000 feet of any residential zone, single- or multiple-family dwelling, church, park, or school. That ordinance was challenged by Playtime Theatres, Inc., and Sea-First Properties, Inc., which purchased two theaters in Renton for showing pornographic films. When they bought the properties, they filed suit in federal court, saying the ordinance violated their constitutional rights.

The case eventually reached the Supreme Court, which ruled in favor of the City of Renton, even though there was no court judgment that the films shown in the theaters were obscene. Justice William Rehnquist, in the opinion of the court, gave four reasons why the Renton ordinance is constitutional:

1. The ordinance is "content-neutral" in that its regulation of time, place, and manner is designed to serve government interest without banning adult theaters altogether or unreasonably limiting alternative avenues of communication.

2. The city's "predominant" concerns were with the secondary effects of adult theaters on the surrounding community, not with the content of adult films. Rehnquist said this finding alone is enough to establish that the city's zoning interest was unrelated to suppression of free speech.

3. The ordinance is designed to serve a substantial governmental interest, namely, preserving the quality of urban life.

4. The two companies have reasonable alternative sites outside the restricted area in which to try to establish their businesses.[7]

These last two Supreme Court decisions, *Ferber* and *Renton*, are especially significant in that they take the emphasis away from the *definition* of obscenity and place it on the *effect* of pornography. The *Renton* decision in particular ignores the question of content and affirms the community's right to regulate its flow, because of its effect on the community. Only time will tell the full implication of these newer cases.

Conclusion

It is amazing, given this history of Supreme Court thinking, that ACLU attorneys and others who know the law continue to maintain that the First Amendment rights of pornographers are in violation. From *Roth* in 1957 to the present day, the Supreme Court has consistently asserted that obscenity is not now and has never been protected speech. Given the sometimes aggressive stance of the Court, we must also wonder why prosecutors and the lower courts have not been more effective in using the laws available to them.

Martin Luther once said that if given the choice between a good king with bad laws and an evil king with good laws, he would opt for the good king with bad laws. For a good king, he reasoned, would find ways of using bad laws for good. But a bad king would find a way to corrupt society even through good laws. If we as Americans who are governed by the people, have good laws, what excuse can we have for the corruption that pornography spreads?

Obscenity is not a constitutional right. The Supreme Court has affirmed this over and over. It is up to the people who govern this nation to see that good laws are enforced.

Notes

1. *Roth v. U.S.*, 354 U.S. 476 (1957).
2. Personal communication with Homer Young.
3. *Hamling v. U.S.*, 418 U.S. 87 (1974).
4. *Paris Adult Theatre I v. Slayton*, 413 U.S. 49 (1973).
5. *Kaplan v. California*, 413 U.S. 155 (1973).
6. See for example *Hamling v. U.S.*, 418 U.S. 87 (1974), *Jenkins v. Georgia*, 418 U.S. 153 (1974), *Smith v. U.S.*, 431 U.S. 291 (1977), and *Pinkus v. U.S.*, 436 U.S. 293 (1978).
7. *Renton v. Playtime Theatres, Inc.*, U.S.——, 89 L. Ed. 2d 29 (1986).

CHAPTER FIVE
Pornography and Public Health

C. Everett Koop

In an ideal world, we shouldn't have that much to say about pornography. There ought not to be enough going on in this subject to fill a chapter, let alone a book. But unfortunately there is, and each one of us—each day—is faced with troubling questions about the presence of pornography in our communal life, in the media, and in the flow of daily commerce: Why does it persist? To whom does it really appeal? What are its true effects? Is it a symptom, or is it a cause?

Pornography is a complex issue in which law, education, public health, and civil order are all delicately intertwined. As a result, the social scientist or the attorney addressing the issue can become very discouraged. It is not only complicated but sometimes thankless work. Nevertheless, we know it's work that has to be done, because—whether by intuition or by the scientific method—we perceive that pornography is a destructive phenomenon. We understand that it does not contribute anything to society but, rather, takes away from and diminishes what we regard as socially good.

Certainly one of the most difficult aspects of our concern with pornography was expressed by Attorney General Edwin Meese. The occasion was his appointment of eleven citizens to the Attorney General's Commission on Pornography. At that time, the attorney general said, "It is abundantly clear that with pornography we are not dealing with one passing incident—one magazine, one play, or one film. We are dealing with a general tendency that is pervading our entire culture—including the culture known to very young children."

That's an important observation. In the past, we've been concerned almost exclusively with the bookstores and the movie theaters that have specialized in pornography. But it's no longer quite that simple.

The hucksters of pornography have invaded cable television, the popular music world, and the whole new field of home video recorders. To them these are new opportunities to expand their markets of sleaze and trash. But to us they are new and complex challenges in the public's battle against pornography.

I want to share with you my concerns about the effects of pornography upon American public health, but I do so with a keen sense of caution.

First, the field of public health is firmly rooted in the sciences, but thus far the literature regarding pornography is still relatively slim. Second, we Americans are very quick to "medicalize" all our worst social problems. As a result, public health planners have been handed such issues as divorce, drunk driving, and teenage pregnancy and they've been asked to "do something" about them.

I think public health people are doing the best they can, even though the problems are not particularly—or even peculiarly—medical problems. Real solutions to those social problems can be generated only when all the different interest groups of society—along with public health— share a sense of proprietorship for those problems.

The Hazard to Public Health

With that caveat, let me say that I believe we have enough evidence to implicate pornography as a serious contributing factor to certain disorders of human health. And I feel strongly that pornography has also been clearly implicated as a kind of "accessory" to antisocial actions that produce grave and profoundly harmful outcomes.

In the past it may have been possible to ignore this evidence or, at the very least, to assign it a low priority in the scheme of public health concerns. But at this stage of our understanding, to ignore the evidence would be to make a conscious decision *not* to see pornography as a clear symptom of stress and disorder. We simply can't do that today.

Pornography seems to have what I would call a "persistent presence" in the following four health areas:

First, there is the field of sexual dysfunction. Pornography intervenes in normal sexual relationships and alters them in some way. It seems to provoke a dysfunctional response among certain people. I think we need to know how prevalent this is and how it works.

Second, one of the more disturbing pieces of information from our National Center for Health Statistics is the rising rate of suicide among young people. Recently, a number of these suicides were judged to have been unintentional, the results of certain autoerotic behaviors in which soft-core pornographic materials apparently played a significant role.

This bears as much investigation, it seems to me, as we invest in many other types of intentional and accidental suicides.

Third, many women are justifiably concerned about so-called "copy-cat" rapes. These are rapes that follow the pattern or "story line," if you will, of a rape shown in a pornographic magazine or dramatized on videotape. While we suspect that many rapists have relied on such displays beforehand, we don't really know how prevalent this is. We also don't know to what extent certain men actually require such instructions in order to commit this vicious crime of violence.

Finally, we need to look at the public health consequences of child pornography, which is a deeply disturbing element in this field. The effects upon individual children are profoundly harmful in physical, psychological, and emotional terms. We suspect that the child who survives being used in this way may never again be able to function in normal human relationships. Tragically, a number of children do not even survive.

Child pornography, once it is released, causes an additional round of profound harm to other innocent child victims, who are used by adults or older children in ways depicted in the pornographic materials.

Pornography is a highly complex area, cross-hatched with social theory, legal theory, and communications theory. But freedom is not paralysis. We act in a manner wholly consistent with our tradition of free inquiry if we search out these and other public health consequences of pornography. The scientific tradition in our society has been scrupulous about pursuing truth but never at the expense of any citizen's freedom or well-being. It is in the spirit of that tradition that I say this.

Four years ago I began to voice my concern over the level of violence in American society. I began somewhat tentatively, as I have here in these remarks about pornography, because our public health experience with violence was still new and evolving.

Nevertheless, I said then—and I'll repeat it now—that acts of assault, rape, marital rape, child abuse, child sexual abuse, and homicide are occurring in numbers far beyond what we might expect even in a big country like ours with its minority of clinically disturbed men and women.

Forcible rape, for example, is very high and increasing. It is now occurring at the reported rate of 165 victims for every 100,000 women. Rape, however, is a crime that is consistently underreported. But even 165 rapes per 100,000 women must be unacceptable in our society.

The outcomes of violence are catastrophic not just for its victims but for the country at large. Our medical and public health and social services people spend years in time and millions in dollars trying to piece together the bodies and the minds and the lives of victims of violence.

This has been my message for the past four years. I've delivered it to professional associations—pediatricians and family medicine practitioners. And I've delivered it to the media, in particular the leadership of the three major networks. Each time, the message has become clearer, and we began to see a sharper focus and direction for our efforts.

Finally I decided not to just talk about this problem but to *do* something about it. I decided to focus the attention of the office of the surgeon general on the problem of interpersonal violence in our country.

I said I thought it was time for people in medicine and public health to come up with what we can do to improve the diagnosis and treatment of victims and also to prevent violence from happening in the first place. To facilitate that, I convened the first Surgeon General's Workshop on Violence and Public Health.

We contacted nearly 150 leading physicians, nurses, psychologists, emergency medicine specialists, victim advocates, and many others who might contribute to such a workshop. The response rate was better than 90 percent. And from the notes that many sent, it seems clear that these colleagues in public health share a strong desire to help stop the violence and bloodshed that is corrupting our national and community life.

In other words, the professionals in medicine, nursing, public health, and social services are strong and willing allies of the general public in its effort to turn back the tides of violence. And I believe that, as the public shares its growing uneasiness about pornography, those same groups of professionals will again step forward, ready to help.

As your surgeon general, and as one who shares with you your deep concern about the effects of pornography on American life, I am approaching this new and complex issue with several points uppermost in my mind:

First, pornography is a problem with important ramifications for the public health. I believe we can recognize that fact without having "medicalized" an otherwise *non*medical social issue.

Second, there seem to be certain specific areas of mental health and social dysfunction to which pornography contributes or, at least, to which it seems to play a strong "accessory" role. These could be legitimate areas for further public health investigation and exploration.

Third, new media and new methods of distribution have provided pornographers with new opportunities to spread their loathsome message to an audience comprising a wider range of age, experience, and sensibility. This, in effect, intensifies the danger to the health and well-being of such vulnerable groups as children and young women.

And finally, I believe that health professionals today are demonstrating not only a greater interest in this kind of issue but also a greater willingness to become involved, without the fear of compromising the canons of free inquiry.

Elsewhere in this book there is much information and insight about pornography—what it is, what it does, and what *we* must do to fight it. It is a long agenda, but much more information must yet come from the field of health. It is essential that health professionals approach the issue of pornography with all the necessary scientific discipline, so that we may lay a strong foundation for future study and action. It is my hope that in the future there will be even more facts unearthed, facts bearing on the relationship between pornography and the physical and mental health of the American people.

I believe there *is* such a connection and I believe it will be more widely understood in the years ahead by the very people who have the greatest need to know: the men, women, and children of America.

Adapted from a speech at the Denver National Conference on Pornography in May 1985.

PART TWO

The New Scientific Research: How Pornography Hurts People

Is pornography harmful? This section describes in detail the most important studies that have sought to answer that question, and provides first-person testimony from persons who say they have been victimized by pornography. The writer is

David A. Scott, a psychotherapist practicing in Toronto, and an authority on social science studies dealing with pornography and harm.

CHAPTER SIX
How Pornography Changes Attitudes

David Alexander Scott

Is pornography harmful? Do people who delve deeply into it become addicts? Does it change men's attitudes about women and sex? Does it incite them to commit rape?

What does happen when normal, well-adjusted people digest a steady diet of X-rated movies? If there are harmful effects, are they permanent? Is there any reliable scientific evidence one way or another?

We are a people who hold scientific evidence in high regard. The 1970 Presidential Commission on Obscenity and Pornography concluded that pornography was harmless, and that it even had potential therapeutic value. It based this judgment on social science research, and thus lent the dignity of academia to what it had to say. When the experts told us in 1970 that pornography was harmless, the floodgates opened. Not only was there more pornography, but during the 1970s hard-core pornography became more sexually explicit, degrading, and violent. By the 1980s, it was shocking and unimaginable to the uninitiated. It is time to look at what the new research shows. But before we do, a word of caution: the social sciences are not as exact as we would like, for good reason. Pornography researchers, for example, want to know the effects of hard-core pornography on adolescents, who as a class see large amounts of it. What they should do as scientists is expose groups of adolescents to large doses and then study the effects. Ethically, however, they could never do this.

Scientists would also like to know precisely what part pornography plays in provoking sexual offenders to commit rape. The best way is to observe offenders who use pornography all the way through an act of rape, and analyze the process. But this kind of research is, of course, unthinkable.

So there are limits. These limits have allowed the defenders of pornography to insist that the research findings are faulty, incomplete, or even nonexistent.[1]

In the next two chapters, then, I have tried to lay out very clearly, and in some detail, the major findings of the most respected social scientists.

Despite its limitations, the best of the social science research has given us evidence that should gravely concern all Christians, and all others who hold traditional moral values. For the new scientific findings paint a clear and deeply disturbing picture.

The Findings from the Battlefront

Actually, many professional people who deal with pornography's victims feel there is already enough evidence to indict pornography as a public health menace. They believe that expensive, meticulous laboratory studies only prove the obvious. For years, these professionals—pastors, counselors, and psychologists—have been saying that the strong forms of pornography now on the market have terrible effects on their clients: distorted perceptions about what constitutes real-life, wholesome sex; ruined relationships with spouses and children (to say nothing of child and spouse abuse); rising guilt and plunging self-esteem. Many of these professionals testified about these sad developments during hearings held in 1985 and 1986 by the Attorney General's Commission on Pornography. Some of this testimony appears elsewhere in this book.

Against this kind of evidence, however, the representatives of the pornography industry try to defend themselves. They say: "So what? This isn't true evidence, just heart-rending anecdotes. The real evidence is what happens or doesn't happen to the millions of satisfied consumers. This is what is truly significant, because these are the vast majority. A few casualties are an acceptable price for preserving free speech."

For this reason, the results of the laboratory studies that follow are very important, for they involve precisely those "healthy" people who haven't been to see a professional counselor about a pornography problem.

Common Pornography and Ordinary People

The most systematic research by social psychologists on nonviolent forms of pornography has been undertaken by Dr. Dolf Zillmann at Indiana University, his colleague Dr. Jennings Bryant at the University of Houston, and their associate James Weaver at the University of Kentucky. The most widely known and quoted research on sexually violent films has been conducted by Dr. Edward Donnerstein at the University of Wisconsin. (He has since joined the faculty of the University of California.) Dr. Neil Malamuth at UCLA, and Malamuth's research associate Dr. James Check at York University in Canada have studied the question of whether men, after viewing pornography, report a greater likelihood of commiting rape or other forced sexual acts, if they could be assured they wouldn't be punished.

Zillmann, one of the most respected psychological researchers in the field, has been studying reactions to various forms of pornography for more than a decade. The results of his work were scrutinized carefully by the Attorney General's Commission on Pornography. Zillmann, as well as Donnerstein, Bryant, and Malamuth, participated on a special committee convened in the summer of 1986 to advise the Surgeon General of the United States on the effects of pornography (see chapter 16).

In 1984 Zillmann and Bryant researched the effects of a quite common variety of pornography, in which there is no violence or degradation. The people portrayed in this variety appear to be enjoying sex, either by themselves, in couples, or together in groups. This is the kind of sex frequently portrayed in commercially released X-rated films and videos (available in the corner video store), and in the pages of magazines such as *Playboy, Penthouse,* and *Hustler.* Depending on how explicit the material is, it could be legally obscene, but the important factor for Zillmann and Bryant was that the participants were not violent toward one another although much of it was degrading.

The first thing Zillmann needed to do was determine exactly what was going on in this kind of pornography. A student of his did a content analysis, and in Zillmann's words, the most common theme is this: "Strangers meet. They look each other over. They are overcome by sexual desire. He is ready to take. She is ready to be taken. . . .

"What then follows is really *the* theme of standard por- ꝏ nography: fellatio, cunnilingus, intercourse in all conceivable positions, including anal intercourse [at least in the newer pornographic movies, this is standard]. What one finds, in addition, is that in less than half of all these cases, 'one-on-one' heterosexual intercourse is depicted. More than half of all these cases feature a third party. Either that, or it is group sex that goes beyond a third party to fourth and fifth parties. That is standard." [2]

This, then, is the content of the most common variety of explicit pornography.

Next, Zillmann created controlled conditions of exposure to pornography. First he selected carefully screened, average male and female undergraduate students from the Universities of Massachusetts, Evansville (Indiana), and Houston. He also drew from the adult population of a midwestern city often used for marketing research because its values and tastes closely reflect those of the nation as a whole. (To preserve its research value, it is not usually named.) In all, he had sixty subjects for the experiment.

He divided them into groups, including a control group, and brought each group in once a week for six weeks. One group was shown six pornographic films per session, one group was shown three pornographic films and three innocuous films per session, and the last group was shown six innocuous films only per session.

A week after the films ended, the critical part of the experiment began. Zillmann brought his subjects back in. He showed them three more movies, and recorded their

FIGURE ONE
**The Effect of Three Types
of Pornography upon Heart Rate**

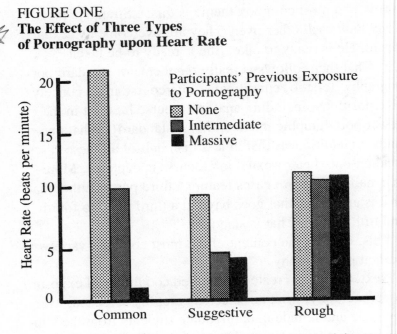

Nature of coital scenes in films shown to participants.

reactions by monitoring changes in their heart rates. One of the movies (see figure 1) portrayed relatively common pornographic scenes of oral and heterosexual intercourse. The second movie was "suggestive," in that all it showed was sensuous, but not graphic, intercourse (similar to an R-rated movie). The third was "rough," in that it showed rough sexual scenes. This included a woman fellating a dog (taking its penis into her mouth), flagellation, and a man urinating into the face of a woman.

The results surprised Zillmann. The graph in figure 1 shows that the group represented by the dotted bar had, in the earlier part of the experiment, no exposure to pornography (they had seen 36 innocuous films). The group represented by the solid bar had been massively exposed (36 pornographic films), and the group represented by the striped bar (in the middle) had seen 18 of each. The three groups of bars represent the three types of movies the subjects were shown.

Notice that the group which had no exposure to pornography during the six-week experiment was quite excited by the common coital scenes, but the group that had been massively exposed to pornographic films was no longer aroused by the common movie. The unexpected finding was that the group that had seen only pornographic movies (the group marked ''massive') for six weeks was greatly aroused by the rough pornography. This finding showed Zillmann that people who are bored by ordinary pornography develop an appetite for stronger, more bizarre versions. This is a highly significant finding. It has since been replicated by Dr. James Check at York University and by Dr. Gene Abel at Emory University in his studies of jailed sex offenders.

Zillmann took other measurements. He asked the subjects about their repulsion or enjoyment of each of the three movies they saw in the second part of the experiment. His questions led him right back to the same conclusion: ''Persons are suddenly dissatisfied with what they are so familiar with. There seems to be an indication that they are now ready to go for more. The usual is no longer good enough, and there has to be more. And this 'more,' of course, means bizarre sex or violent sex.''[3]

(Zillmann and Bryant confirmed this finding in a separate study with a separate group of people whom they had massively exposed to ordinary, nonviolent pornography. After the exposure, they provided the group with videos they could select and watch privately. The material ranged

FIGURE TWO
**How the Occurrence of Unusual
Sexual Practices in Films Is Perceived**

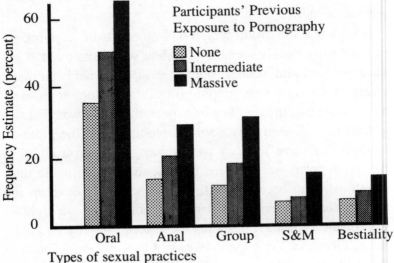

Types of sexual practices
in films shown to participants

from innocuous, sexual content to rough, bizarre forms of sex. The researchers secretly recorded which videos the subjects selected, and they found by a convincing margin the subjects preferred the bizarre sex. They found that it was true for women as well as men in the group.)

Two weeks after the experiment ended, Zillmann brought his subjects in once again. He showed them yet another round of movies, one with common, one with suggestive, and one with rough sex scenes in it. He took another round of measurements. He found that the effects were basically the same.

Three weeks after the experiment, he brought them in yet again, to see if their changed attitudes and preferences would still show up. They certainly did. Zillmann interviewed the subjects about how frequently they believed people engaged in unusual or bizarre forms of sex. You can see the results in figure 2.

The group that had been massively exposed to the pornographic films thought that each unusual sex practice listed in the chart was more commonly practiced than did the other two groups. (The unusual sex practices about which they were asked were: oral [including fellatio and cunnilingus], anal sex, group sex [orgies], sadomasochistic sex, and sex with animals [bestiality].)

These findings show clearly that the use of common pornography leads people to grosser forms, and that it changes their attitudes about these sex practices. Perhaps the most alarming findings were the responses to two other questions Zillmann asked the group three weeks after the original six-week experiment had ended.

The massively exposed group was far less concerned about the harmful effects of pornography on society than was the group that had seen no pornography during the experiment (see figure 3). The massively exposed group thought that pornography was less offensive and that there was less need to restrict minors' access to it and to restrict broadcasting of it.

Callousness toward Rape

Finally, Zillmann asked his group to undertake what he said was an investigation for the American Bar Association. The group learned the facts about a (fictitious) rape case, in which a jury had heard evidence and convicted the rapist. Zillmann's group was asked to decide an appropriate jail

FIGURE THREE
**How Pornography Influences Opinions
about Its Harmful Effects on Society**

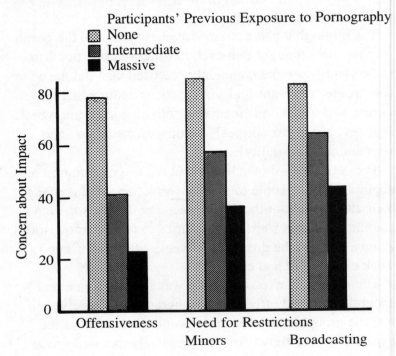

Participants' Previous Exposure to Pornography
None
Intermediate
Massive

term for the rapist. The results of these decisions are in figure 4.

The group which had been massively exposed to the pornographic films was decidedly more lenient than the other two groups. Of this finding, Zillmann said: "As you can see, men who had been massively exposed to pornography came to look at rape as reasonably trivial. In many cases they assigned the minimal term that was allowed under the circumstances. To many of them, rape was no longer a crime at all. Most of them, however, continued to judge it as a crime. But it was clearly a lesser crime. The thing that

FIGURE FOUR
**How Pornography Influences
Opinions about Rape Victims**

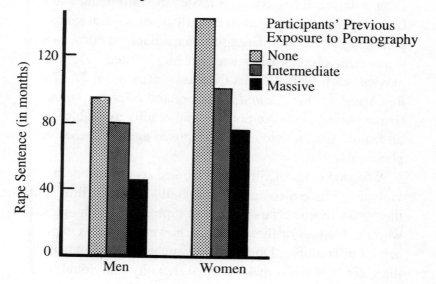

shocked us the most was that we found a similar effect among women. *Even women who had been massively exposed to standard pornography came to look upon rape as a trivial offense"* (emphasis Zillmann's).[4]

Zillmann's overall conclusion from this experiment was that "Whatever the specific contents of standard pornography, there can be no doubts that effects are created, and consistently so. There can be no doubt that pornography, as a form of primarily male entertainment, promotes the victimization of women in particular."[5]

How Violent Pornography Affects People

In 1984, at a symposium on pornography and media violence in Toronto, psychologist Edward Donnerstein of the

University of Wisconsin reported the preliminary findings of his three-year National Science Foundation project. Donnerstein and his associates, Steven Penrod and Daniel Linz, had been interested in the effects of several kinds of pornographic films, many of them available at corner video stores. One class of films was violent, R-rated "slasher" movies, such as *The Texas Chainsaw Massacre, The Tool Box Murders, Vice Squad, Maniac,* and *I Spit on Your Grave*. All of these are popular and readily available, and all feature graphic violence juxtaposed against scenes of pleasurable sex.

A second class of films was labeled by Donnerstein "X-violent." These also are commercially released films, but they carry more scenes of violent rape and assault against women. Neither of these classes, however, shows explicit acts of intercourse. Donnerstein wanted to know whether these kinds of films make normal, healthy individuals more tolerant of sexual violence.

A third class of films was nonviolent, X-rated, such as *Debbie Does Dallas*. These films do contain explicit acts of intercourse, cunnilingus, fellatio, and some anal sex, but they do not contain violence.

(Donnerstein's work is often quoted by the pornography industry in support of its contention that it is the violence in pornography and not the sexual explicitness that is harmful. It is important to note, however, that in his research, Donnerstein has never studied films in which extreme violence and explicit sexual penetration are shown together. This is what is generally known as violent, hard-core pornography. Therefore his research cannot be used to show that violent pornography is more harmful than nonviolent pornography.

In fact, Donnerstein did conduct one study in which he

compared the effects of sexually violent, R-rated films and nonviolent X-rated films. [The difference is that the first group of films is sexually violent but does not show explicit sexual penetration. The second group does show consenting, explicit penetration but without violence.] Donnerstein found that there was greater harm in the nonviolent material than in the violent. This contradicts statements that it is the violence and not the sex that is harmful.)

The Findings

In his research, Donnerstein carefully screened and selected a group of 156 male college students and divided them into smaller groups at random. He showed each group one of the feature-length films each day for five days. He juggled the sequence so that one group might see the R-rated film the first day of the experiment, and another group might see that film the last day.

Donnerstein found that different groups saw different things in the films, depending on the sequence in which they viewed the films. For example, the group that saw the R-rated film on the first day of the experiment reported seeing more scenes of violence than the group that saw that same film on the fifth day (see figure 5). The group that saw a film on day one also reported that the violence was more gory, more graphic, and that the movie had more overall violence, than the group that saw the same film at the end of the week. The point is that by the end of the week the group had become desensitized to violence.

He found other noticeable differences between the group that viewed the R-rated material on day one as opposed to day five. The day-five group found the violent film more

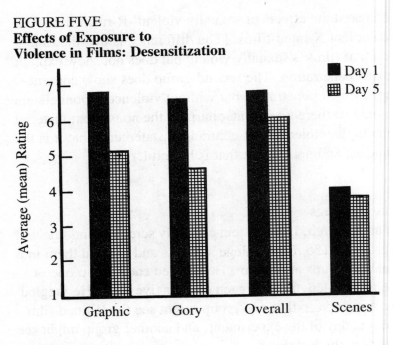

FIGURE FIVE
**Effects of Exposure to
Violence in Films: Desensitization**

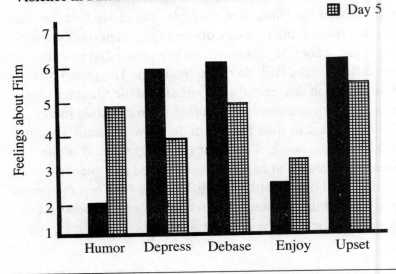

FIGURE SIX
**Effects of Exposure to
Violence in Films: Emotional Reactions**

FIGURE SEVEN
**Effects of Exposure to Violence in Films:
Perception of Violence toward Women**

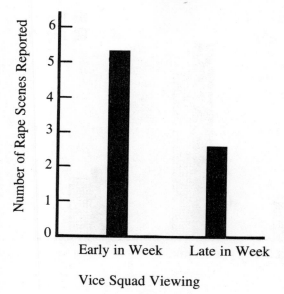

Vice Squad Viewing

humorous, less depressing, less debasing, more enjoyable, and less upsetting (see figure 6).

One of the R-rated films, *Vice Squad,* depicts a large number of brutal rape scenes. Subjects who saw that film at the end of the five-day experiment only remembered seeing about half the number of rapes as did the group which saw that same film the first day, before the group was desensitized to the violence (see figure 7).

Donnerstein found the same pattern when he asked his groups how degrading they thought the films were toward women (figure 8).

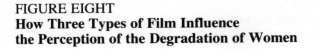

FIGURE EIGHT
**How Three Types of Film Influence
the Perception of the Degradation of Women**

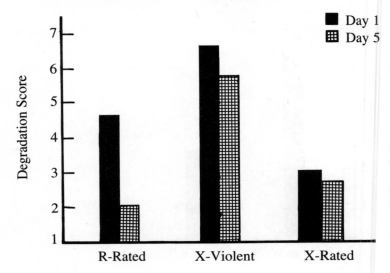

Note particularly the pair of bars on the left. The group that viewed an R-rated movie on day five saw less than half as much degradation toward women as did the group which saw it on day one. Remember, these R-rated movies are highly violent, but Donnerstein found that his subjects were just as sexually *aroused* by the films at the end of the experiment as they were at the beginning. What they were desensitized to was the *violence* and the *degradation* of women portrayed in the films.

After the experiment ended, the subjects were taken to the University of Wisconsin Law School. They were asked to view a one-and-one-half-hour reenactment of a rape trial

FIGURE NINE
How Violent and Por   **phic Film**
Influence Perceptions   **ape Victims**

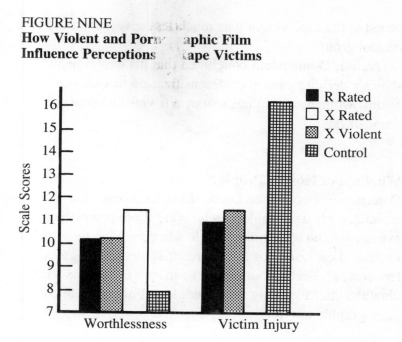

and then, acting as the jury, to evaluate what they saw. They were given questionnaires that asked the subjects about how much the woman suffered, the extent of her injuries, how much pain she experienced, and whether she was humiliated greatly during the rape.

A control group, which was not involved in the earlier movie-viewing experiment, also saw the same rape trial reenactment and also evaluated it.

Figure 9 shows the results.

Those who saw the different varieties of pornographic movies rated the rape victim as much more worthless than did the control group. They also perceived that what happened to the rape victim was much less severe than did the control group.

Overall, Donnerstein concluded that his experiment shows a definite pattern of desensitization to violence against women, and in particular, a trivialization of the crime of rape.

What about Hostile People?

Donnerstein's colleague Daniel Linz has completed research with sixty subjects who were more prone than the average person to become hostile when viewing these movies, based on results of test scores that measure aggressive tendencies.[6] Here, in summary form, are the results Linz obtained after exposing these people to only two violent pornographic movies:

—Less interest in love and affection as a motivation for sex.
—A greater tendency to fantasize about the use of force in sexual relations.
—Less positive evaluation of conventional sexual activities.
—Greater self-reported likelihood of participating in unconventional sexual activities such as rape and pedophilia.[7]

These subjects were exposed to fewer R-violent or X-violent movies for far shorter periods of time than the normal young adults that Donnerstein reported on. Nevertheless, they were affected more quickly, more intensely, and by far less exposure than normal subjects.

This research found that "viewing only *two* violent movies containing approximately twenty violent acts over a three-hour viewing period is sufficient exposure to obtain a desensitization effect previously only obtained after view-ing *five* of these films. Far faster desensitization to filmed violence occurred with these subjects than was previously thought possible.'' [8]

Linz stated: ''Experimental evidence suggests quite strongly that there is an identifiable, indeed quantifiable, harm arising from exposure to this material. The research conducted to date defines the specific type of material likely to incite aggression against women to be portrayals of rapes, or other forms of sexual assault which show the female victim becoming involuntarily sexually aroused, or otherwise responding positively to sexual aggression.'' [9]

He noted the specific effects of exposure to the material:

—Greater sexual arousal to subsequent depictions of sexual violence against women.
—A greater tendency to endorse deprecatory beliefs about women
  (e.g., women enjoy sexual violence, women are often responsible for their own rapes, etc.).
—A greater tendency [in a laboratory situation] to punish
  females.

Linz found that ''the probability is definitely increased (if only to a small extent) that an individual will be moti-vated to reenact what he has seen depicted in a film.'' This is what the Donnerstein researchers term ''an incitement effect.'' [10]

The research also suggests that violence against women need not occur in a sexually explicit context for the images to have an impact, and neither will the impact necessarily be immediate.

''This lesson is not easily forgotten,'' he wrote. ''It does not have to be acted upon immediately. The message may be retained and acted upon later."[11]

The brunt of Linz' research is simply that violent pornographic films are especially volatile material for people who are more prone to respond to aggressive images than average people. The implications of this research are clear.

It was this research by Zillmann and Donnerstein and their colleagues that helped the Attorney General's Commission on Pornography to conclude in 1986 that degrading pornography—both violent and nonviolent in form—is harmful.

The Harmful Effects of Nonviolent Pornography

In 1984, a Canadian researcher from York University, James Check, conducted an experiment in which he used 436 male subjects.[12] He divided them into groups, including a control group, and showed each group films depicting three kinds of sexual material: simple erotica (such as used in sex education programs); nonviolent, dehumanizing material (such as a man sitting atop a woman ejaculating into her face); and violent pornography (such as a man forcing an oversize plastic penis into a woman while she is strapped to a table). He wanted to see the effects of violent versus nonviolent forms of pornography.

What he found was startling. He performed the normal kinds of post-test evaluations. He discovered that the nonviolent pornography increased the likelihood that subjects would commit rape and other forced sexual acts to the very same extent that the violent pornography increased the tendency to commit rape and other forced sexual acts. This was significant in that while Zillmann had been studying nonviolent pornography, and Donnerstein had been specializing in the violence in some forms of pornography, Check directly compared the two in the same experiment. He found that nonviolent pornography has as many harmful implications as does violent pornography. Weaver, at the University of Kentucky, has replicated the Check findings, an important step in the substantiation of scientific research.

In commenting on the significance of Check's research, Zillmann had this to say: "The investigation by Check has obvious implications for public health. It shows that, on the whole, common, nonviolent pornography has the strongest influence on men's willingness to force intimate partners into forms of sexuality that are not necessarily to their partners' liking, and on the propensity to force sexual access. Violent pornography apparently has the same power to increase rape proclivity, although its influence on the coercion of specific sexual acts is limited if not negligible."[13]

Both Zillmann and Check believe that the future of pornography research will be centered in nonviolent pornography. This is because nonviolent pornography is growing ever more degrading as the industry seeks to titillate its jaded clientele. For example, a common theme in this kind of pornography is that of a man ejaculating and a woman pleasurably ingesting the sperm. While they are not violent, these acts are degrading, and the potential for lasting effects on the audience is a growing matter of concern.

And there are other problems with nonviolent pornography, even the milder versions. Generally, *Playboy, Penthouse,* and, to a lesser extent, *Hustler,* escape much of the criticism leveled at hard-core pornography. These three magazines are mass circulation periodicals, and depend on widespread newsstand sales. To remain acceptable, therefore, they must reign in the natural tendency to show their audience ever rougher material. Yet what they show by implication is troubling.

Judith Reisman, a researcher at American University, recently completed an exhaustive study in which she and her researchers analyzed the extent to which sex involving children was presented in every issue ever published of these three magazines between 1954 and 1984 (in all, 683 issues).[14]

She found that from the first issue of *Playboy* in 1954, children in cartoons (or photographs of adults dressed to suggest children) have appeared in sexual contact with adults, and the frequency and intensity of these contacts has increased through the years. Reisman concluded that the dominant impression was that child/adult sex is glamorous, thereby enhancing the impression that these activities are harmless. In all, her team counted 6,004 images linking children with sex, or an average of 8.2 times in each issue of *Playboy,* 6.4 times in each issue of *Penthouse,* and 14.1 times in each issue of *Hustler.* (This compares to 15,000 images of crime and violence, 35,000 female breasts, 3,000 genital and 9,000 gynecological images in these same magazines.)

What this means is that magazines can escape the letter of child pornography laws while still implying that sex with children is desirable and readily available. And these magazines, of course, are sold in the open.

The Effects of Pornography on Family Values
The results of Zillmann and Bryant's 1984 research into nonviolent, common pornography led them to clear conclu-

sions: Exposure to milder forms led people to tolerate it and desire more bizarre kinds. Heavy exposure to pornography also made the crime of rape seem more trivial, both for men and women.

They continued to wonder about pornography and its effects on people. The content analysis in their 1984 study had told them that common, nonviolent pornography focuses almost exclusively on chance encounters between strangers, who suddenly arouse themselves to heavy, immediate sex, but without kindness, and without enduring emotional relationships. Never, in pornography, is there a hint that sexual intercourse produces children, whose rearing requires commitment and financial sacrifice on the part of the parents.

"Essentially then," Zillmann and Bryant theorized, "pornography projects access to some of the greatest unmitigated pleasures known, without indicating any restriction in freedom. . . . Adoption of the values permeating pornography thus could undermine the values necessary to form enduring relationships in which sexuality, and, possibly, reproduction, are central."[15] Zillmann and Bryant set out to discover the effects of pornography on attitudes toward committed love, marriage, and raising children.

The Tragic Effect on Values

They established a research framework in which they would expose one group of subjects to one hour of pornographic films each week for six weeks, and another group (the control group) to the same number of innocuous films. They selected undergraduates from two universities, and adults who lived in a mid-size midwestern city. The city is often used for marketing research because its values and tastes closely reflect those of the nation as a whole. Equal numbers of men and women, students and nonstudents, were put into each of the two groups. The total number of participants was 160.

The subjects that were exposed to pornography saw six hours' worth of X-rated movies purchased in typical video stores. The sex in them included explicit scenes of fellatio, cunnilingus, coitus, anal intercourse, but no violence, homosexuality, or bestiality. The control group saw six hours of situation comedy taken from prime-time television programs.

To deflect attention from the true purpose of the study, the subjects filled out questionnaires after each session in which they were asked about technical aspects of the tapes, such as the quality of lighting, the use of sound effects, etc.

In the seventh week, the participants were told the film evaluations were over and a new experiment would begin, this one seeking their views on societal institutions. The institution their particular group would consider was marriage. They were given three questionnaires which asked them to rate their views on a variety of attitudes toward marriage and sexual practices. This, of course, was the purpose of the entire experiment.

Zillmann and Bryant discovered profound attitude differences between the group that had seen six pornographic videos and the group that had not. Here are some of the results:

1. The group exposed to the pornographic films believed that extramarital affairs occurred twice as often as the control group believed they occurred.

2. Members of the group exposed to pornography were

twice as likely to accept sexual infidelity in their own marriages or committed relationships as was the control group.

3. The exposed group was almost half as likely (38.8 percent) to view marriage as an essential institution as was the control group (60 percent).

4. The exposed group was much less likely to find sexual infidelity as grounds for breaking up a marriage or an intimate relationship as was the control group.

5. The exposed group was nearly half as desirous of raising children as the control group. The group particularly did not want daughters. (Women in the exposed group were much less likely to want daughters than were women in the control group.)

6. The exposed group accepted male dominance over females *twenty times* more than did the control group. (This applied to women as well as men, although women less so.)

In the conclusion to their study, Zillmann and Bryant had this to say: "The findings leave no doubt about the fact that repeated exposure to common, nonviolent pornography is capable of altering perceptions of and dispositions toward sexuality and relationships formed on its basis."

Exposure to pornography, they said, clearly makes people more likely to believe that:

—The greatest sexual joy comes without enduring commitment.
—Partners expect each other to be unfaithful.
—There are health risks in repressing sexual urges.
—Promiscuity is natural.
—Children are liabilities and handicaps.

One finding in particular surprised Zillmann and Bryant: "The diminished desire of female respondents to have female babies is surprising. This finding would seem to suggest that there is something in pornography that makes females appear undesirable in the eyes of females. Although it remains unclear exactly what aspect of pornography creates this effect, the findings can be considered supportive of the allegations of feminists that most pornography debases women."[16]

The researchers said that those who endorse a sexually open society may well embrace their findings, while those who believe enduring sexual relationships are critical for a well-functioning society will be alarmed.

"Our intention is not to take and support the one or the other value position. Rather, it is to demonstrate the impact of pornography consumption in hopes that those with strong value positions and ambitions to influence policies regarding the dissemination of pornography might take notice, ponder the questions, debate the issues, and come to resolutions that benefit the greatest number."[17]

Pornography and Sexual Happiness

Zillmann and Bryant were not finished yet. They wanted to find out what effect pornography might have on people's satisfaction with their own sex lives and their sexual partners. Given the fact that in pornographic films actors are unfailingly shown to be enthusiastic, orgiastic, athletic, and obviously delighted with their activities, people who view the films might become disenchanted with their own sexual partners and habits.

They conducted another carefully controlled experiment in 1986 similar to the one just described. They chose participants from the same university and city locations as before, and divided equal numbers of males, females, students, and nonstudents into two groups. One group was shown pornography for six weeks, the other was shown innocuous movies. As before, the subjects were examined by questionnaires.

Here is a summary of the findings:

—Exposure to pornography diminished satisfaction with the physical appearance of the respondent's sexual partner.
—It reduced satisfaction with the partner's affection, sexual behavior, and sexual curiosity and innovations.
—It reduced the overall satisfaction with the respondent's present intimate relationship.
—It enhanced the importance of sex without emotional involvement.[18]

The researchers found that the subjects' assessments of their personal happiness outside of the sexual realm were not influenced by the pornography. The impact of the films was limited to sexual attitudes.

They found, furthermore, that after viewing repeated pornographic films, sexual dissatisfaction increased just as much in women as in men, and for students as well as townspeople (who were on the whole older and presumably had more sexual experience). "The cliche that males are attracted to erotica and that only they might become disenchanted with the looks and sexual performance of their opposite-gender partners is apparently in need of correction," the researchers said. [19]

The studies of Zillmann, Bryant, and Weaver; Donnerstein and Linz; and Malamuth and Check, taken together, constitute valid "laboratory" evidence, closely controlled and scientifically sound, that pornography, nonviolent as well as violent, alters perceptions and influences the attitudes of people.

One might conclude that all of the foregoing was a lot of work and expense to prove the obvious. After all, if people who embrace Marx's works learn Marxist values, and people who embrace religious works learn religious values, shouldn't one assume that people who embrace pornography learn pornographic values? Yes, and more: The studies by Zillmann and Bryant show that subjects who are only exposed to repeated doses of pornography, whether or not they ever assent to its messages and values, have their attitudes shaped accordingly.

The next question is the relationship between attitudes and actions. If someone believes something, does he necessarily act on it? What part does pornography play in the incitement of violent behavior, such as rape and child molestation? The next chapter deals with that question.

Notes

1. Barry Lynn of the American Civil Liberties Union purports that no research exists showing the harmful effects of pornography. In the July 1986 issue of *Forum* magazine, he said, ". . . no data whatsover comes close to demonstrating that sexually explicit material directly or indirectly causes crime" (p. 16). He made a similar statement on the ABC-TV "Nightline" program aired 29 June 1986.
2. David Scott, ed., *Proceedings of the Symposium on Media Violence and Pornography,* (Toronto: Media Action Group), February 1984, 96.
3. Ibid., 105
4. Ibid., 111
5. Ibid., 115
6. Daniel G. Linz, *"Sexual Violence in the Media: Effects on Male Viewers and Implications for Society,"* Ph.D. diss. (University of Wisconsin at Madison), 1985, 38-41.
7. Ibid., 31
8. Ibid., 65
9. Ibid., 126
10. Ibid., 136

11. Ibid., 127

12. James Check, "The Effects of Violent and Nonviolent Pornography," (Ottawa: Department of Justice for Canada, Department of Supply and Services contract 05SV.19200-3-0899. Submitted June 1984), 1.

13. Dolf Zillmann, "Effects of Prolonged Consumption of Pornography," a paper prepared for the Surgeon General's Workshop on Pornography and Public Health, Arlington, Va., 22-24 June 1986, 25. See also Dolf Zillmann, "Shifting Appetites in Pornography Consumption," *Journal of Communication Research,* Summer 1986.

14. Judith Reisman, unpublished testimony before the Attorney General's Commission on Pornography, Miami, 21 November 1985.

15. Dolf Zillmann, and Jennings Bryant, "Effects of Pornography Consumption on Family Values," 1986, 7 (to be published in *Journal of Family and Marriage*).

16. Ibid., 32.

17. Ibid., 33.

18. Dolf Zillmann, and Jennings Bryant, "Pornography's Impact on Sexual Satisfaction," 1986, 15 (to be published in the *Journal of Applied Social Psychology*), 1986.

19. Ibid., 16.

CHAPTER SEVEN
Pornography and Violent Behavior

David Alexander Scott

In the spring of 1941, four crack German *Einsatzgruppen* batallions (mobile killing squads) containing 500 to 900 men each, fanned out across Eastern Europe systematically murdering Jews, gypsies, and political commissars in town after town. In a matter of months, fewer than 3,000 men killed more than one and a half million men, women, and children.[1]

Although many members of the *Einsatzgruppen* squads had been experienced killers before their transfer into the elite batallions, new recruits were able to kill with surprising ease as they became desensitized by the *Einsatzgruppen* experience.

As they drove into the Baltic States, White Russia, the Ukraine, the Crimea, and the Caucusus, the *Einsatzgruppen* commanders encountered no difficulty replenishing their ranks from among Ukrainian, Latvian, Lithuanian, and Estonian "collaborators." The victims' own countrymen became the killers.[2]

The elite squads were indoctrinated with the "necessity to exterminate subhumans threatening the life of the Reich." They were told, essentially, that murder was a civic duty.

In his study of mass executioners, one authority succinctly described the process: "Tentatively at first, then callously, and finally quite easily, they performed these terrible massacres."[3]

The transformation of the *Einsatzgruppen* recruits into callous killers has been continuously researched for four decades. The psychological processes that enabled these Europeans to kill their own countrymen are the same ones by which people perpetrate—and justify to themselves— horribly violent crimes today. They are of especially grave concern to forensic psychiatrists, who study how criminal gangs form, and how sexual perversion and addiction can drift into rape and murder.[4] More and more they are studying the role played by pornography, especially nonviolent pornography, in the processes that lead to those crimes.

One of the persistent arguments emanating from the pornography industry is that there is no proof that pornography is causally related to sexual crime. In other words, pornography may change attitudes, but no one can prove that anyone is actually harmed by it.

This much is conceded: There will never be a social science study that proves the link between pornography and rape until researchers employ actual rapes in their laboratory and field studies. There will never be a social science study that proves the causal link between pornography and child molestation unless researchers are permitted to conduct actual child molestations in their inquiries, and then analyze the process. These ideas, of course, are absurd, just as absurd as for the pornography industry to continue to deny the possibility of harm until the causal link is proved.

The significance of the *Einsatzgruppen* study is that it shows how people *have* perpetrated hideous crimes—more hideous than the crime of rape—when they have been able to perceive those crimes as socially acceptable, and when they can mentally accommodate those crimes through self-deceiving mechanisms.

In a prominent university textbook on social learning theory,[5] Stanford University psychologist Albert Bandura describes how people who are disposed to commit violent crimes, whether sex crimes or murder, justify their actions. He calls the process the "disinhibition of aggression."

First, they gradually become desensitized to a violent act by seeing it portrayed time and again. Bandura writes: "Graduated desensitization is a gradual change from compassion to aggression in which the participants may not fully recognize the change they have undergone. Discomfort and self-reproach are gradually extinguished by repeated performance. The level of aggression is progressively increased until eventually gruesome deeds, originally regarded as abhorrent, can be performed without much distress."

(Bandura adds that a similar process affects people who only observe the commission of violence: "Seeing victims suffer punitive treatment, for which the victims are held partially responsible, leads observers to devalue them. This, in turn, provides moral support for even more brutal acts by aggressors." If a victim defends himself, the aggressor can then vindicate his behavior by interpreting the defense as the original incitement. After fixing blame this way, victims themselves may even begin to believe they are to blame.)

Pornography and Sex Offenders

What has all of this to do with pornography? The same core processes Bandura described are used by sexual offenders to justify and perpetrate their own crimes. Some startling new research presented to the Attorney General's Commission on Pornography in 1986 suggests that a substantial number of rapists and child molesters may be using pornography to start the process that triggers the crime.

This research was undertaken by William Marshall at Queens University in Ontario and by Gene Abel at Emory University.[6,7]

Over a six-year period that ended in 1985, Marshall undertook a detailed study of sexual deviants (child molesters and rapists) who were patients at his Kingston (Ontario) Sexual Offenders Clinic. He compared their use of hardcore pornography with a control group of men who were sexually normal. His study encompassed 89 deviants, including 33 heterosexual child molesters, 18 homosexual child molesters, 15 incest offenders, and 23 rapists. His control group consisted of 24 men with no history of sexual offense, but whose ages, intelligence, and socioeconomic classes matched those of the patients, to the extent possible.

During the course of his investigation, Marshall found something he was not looking for. It was a discovery that suggests there is much more harm in nonviolent pornography than has been previously known. Here is what he found:

Out of the 23 rapists in Marshall's study, 19 of them used hard-core pornography—some occasionally, some frequently. During the course of an interview, one of the rapists told Marshall that he used pornographic pictures of people enjoying sex with each other in order to get aroused enough to rape. The reason he did not use pornographic pictures of rape scenes, he told Marshall, was that in these scenes the women obviously were acting, and, in the rapist's words, "Who would want to rape a willing participant?"[8] After hearing this, Marshall questioned the other rapists in the study. Five more made similar claims. Altogether, 10 of the 19 rapists who used pornography used pictures of consenting sex acts to fantasize about rape (although some said these fantasies did not always end in acts of rape).

The rapists believed, quite uniformly, that the "girl next door" depicted in the nonviolent pornography would not want to be raped, and that she would resist. This, then, triggered their rape fantasies (and for almost 40 percent of Marshall's subjects, it triggered actual rape).

There has been much criticism about explicit pornography depicting rape, because it is degrading to women and portrays violence. But for a substantial number of rapists, according to Marshall's study, it is these images of *consensual* sex—pictures of people *enjoying* sex—that starts the process and triggers the crime. This is the very kind of pornography that the pornography industry constantly claims is harmless. It is only by flatly ignoring Marshall's findings that the pornography trade and the American Civil Liberties Union can assert, as they do time and again, that there is absolutely no evidence connecting pornography with harm.

Marshall uncovered a similar trend with the child molesters in his study. Nearly all of them used pornography at

FIGURE ONE
**The Use of Hard-Core Pornography by
Various Sexual Classifications of People**

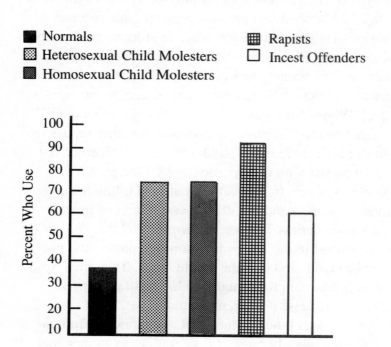

least occasionally, and 14 of the 33 used it to instigate sex
crimes (5 said they did so usually, and 9 occasionally).[9]

Incidentally, Marshall's study found that sex offenders
used hard-core pornography much more frequently than did
the control group of normal males. Figure 1 illustrates this.

Marshall concluded in his report that ''the present data
tends to support suggestions that restrictions be placed upon
the availability of the kinds of pornography described in

this paper. Highly explicit sexual depictions, particularly those depictions involving forcefulness or children, affect the behavior of vulnerable males, although even explicit versions of consenting sex between adults appears to negatively affect some sexual offenders."[10]

Many commentators who have had no clinical experience with sex offenders as patients argue that the consumption of pornography is somehow "cathartic," that is, it releases tension in a nonharmful way. Recent research by University of Missouri psychologist Russell Geen and recent testimony by Dr. Gene Abel before the Attorney General's Commission on Pornography counters this argument.

In his studies with sex offenders, Abel, of Emory University, found that once an individual begins to engage in deviant behavior, he begins using pornography to sustain his fantasy between crimes. Abel found that pornography enables a deviant to sustain his fantasy longer than he otherwise could. "In this way," he observed, "the use of fantasies, or stuff they purchase or look at, maintains their deviant arousal over time because deviant fantasy is paired with more orgasm [as they masturbate]. Because they maintain their arousal longer, they are more prone to perpetrate crimes," Abel said.[11]

When "Catharsis" Backfires

Abel has found that many times sex offenders use pornography for masturbation instead of actually commiting a sex crime, for fear of being caught. There is, then, a temporary subsidance of their urge.

But there is a price to be paid. Abel said, "When they

use the fantasy, it does transiently reduce the risk of their committing the crime, but they have to pay the price, and the price is [that] it maintains their arousal over time, and therefore greater opportunities to commit further crimes occur."[12]

During his testimony before the attorney general's commission, Abel acknowledged that when sex offenders employ pornography to temporarily reduce their urge, over the long term there is a likelihood of an increase in antisocial behavior.

Abel has found that sex offenders who do not use pornography commit slightly more sex offenses in their "careers" than those who do use pornography. But he also found that offenders who use pornography maintain their activity far longer than nonusers.

"Would You Like Your Mother to See This Picture?"
Child molestation is a particularly ugly brand of sexual deviancy. Molesters prey upon the most innocent and immature of victims. There is increasing evidence to show that pornography is used by molesters for far more than simply arousing themselves to commit sexual crimes.

Some of this evidence was reviewed for the Attorney General's Commission on Pornography by Dr. Ann Burgess, a professor of nursing at the University of Pennsylvania.[13] Since 1972, she has been studying and treating victims of sexual violence, mostly at Boston City Hospital. She has authored or edited numerous books and scores of academic articles on the subject of sexual abuse.

She said that the passage of a federal law in 1978 to protect children against sexual exploitation has, among other
things, produced a wealth of information about child sex
rings and the use of pornography by molesters to entice
children. She said that there is now ample evidence to suggest that both adult and child pornography are essential
components in the sexual victimization of children.

Her report to the attorney general's commission is worth
quoting at length:

Entrance into a sex ring introduces children to an elaborate
socialization process that not only binds them to the ring but
locks them into patterns of learned behaviors. The maintenance
of children in the ring is through a distortion of a belief system
that convinces the child the activities are "normal" and strongly
discourages any challenges to the behavior. This explains, in
part, why children do not reveal their involvement to parents and
authorities ("I was scared not to do what he said") and why it
was so difficult to leave ("All the kids were doing it"). . . .
In the organized rings the sexual abuse of children by the adult
is compounded by the adult's supporting the children's exploitation of each other. The adult acts benevolently and pits the group
members against one another . . . , and vicariously enjoys the
peer sadism. There is a definite hierarchy within the group and
the older, stronger children in the ring harass and abuse the
smaller, weaker and more vulnerable ones.
In *all* rings adult pornographic books are used for instruction.
[That is, the pornography is used to show children "what
mommy and daddy do."] The introduction of child pornography
into a ring further links the child to the group and its lucrative
outcome is a powerful reinforcement to the group. Pornography
is also important to understanding the betrayal of the group
("Would you like your mother to see this picture?"). . . . Pornographic materials found in the home of a thirty-one-year-old
ringleader included videotapes of three teenage boys doing pornographic commercials, twenty-two photographs of a ten-year-
old boy undressing, and hundreds of photos of young boys
kissing and fondling each other while dressed as women.[14]

Burgess said that when children are used in pornography and are in a sex ring for more than a year it is very likely they will develop deviant sexual attitudes and behaviors.

Sexual Suicides

There is evidence that shows people are actually killing themselves accidentally as they attempt to arouse themselves by cutting off oxygen to their brains. Burgess reviewed for the commission the results of a study conducted by the Behavioral Science Unit of the FBI Academy on 157 cases of suspected "autoerotic" deaths.

She said that in a sizable proportion of cases, bondage pornography was found in the possession of the decedents, leading some experts to believe that the practice was learned from pornography.

In commenting on the FBI study, Burgess reported that:

The presence of commercial erotica was mentioned in official reports in forty-four cases and was found either at the death scene or at the victim's home. Reported titles reflected a diversity of interests, and included: *Playboy, Oui, Forum, Hustler, Drummer, Male Lovers, Gay Stud, Boy Friends, Gay Orgy, Bound Beauties, Bondage Beavers, Hog Tie, Knotty, Oralism, Hot Tongues, Hardened Leather,* and *Master and Slave.* One wife volunteered that the bondage magazine found by her husband's body was open to his favorite bondage picture. She said he replicated to exact detail every knot and tie in the picture. . . .

Photographs at the death scenes included those of the victim as well as those of others. One victim had taken photographs of friends and relatives and superimposed them on nudes in pornographic magazines. In another case, a movie projector threaded with a pornographic film was found, indicating the victim had been watching the film prior to or during his final autoerotic act. One man, found bound and hanging with mirrors arranged such that he could view himself, had been watching an explicitly sexual movie on cable television.[15]

Experts such as Burgess, Marshall, and Abel make it clear that pornography, even the nonviolent, consensual variety, actually causes physical harm to people. It is increasingly hard for the pornography industry to deny this, but it continues to do so.

What Does the Pornography Industry Say?

There is hard evidence, then, linking pornography with crime. It is not conclusive and it is not overwhelming, but that is only because it is new. In coming years, researchers will be conducting many more studies. Nonetheless, the evidence is there. It exists. And as we saw in the last chapter, there is other evidence to link pornography with destructive attitudes about sex, rape, and marriage.

So how does the other side handle all of this? What does the pornography industry say in its defense? When spokesmen for the industry try to defend themselves, they say as little as possible. They prefer to talk about the First Amendment and free speech, even though chapter 4 shows why their constitutional arguments are not valid.

When they are forced to address the social science evidence, the pornographers generally rely on a few particular studies that lean their way. For example, they point to the outdated report of the 1970 Presidential Commission on Pornography, and to a more recent Canadian study, which we will examine shortly. Both of these reports generally exonerate pornography by concluding that there is no evidence showing it to be harmful.

The most recent examples of this kind of a response came during the Attorney General's Commission on Pornography hearings during 1985 and early 1986. Burton Joseph, counsel for Playboy Enterprises, Inc., submitted evidence from the Canadian study, as did John Weston, counsel for the Adult Film Association, and Alan Dershowitz, counsel for *Penthouse* magazine.[16] References to this testimony also appear in the 1986 book entitled *United States of America v. Sex: How the Meese Commission Lied about Pornography* by *Penthouse* editors Philip Nobile and Eric Nadler. The book was published by Minotaur Press, Ltd., a Penthouse company.

The Canadian Study

The so-called Canadian study is worth examining in some depth because it is so frequently cited by the defenders of pornography. It was prepared in 1984 for a Canadian government committee that looked into the issues of pornography and prostitution. That committee was called the Fraser Committee, after its chairman, Paul Fraser, a Vancouver attorney. One of its major study documents was prepared by two researchers, H. B. McKay and D. J. Dolff. It is this report that has come to be known as the Canadian study. The Fraser Committee leaned heavily on the McKay report for its findings and issued its own final report in 1985.

The McKay report provided the Fraser Committee with its major review of scientific research into the effects of pornography. What did the McKay report conclude? Here are several of its findings:

—There is no persuasive evidence that the viewing of pornography causes harm to the average adult.
—There is no persuasive evidence that exposure to pornography causes the average adult to harm others.
—There is no evidence to suggest that exposure to pornography causes the average adult to alter established sex practices.

—There is no systematic research evidence available which suggests a causal relationship between pornography and the morality of Canadian society.

What is going on here? The preceding chapter dealt in detail with studies that clearly show harmful effects of pornography, both soft- and hard-core. How could the Canadian research come to such opposite conclusions?

The McKay Report is 95 pages long with 109 additional pages of annotated bibliography. Some 45 times in those 95 pages, McKay cites the work of feminist Thelma McCormack, a sociologist at York University in Canada. He cites the work of feminist Susan Gray, a sociologist at Fordham University, 21 times in those same pages.

In his study, McKay quoted extensively from McCormack's 1984 paper entitled *Making Sense of Research on Pornography*, which in turn relied heavily on a 1982 paper by Gray.[17] Without question, McCormack's work was the major influence on McKay's work.

McCormack simply ignored much of the major research. She did not refer at all to William Marshall or Gene Abel, who are perhaps the world's leading experts on sex offenders' use of pornography, nor did she draw from the work of Ann Burgess of the University of Pennsylvania. McCormack ignored Zillmann, Bryant, and Check completely, and referred only one time each to the work of Donnerstein and Malamuth, two of the major investigators in their fields. But she did so only to criticize harshly their methods and findings (although neither McCormack nor McKay have themselves done research in the field).

McCormack became well known in Canada in the 1970s for her feminist views. This bias is noticeable in her 1984 work. For example, in commenting on what she found in her review of research, she wrote that "there were strong suspicions that feminist sentiments were being manipulated by ambitious district attorneys, that the present hysteria about child pornography, for example, might be a smoke-screen diverting attention from various abuses by law enforcement agencies; beyond this, [it was questionable] whether all of this male solicitude was not a further example of patriarchy with no real transfer of authority to women."[18] This is loaded language. It is not the sort of professional, scientific writing one frequently encounters in a research paper.

In the introduction to her report, McCormack states frankly her bias: ". . . I will indicate, wherever appropriate, a feminist critique of the way the research has been conceptualized, its methodology and the interpretation of its results." There is nothing wrong with a feminist having feminist views, and stating them forthrightly. But McCormack hardly takes a neutral view as she interprets the research and selectively ignores the work of most of the major researchers.

McKay closely allied himself with McCormack's feminist views in his own report to the Fraser Committee, in which he said, "In one of the most thoughtful, careful, and constructively critical reviews (in a field where such work often remains unpolluted by logic) Thelma McCormack refers to the '. . . mindlessness of this research . . . ,' a view we share and applaud."[19]

In 1983, Thelma McCormack and I were members of a subcommittee on pornography of the Metro Toronto Task Force on Violence Against Women. I was asked by the subcommittee to review the literature so that the subcommittee could base its recommendations on the most current research available. In response I submitted a research summary of the 1,200 most relevant research articles. It was accepted and approved by the subcommittee. Late in the spring, Ms. McCormack, independent of the task force review process, prepared her own review. She submitted it to the subcommittee after the subcommittee report was finished. The members found her paper to be so flawed that they rejected it. Nonetheless, McKay depended heavily on it as he prepared his work for the Fraser Committee.

Actually, the Fraser Committee didn't have to depend on someone else's review. On February 4, 1984, the day before the Fraser Committee opened its public hearings, sixty of the most highly regarded researchers in the field, including Zillmann, Donnerstein, Burgess, and Malamuth, presented their most recent findings at a symposium I organized in Toronto. Although members of the Fraser Committee and its staff were in the audience that day, none of the research presented was considered by the Fraser Committee in its final report, or saw the light of day in a single footnote or reference.

The Fraser Committee ignored the proceedings of the Toronto symposium, the report prepared by William Marshall in 1983, and the report prepared by James Check in 1984 (see chapter 6). Given all this, it is no wonder that the pornography industry embraces the Fraser Committee's work, and the McKay study which so heavily influenced it. When the pornography trade claims that pornography is not harmful, the Canadian study is usually close at hand.

Notes

1. L. Dawidowicz, *The War Against the Jews: 1933-1945* (New York: Holt, Rinehart, Winston, 1975).
2. J. Gilbert, *The Holocaust: A History of the Jews of Europe During the Second World War* (New York: Collins, 1986).

3. R. Hillberg, *The Destruction of the European Jews,* vols. 1 and 2 (London: Holmes and Meier, 1985), 271-279, 301-390.
4. D. A. Scott, *Pornography: Its Effects on Family, Community and Culture* (Washington, D.C.: Free Congress Foundation, 1985), 4 (see footnotes 50-54).
5. A. Bandura, *A Social Learning Theory* (Englewood Cliffs, N.J.: Prentice Hall, 1973), 155-158.
6. W. Marshall, *Report on the Use of Pornography by Sexual Offenders.* Prepared for the Federal Department of Justice (Ottawa, Canada, 1983).
7. G. Abel, D. Barlow, E. Blanchard, and D. Guild, "The Components of the Rapist's Sexual Arousal," *Archives of General Psychiatry* 34 (1977): 895-903. See also: G. Abel, E. Blanchard, and J. Becker, "An Integrated Treatment Program for Rapists," in *Clinical Aspects of the Rapist,* ed. R. Rada (New York: Grune and Stratton, 1978); and G. Abel, J. Becker, W. Murphy, and B. Flanigan, "Identifying Dangerous Child Molesters," in *Violent Behavior, Social Learning Approaches to Prediction, Management, and Treatment,* ed. R. Stuart (New York: Bruner-Mazel, 1981).
8. W. Marshall. Testimony submitted to the Attorney General's Commission on Pornography, Houston, Texas, 12 September 1985.
9. Ibid.
10. Ibid.
11. G. Abel. Testimony submitted to the Attorney General's Commission on Pornography, Houston, Texas, 12 September 1985.
12. Ibid.
13. A. Burgess. Testimony submitted to the Attorney General's Commission on Pornography, Washington, D.C., 20 June 1985.
14. Ibid.
15. Ibid.
16. Each of the following three presentations came in as unpublished testimony before the Attorney General's Commission on Pornography: Burton Joseph on July 25, 1985; John Weston on October 16, 1985; and Alan Dershowitz on January 22, 1986. Joseph submitted other evidence to the commission. He provided summaries of all published research in the field from 1970 to 1985. Many of the studies simply were not conclusive because of testing deficiencies (i.e., some had no control group, some used volunteers rather than randomly selected subjects, some depended on subjects' own recollections of past thoughts and activities rather than laboratory testing). A few studies, particularly the older ones from the 1970s, supported the notion that pornography is not harmful. But newer studies by the major researchers were not neglected (to Joseph's credit) and they present a more damaging picture: violent pornography trivializes men's attitudes about sexual aggression against women.

   Indeed, one of the summaries reviewed a study by Neil Malamuth and Barry Spinner, published in the *Journal of Sex Research* in 1980. It analyzed the contents of pictures and cartoons in *Playboy* and *Penthouse* between 1973 and 1977, to test the validity of speculation that sexual violence was increasing in these two generally soft-core publications. They found a 10 percent increase in violent depictions (most of it in *Penthouse*), prompting the researchers to conclude that the magazines may be contributing to a climate of violence against women.

A review of the summaries submitted by *Playboy's* Joseph suggests a changing picture about the effects of pornography. Older studies that researched pornography available in the 1970s find less evidence to conclude that pornography is harmful. But the newer studies, particularly those dealing with the violence-prone pornography of the 1980s, present a much more disturbing picture. And this is evidence submitted by *Playboy* itself.

17. S. Gray,"Exposure to Pornography and Aggression Toward Women: The Case of the Angry Male," *Social Problems* 29 [1982]: 387-398.
18. T. McCormack, "Making Sense of Research on Pornography." Mimeo. *Women Against Censorship*, ed. V. Burstyn (Vancouver and Toronto: Douglas & McIntyre, 1985).
19. H. B. McKay and D. J. Dolff, "The Impact of Pornography: An Analysis of Research and Summary of Findings," in *Working Papers on Pornography and Prostitution* 13 (1984): 91. Ottawa Department of Justice, Policy Programs and Research Branch, Research and Statistics Section.

CHAPTER EIGHT
The Victims Speak

The Attorney General's Commission on Pornography heard tragic testimony during its six public hearings about the effects of pornography on its victims. Some examples of that testimony are excerpted here.

Ann

When I met Tom we were twenty-one years old. I came from an abusive background, but had no exposure to pornography. In fact, my parents were very strict about the issue of sex and sexuality.

In 1972, the year we first met, Tom introduced me to pornography. He first brought to my attention the variety of magazines that were available as "resource material." He treated this information as though it were normal for everyone to read it, and so I began to read some of the magazines. I naturally assumed Tom was just reading them and could never have guessed what he was really doing with those magazines. We discussed some of the techniques described in the magazines, and eventually Tom began tying me up for sexual purposes. I found this to be very frightening and thought something was wrong with me because I was not receptive to this new experience. Tom's approach was ''I'd get used to it and don't worry about it too much.'' For the next eleven years I would wonder what was wrong with me sexually.

In the fall of 1975 I found out Tom was having sex with many of our friends. Each one of them had been told that she was the ''one'' in his life, aside from me. During this time I felt rejected, and because I had a very low self-image, I felt even more that I had a personality flaw or that something else was wrong with me. Why else would a husband bed with so many unattractive women? . . . Tom swore he did not use prostitutes, but he [admitted he] did fantasize quite a bit with magazines, and I thought: *What's wrong, that my husband can have sex with magazines but not with me?*

Once in this sexual dry spell, Tom tried to get me to have sex with one of my friends (his lover). I was so dead inside that all I could do was watch the two of them and feel disgust and contempt for myself because I had allowed my marriage to get to this point.

In 1981 we moved back to Houston, after Tom could no longer function in his job. I thought at the time that his boss was mean to him and that he was overworked. Now I know that he could no longer partake in the daily and hourly use of pornographic magazines, theaters, and shops that he had been addicted to for many years. Because he had to account for his time, and he was being supervised, he could not escape into his anonymous world of porno.

In August 1981, my daughter and I were in a car accident and I began what was to become a nervous breakdown. The years 1981-82 were also the beginning of our financial downfall. Money had disappeared mysteriously over the years. Tom would not let me have access to our finances. I thought he was telling the truth when he said he liked to pay the bills and keep the records. Since I was extremely suicidal and depressed, I really didn't pay any attention to our finances for over an entire year.

It was after I completed therapy that Tom's use of pornography and movies became most intense. According to him, all of his time and energy was spent on some form of acting sexually with the use of pornographic material. Much of our joint income was spent on sex in porno houses, porno magazines at $10 per copy, and the hotel rooms and movie theaters that he frequented.

I lost the home I had worked so hard for. I lost the ability to buy another home because my husband would rather spend time having sex with a magazine than work to pay the mortgage and other bills. More publicity about the negative effects of pornography would have certainly opened my eyes sooner, and those bills would have been paid. Instead, our money was spent on something that cripples the mind and body. It warps a person's perception of himself and others.

There was an enormous void spiritually. I have learned how important spirituality is. Pornography and spirituality do not coexist. If a person is spiritually aware, he has respect for himself and others. Pornography sells and feeds off of disrespect for self and others.

It has been two and a half years since I divorced my husband. I am a single parent who has a lovely child. I am afraid of relationships with men, but like to believe I'll find someone to love and trust, and who will feel the same about me.

Tom is getting ready to remarry, and I am not upset or jealous of his bride-to-be. I would love to tell her about Tom, but I know she wouldn't believe me.

SARA

I was one of the many girls who ran away from home during the 1960s. I was thirteen at the time. The first night out, I was raped. On the second night, I was gang raped. The third night I wandered around the streets in a daze, when a man befriended me.

I told him my problems and he offered to take me in. During my stay with him, he treated me relatively well. He was kind to me, he fed me, he said he cared about me. He also kept me drugged and took nude photographs of me. After a few weeks he sold me to a pimp named Bob. Early on, Bob tried to seduce me. I resisted. He raped me and told me I would work for him as a prostitute.

During my initial imprisonment he stole my identification, jewelry and clothing. I was repeatedly beaten and raped. To keep me in line, he threatened my life and the life of my family. He would also threaten to turn me over to the police, who he said would lock me up until I was twenty-one. And there were times when he threatened to contact my family and tell my mother I was a prostitute. He said the scandal would destroy my family. I was so frightened, I believed everything he told me. I know now that I was totally traumatized by my imprisonment, rapes and the beatings.

I tried on many occasions to escape my pimp. But my inexperience in the city made it easy for him to track me down. Each time I escaped, he forcibly brought me back to his apartment. He would drag me through streets, out of restaurants and into taxis, all the time beating me while I cried for help. No one came to help. No one wanted to get involved.

Many of the men my pimp sold me to were prominent entertainers and government officials. Most of them were in their fifties and sixties. They had daughters and granddaughters my age. They knew a child's face when they looked into it. It was clear to them that I wasn't acting on my own free will. It was even clearer that I was sexually inexperienced. So they showed me pornography to teach me about sex, and then they would tell me to act like the women in the pictures.

One of the men I saw regularly had a vast collection of both adult and child pornography. He had video equipment in his home long before it was mass produced. Every time he saw my pimp he would show him pornographic pictures of me. He also made videotapes of the sex I had with him. I saw him on an average of once a week for about a year.

My pimp also made me work stag parties. At these parties ten to twenty men got together to view several pornographic films. Afterward another woman and I would be forced to have sex with some of the men. These parties took place in public places, like catering halls, bars, and union halls.

I was also forced to work conventions. These were weekend affairs held at major hotels in New York, and attended by hundreds of professional men, like doctors and lawyers. The sequence of events was always the same. Pornographic films were shown, followed by myself and other women having sex with various men. Most of the films shown set the tone for the types of acts we were expected to perform.

There was an apartment on the west side of New York I was sent to often. There were usually two or three men there. After I had sex with them, they would take pictures of me in various pornographic poses. When I was a young girl, I didn't have the vocabulary to call them pornographers. I used to refer to them as photographists.

It was only in retrospect as an adult that I realized the studio apartment furnished with a bed and professional photography equipment was an illegal pornography production firm.

On another occasion another girl and I were taken to an apartment in New Jersey to meet some men. We were told they were gangsters and we should be nice to them. When we arrived, we were taken into a room that had a large set served by lighting and filming equipment. We were told to act out a lesbian scene.

After fifteen minutes, we were told to get dressed and we returned to New York. Again, it was only later that I realized I had been used for the illegal production of pornography.

Some might want to ask why I didn't turn to the police for help. I didn't have to walk all the way to our local headquarters to speak to the police. They were at our apartment every week for their payoff: me.

It soon became clear that both the police and the social service community were unprepared to protect me. Authorities not only wouldn't help me, but were also my exploiters. When I was sixteen, I was sent to juvenile detention by the courts. My incarceration was a nightmare of sexual abuse at the hands of the male employees of the facility. One young girl complained to her parents about abuse on visiting day. That night after they left she was made an example of. We heard her cries and pleading all night long. The "official" story the next morning was that she had tried to run away, was caught, and was being held in isolation.

In time, I was transferred to a facility upstate. When I saw my opportunity, I escaped. There was no place to go except back to prostitution.

My last pimp was a pornographer and the most brutal of all. He owned three girls or women at any given time. Every night we would set up a screen and run a series of stag films. Then he would become aroused by that and force us into sex with him.

This pimp made pornography of all of us. He also made tape recordings of our screams and pleadings when he gave us brutal beatings. During these times, it was not unusual for him to threaten us with death. He would later use these recordings to humiliate us by playing them to his friends, for his own sexual arousal, or to terrorize us or other women he brought home.

One morning I came in from working all night to find the walls of our bedroom literally covered with blood and a semiconscious woman lying on the floor covered with bruises and welts. Her eyes were swollen shut and there was blood running down her legs. My pimp had brutally raped her with a broom. I was told to guard her so she wouldn't escape. When he fell asleep, I freed her.

I paid dearly for that. He beat me with a riding crop and raped me. He made a tape recording of that entire evening and delighted in playing it for us over and over.

The way this man got women into prostitution was to advertise in the newspaper for models. When a girl or woman answered his ad, he would offer to put her portfolio together for free and be her agent. All in all, he promised to make her a star. It was an easy next step to convince her to pose for soft-core porn. At that point he would smooth-talk her into prostitution. Just long enough, he would say, to get enough money to finance her career as a model. If the sweet talk didn't work, brutal beatings, starvation, captivity, and blackmail did. She became one of us.

I escaped prostitution quite by accident. I had been taking drugs regularly doled out by my pimp. I accepted them because they helped my physical and emotional pain. As I destroyed myself with heroin, I was no longer useful to pimps for tricks, so I was set free. At eighteen, after five years of prostitution, I was penniless, homeless, and addicted to heroin.

I was in my early twenties when I kicked the heroin habit for good. A few years later I met and married my first husband. In short, the relationship was hell. He was an alcoholic and a bad one. The tone of my relationship was frighteningly like my life in prostitution. He couldn't hold a steady job so I supported us. He would fly into rages and beat me mercilessly. After the beatings, he demanded sex.

The current issue of *Playboy* and other soft-porn materials were ever-present in our home. Once he insisted that we go see an X-rated movie together. The viewers openly masturbated. I remember feeling humiliated and frightened. I kept my eyes glued to the screen and prayed for it to be over soon. When we got home he demanded sex.

Before he turned twenty-five, my husband died in a car accident. He was drunk at the time. A few months ago I learned something that explained his low self-esteem, his alcoholism, and his avid consumption of pornography. He too was exploited; as an adolescent he had appeared in pornographic material.

It has taken me close to twenty years to undo what was done to me by pornography and prostitution. I am now an undergraduate student at a major university and plan on counseling women who are going through what I have experienced. I have the support of a loving husband, mother, and sisters. Most women who have shared my experiences are not as fortunate as I am. But I still have lasting wounds. My thighs are permanently scarred from the repeated beatings with wire coat hangers. And the pornography I was forced to make still exists. I know the men who made it; I know where they are; and I know that there is nothing I can do about it. I live knowing that at any time my past can surface and be used to humiliate me and my family. I know it can be used to ruin my professional life in the future. I also know what happened to me will continue to happen to other girls and women like myself. They will continue to be used and hurt in the way that I was used and hurt by pornography; and if they should be fortunate enough to escape, like I was, then they will live under the same threat of exposure and blackmail that I do.

BONNIE

I am the thirty-one-year-old mother of two daughters, Debbie, age thirteen, and Michelle, age eleven. My daughters and I were physically and sexually abused by both my first and second husband.

Leon, my first husband and the father of my girls, had a

large collection of pornographic material. He could not have sex with me without first getting aroused by looking at pornography. Most of the magazines consisted of either homosexual couples or small children in various acts of sex and violence. Often he would be high on drugs or alcohol and force me into violent sexual acts. And all the time he would be leafing through pornography.

Once when I went out briefly, he tied both of my daughters to their beds on their stomachs and put his finger into their rectums. When Debbie and Michelle told me, I believed them immediately because Leon had done the same to me. Shortly after that I decided to divorce Leon; I sought help from the Domestic Violence Unit. When I told them about the sexual abuse, they didn't seem to believe that a man would sexually molest his daughters. Because of this, the divorce complaint didn't mention my daughters' sexual abuse, just the physical abuse.

I married Paul in 1980. I must say I was leery about remarrying. But Paul promised he would be a good husband and a good father to my daughters. He was also a prominent businessman in our community. On the outside, Paul appeared very average; he was always well dressed and looked clean cut. The prospect of security and the chance to be happy prompted me to marry him.

Paul had a large collection of bizarre S&M [sado-masochistic] and bondage pornography that he kept in the nightstand drawer. I feel that Paul was obsessed with pornography and violence. His magazines ranged from kinky violent pornography to child pornography. Many times he would show me pornographic pictures and say, ''Why don't you do this?'' or ''Pose like this.''

He couldn't perform sexually without first getting

aroused by looking through magazines or a deck of cards he had that show men and women doing things to each other. One night he wanted me to agree to be bound and tied like the models in some of his pornographic magazines. When I refused, he forcibly tied me to our bed and sodomized me. He often asked me to accompany him either to an X-rated movie or an adult bookstore. I always refused to go.

It was about one month after we were married that he started physically abusing Debbie and Michelle. This would happen when I left him alone with them. At around that time he also started "tickling" Michelle on or near her genitals. He would make crude remarks to Debbie about her body parts.

The molestation of the girls occurred in the bathroom, bedroom, or car. But Paul also was bold enough to molest them in church. I feel that the bathroom molestation can be linked to some of the child pornography Paul had. This material depicted young nude females in bathtubs in sexually provocative poses.

He seemed to enjoy showing them pornographic material. The girls remember specifically a time when Paul showed them a picture of a "naked lady dressed in the bottom of a leopard skin outfit and holding a whip." He asked them what they thought of it. Both children said they were disgusted at viewing the picture.

My daughters told me a while back that Paul asked them if they wanted to be photographed like the girls in the magazines. The girls also told me that Paul sometimes played a game with them in which their feet were tied up tightly with a rope. The molestations included "bad touching" and exhibitionism by Paul, but did not involve actual penetration.

When Debbie started maturing sexually Paul often teased her, using very obscene language. Also, whenever Debbie was bathing, or if she or Michelle was in the bathroom, he would just walk in. I fought many times with him about this and requested that locks be put on the bathroom door. But he refused to let it be done.

Whenever I would have to leave the house at night or on his days off, or to spend time out with my mother, he would insist that I leave both girls home. At times, when I hadn't driven myself, he would pick me up to go home. Michelle would be curled up in a fetal position in the back-seat of the car. If I questioned either her or Paul about what was the matter, Michelle would look scared at Paul and say, "Nothing's wrong, Mommy." Paul would usually say she was "naughty, isn't that right, Michelle?" Michelle would nod yes.

After I left Paul, Michelle told me why she never said what was wrong. If she had told, Paul threatened to put her in a large garbage bag and dump her in a lake.

Even as an adult, I can relate to my daughter's fear. At first I was afraid to report him. If I turned him in, he said he would take my children and put them in a home or do something to them.

But finally I did report him on several occasions to Child Protective Services for physical abuse. Yet my problems continued. Although immediate action was taken, and Paul was removed from the house within four days, the criminal justice system fell short in accommodating my needs and those of my two daughters. Paul was, and still is, a prominent businessman in the community. Because of his status, I had difficulty obtaining a lawyer to represent me.

The case was submitted to family court where the judge

was a college friend of Paul's. Incredibly, the case was dismissed because the judge didn't believe Paul could do such a thing to his stepdaughters. In criminal court things fared slightly better. Paul was put on probation.

But the damage has been done. My beautiful daughters are very wary and frightened of men now. Both Debbie and Michelle say quite often they don't want to get married or date when they are old enough. Michelle still suffers from headaches, nightmares, and doesn't like to walk anywhere alone.

I personally am afraid to even date anyone. I find it very hard to trust most men. I am having difficulty making friends at the college I am currently attending. I can't stand to watch any movies or pictures of naked men or women. They frighten me. It just doesn't seem normal to me anymore. I just don't feel normal.

Paul is an influential member of this community in New York state. Most of the attorneys available for divorce cases knew Paul and disbelieved the charges of sexual and physical abuse. To date, the divorce has not been finalized.

DAN

I am a successful professional man with management-level responsibilities. I am married, and I have children. And I have been a porno addict for more than forty years. But I was not born with this addiction. I was introduced to it as a child.

At the age of nine, I spent my summer afternoons swimming at the local YMCA. That was where I met a young man in his early twenties. He befriended me and quickly won my confidence. About a week after we met, he talked me into going to a movie one day instead of swimming. After the movie, we walked down by the railroad track and climbed into an empty boxcar. He took some little cartoon books out of his pocket and showed them to me. I had never seen anything like them. They showed several cartoon characters in various stages of fornication and oral sex. While we both looked through the book, he began to masturbate and encouraged me to do the same. Later, he performed fellatio on me. From that day on, through the remainder of the summer, that same scene was repeated at least three times per week; he warned me never to mention it to my parents.

He left town after I started back to school, and I never saw him again. But by then I was conditioned to associate pornography with masturbation.

During the next two years, I do not recall masturbating. I attribute this to the absence of pornography in my life. I did, however, at some time during my early teen years, acquire several of those pornographic cartoon books from my friends at school. They were readily available at ten cents each, or three for a quarter. When I was around fifteen, I suddenly lost all interest in them and threw them away. I suppose it was because I was beginning to take notice of girls.

It was during my military tour of duty in Europe that I had the opportunity to purchase actual photographs, books, and magazines depicting explicit sex acts. I then resumed my former habit of stimulation and masturbation through pornography. This continued for two years until I met and married my wife. After my marriage, I once again stopped buying sexually explicit material and again disposed of all the material I had collected.

However, the demon which had invaded my mind in that railroad car so many years ago would not let me alone. Without any consciousness on my part, I had been thoroughly conditioned to relate pornography with my own sexual experiences.

In addition to my sexual dependency on pornography at age twenty-two, I began to experience problems with social behavior. I avoided close friendships with males. There were periods when I was unable to concentrate my thoughts on anything other than mental images of sexually explicit material. I blame this on my past experiences with pornography.

Then I remember going into a newsstand to purchase a paper one day and saw the first issue of *Playboy* magazine ever printed. It was like a magnet compelling me to buy a copy. I felt I had no choice in the matter. After buying that first issue of *Playboy*, I bought every issue that followed. The whole process began all over again, and I realized I was hooked on sexually explicit material.

After the court battles with *Playboy* were over, and *Playboy* won, other publications began to appear; I bought all I could get my hands on. Over a three-year period I managed to collect more than 200 books, magazines, and films.

It became increasingly difficult to keep them concealed from my family. So I occasionally disposed of materials, all the time telling myself I was going to stop buying them. But it was only a matter of time until I purchased new ones, which provided a fresh stimulus.

By this time in my life, the industry of sexually explicit material was becoming bolder and bolder. More and more, the publishers and distributors were challenged in the courts with obscenity laws; the courts lost. I was no longer forced to settle for simple nudity magazines; hard-core stuff was plentiful, in good quality, and in full color.

During the sixties and seventies, I purchased thousands of explicit sex materials, including books, magazines, and 8-millimeter movies. I saw hundreds of films at adult movie theaters. I tried many times to stop my habit and would often dispose of everything I had collected. I would burn the material, hundreds, even thousands of dollars going up in smoke. Only it never stopped. Eventually the urge would come over me, and it would start all over again, each time my appetite becoming more bizarre.

Yet as bizarre as it had become, I had some so-called standards. I never went into an adult bookstore. I never purchased materials which involved children, animals, bondage, S&M [sadomasochism] or homosexuals. I felt these things were subhuman and revolting. But I also knew it could be just a matter of time until they too became a stimulus. I don't think I could have gone on living had I become involved with a child or another male.

It was at this point I realized I needed professional counseling, which I received. Through professional help, I came to realize that sexually explicit material is very much like substance abuse. The user becomes dependent upon material to satisfy a mental and physical demand. It exercises tremendous control over the mind. Fortunately for me, I was able to recognize my problem and had the desire to overcome it.

In no way is this to suggest that I am cured. What it does mean is I am in control of my habit. I have not purchased sexually explicit material for over four years. But the demon is still there, just waiting for the opportunity to regain control. It requires constant vigilance on my part to keep him under control.

I cannot allow myself to be in a situation where I might

weaken and once again fall prey to pornography. I cannot and will not patronize a store that displays and sells any type of sexually oriented material. I must carefully select the television programs I watch and the movies I see. Sometimes I am caught off guard when someone leaves a copy of *Playboy* or *Penthouse* lying around. I must leave as quickly as possible, because I know if I took so much as one little peek, it would start all over again. I cannot afford to let that happen.

There are thousands, perhaps millions, of men and women just like me who have been enslaved by sexually explicit material—and their number continues to grow with increasing availability of X-rated video cassettes and the accessibility of pornography. I personally know many users myself. They may think it is harmless and simply adds a little spice to their sex life, but in reality, they are playing around with dynamite. Sooner or later, most of them will be hooked just like I was.

GEORGE

I had been acting in porno films for over two years. I got into the industry somewhat gradually. At nineteen, when I was in college, I started out with dancing and nude modeling. That was in New York. After awhile I was approached by a couple of different magazines. I was almost twenty-one when I finally got involved with X-rated movies—my goal. I got into it as an ego trip. At first it was pretty much glamour, like you hear about all the time. You know, you get paid to have sex with all these really pretty women. Life in the fast lane. Easy work. It was a real head trip. And it was easy money.

And anyway, it was my chance to become an actor. But the reality of what ''acting'' really meant hit me pretty fast. In the industry, you're not paid by the number of lines you have; you are paid per sex scene; that's how they quote it to you. If you have one sex scene a day you get $200 to $250. If you have two sex scenes, you may get $300 or $400. You are paid more for anal; girls are paid more when they are working with two guys.

So the people who say they are getting paid to act only say it to keep their jobs. That way they make it sound all very legitimate. Yet anybody in the industry knows you are paid per sex act—and not for acting.

One thing to always keep in mind is that the producer and director just have to get a product out. They really don't care about developing a ''skill.'' Oh, they may claim they are producing art and creating jobs for a lot of people. But they are nothing but pimps. All they are out to do is make money. They don't give a hoot about the girls or guys.

They really don't care what it costs anybody else. They don't care about anybody in the industry no matter what they say in public. Just take insurance, for instance. It doesn't exist. There are no health plans in the porn industry. I personally saw my doctor every one or two weeks. Yet it cost me about $45 a visit. Then if you do catch something, like herpes, and it gets around, the other models are going to refuse to work with you. My point is, you just don't see people in the industry helping people who have been hurt.

The whole disease thing is one reason I decided to get out of the business. I personally have been pretty lucky only to have gotten gonorrhea a couple of times. I never caught herpes, but it was scary. The diseases are really rampant out there. Then there's the AIDS scare. If you have one person with AIDS, the whole industry can be infected.

Another reason I got out had to do with the way it dehumanizes you and the young ladies you work with. I have been friends with a number of porno "actresses" over the years, and I hate seeing what it does to them.

It really bothered me the way women were treated. Directors and producers would often, amid a lot of shouting and—sometimes—throwing of objects, tell them they'll never work again if they don't do a certain scene. I have seen a lot of producers, directors, and photographers either badger or almost force the girls into doing things they would really rather not do.

I have been on a couple of sets where the young ladies have been forced to do anal sex scenes with guys who are rather large; I have seen them crying in pain. It just destroys their personalities when they are forced to do things like that.

If a girl doesn't want to do a certain scene, the director will call up her agent and say, "Give us somebody who will." He also may pay an extra $50 or $100 to get the girl to do it. But when she gives in, she always regrets it afterward.

I have seen real nice, sweet eighteen-year-old girls go through total changes in personality and life-style. The industry affects them in really bad ways. And once they get into it they find it real hard to get out, because many of them have a drug or alcohol habit to support. I would say about 80 to 90 percent of the models delve into cocaine, and definitely use pot and alcohol.

And while some producers and directors are against drug abuse, they are all out for a profit first. I have seen producers, directors, and photographers hand out coke on the set to relax the girls—to entice them into doing scenes they don't really want to do. And many of the models themselves bring drugs for relaxation between scenes.

Porno actors and actresses also get hooked on the money. I personally worked up to $1,000 to $2,000 per week. For the women, especially, it's the only way they can make a couple of thousand dollars a month without actually getting into street prostitution.

Of course, they could try straight work. But the only jobs most of these women could find would be waitressing or secretarial work—something that makes three or four times less than what they're used to making. Many of these women also have boyfriends sponging off of them and pushing them to stay in.

Now that I'm finally out of the industry, I thought I could pretty much leave it all behind me. But it keeps creeping up. I almost lost my current job because my boss found out about my past. It even destroyed my family life. My parents aren't talking to me anymore. My wife divorced me because of this. What seemed like a great thing at the beginning (making a lot of money, being with beautiful women, getting to act) is going to hurt me for the rest of my life.

George had the following to say about the impact of his family background: My daddy always had magazines, like *Playboy*, around the house. He also had quite a few X-rated publications. Even as a small child, I would find them and read them. Then as I got a little older, like junior high, my daddy would finish his magazines and throw them on my bed for me to look through. At that time, he would also take me to see *Naughty Nurses* and other R-rated movies at the drive-in.

My home life definitely had an impact on me. If I hadn't been exposed to so much pornography, I really wouldn't have had that much interest in becoming a pornographic actor. If I hadn't had that influence growing up, I definitely wouldn't have gotten into this.

PART THREE

How the Battle Is Being Won

In a growing number of communities across the country, people are learning how to close down pornographic outlets, through citizen action and effective prosecutions. This section shows how that has been accomplished in three cities, and describes effective tactics and strategies. It also explains the growing problem of cable and video pornography. The writers are

Beth Spring, Washington, editor of *Christianity Today.*

Hinson McAuliffe, retired Fulton County (Atlanta) solicitor.

Randall Murphree, editor, *NFD Journal.*

Richard McLawhorn, executive vice president and general counsel, National Coalition Against Pornography.

CHAPTER NINE
Victory in Virginia Beach

Beth Spring

The Rev. Frederick H. "Fritz" Stegemann, pastor of
the Open Door Chapel in Virginia Beach, Virginia, holds
services inside a converted movie theater where spiritual
messages are posted on the aging marquee. Church ministries—a day school, a coffee shop, a thrift store—occupy
abandoned shops that wrap around both sides of the sanctuary. It is a place to which people are drawn "when they feel
they won't fit in anywhere else," Stegemann explains. A
former alcoholic from New York, and a former Virginia
politician, Stegemann counsels, cajoles, and presents the
gospel to people whose lives are marred by incest, drugs,
alcohol, and immorality. Stegemann's sensitivity to these
effects and expressions of sin equipped him to lead a successful community-wide fight against pornography. But the
reason it succeeded, he says, is because "God got mad."

Over the course of a year, Stegemann and an unlikely
assortment of community members convinced their local
cable television company to drop the Playboy Channel from

its lineup. The effort required prayer, relentless persever-
ance, and a rare sense of team spirit among very dissimilar
church leaders. Stegemann organized mainline Methodist
pastors and independent Baptists, and he enlisted the support of the Roman Catholic Bishop of Richmond, Virginia.
They concentrated their efforts on this single issue, without
getting sidetracked in other agendas.

The First Action Fails
Playboy was on the air for two and a half years in Tidewater, a coastal region of Virginia that includes Norfolk,
Virginia Beach, Portsmouth, and Chesapeake. It is an
optional channel that subscribers must pay extra to receive,
just as they do for Home Box Office or the Disney Channel.
But it did not take long for Cox Cable's subscribers to discover a problem the cable company had, called ''bleedthrough.'' Households with cable could occasionally pick
up the Playboy signal even if they did not want it; and teenagers throughout the community devised ways to jimmy
their cable boxes and pull in the channel regularly.

A newspaper reporter, disgusted by the bits of movies he
saw on the channel, approached a pastors' group about the
problem. ''You have to do something,'' he told the preach-
ers, and Stegemann felt a tug at the edge of his conscience.
That feeling was reinforced when a friend who serves on
Virginia Beach's city council, H. Jack Jennings, invited
Stegemann and several other pastors to a private meeting
with Roger M. Pierce, vice president and general manager
of Cox Cable.

Jennings explained, ''We tried to bring [the bleedthrough problem] to the leadership of Cox in a private,
mature way, and convince him Cox could gain a tremen-

dous public relations advantage by just removing it with no public outcry.'' Pierce was reluctant to drop a popular item from his cable service without doing a survey to sample community opinion. Because of the standoff, Stegemann and the other pastors launched a letter-writing campaign in February 1984. It failed dismally, Stegemann admits, because he knew nothing about the programming the channel offered.

''I don't subscribe to *Playboy*, and most Christians don't. I was not aware of how horribly bad it was.'' It appeared that the Playboy Channel would continue being broadcast over cable channel 27 with barely a whimper of protest. Then some newspaper headlines caught Stegemann's attention.

The Second Attempt Fails

''I started to notice reports of rape, assault, and incest in the paper,'' he said. He was especially alarmed to learn that there were 60 reported cases of rape in 1983 in Virginia Beach, and 127 in 1984—a 112 percent increase. Stegemann wondered whether a connection exists between pornography and violent crime. He found out that a U.S. senator from Virginia, Paul Trible, has a legislative aide working on the issue of pornography, so Stegemann wrote him a letter. The senator's aide put Stegemann in touch with Citizens for Decency through Law, an Arizona group. ''They started shipping information to me by the ton,'' Stegemann recalls. As he sifted through it all, he learned that in cities where pornography is readily available, there tends to be an increased rate of sexual crime and violence.

He was disturbed as well by reports from some of the

people he counseled. One forty-year-old woman came to him saying her husband ignored her and she feared her marriage would break up. She discovered that her husband stayed up late night after night to watch Playboy movies and had no interest in normal sexual relations. A teenage boy told Stegemann his girlfriend wanted him to run away with her because her father, who was separated from his wife, kept her up late at night to watch Playboy movies with him.

When hearings were scheduled before the city council to consider a rate increase for Cox Cable's 112,000 subscribers, Jennings alerted Stegemann. The cable company's charter said programming content could be reviewed at any time a rate increase was considered. Jennings, who shared the concerns of the pastors, urged Stegemann to set aside his earlier disappointment and prepare for another battle. Armed with all the data he had collected, he prepared an information packet for the city council. An antipornography group in Memphis sent him a ninety-minute video cassette tape of Playboy film clips, and he took it to his friend, Paul A. Sciortino, Commonwealth's attorney and a veteran prosecutor in pornography cases.

No longer half-hearted about pornography, Stegemann fought back tears when he met with city council members before the hearings and arm-twisted Sciortino to watch the video. For the second time, the pastor's attempts appeared to fall flat. The council paid scant attention to his information packet. Sciortino dismissed the tape without watching it, because he thought he knew what it contained. He told his friend the Virginia obscenity law was too vague to use in prosecuting a cable television case. "There is nothing we can do," Sciortino said.

A Different Approach

As the weeks before the scheduled hearing wore on, Stegemann got into the habit of kneeling by the side of his bed
each morning and praying with his wife, "Lord, give us
wisdom. We don't know how to approach this." Feeling as
if he had struck out again, Stegemann asked God for wisdom and believed he received an answer: "Contact all the
pastors in this city." He recruited fifteen parishioners to
spend all day on a Friday and Saturday calling every
clergyman in town. "There was no pressure put on them to
join an army to march on city hall," Stegemann said. "We
just asked if they would pray about an effort to rid this city
of the pornography channel. We formed no organization
and requested no commitment to action."

His telephone volunteers heard the same response over
and over: "We're with you 100 percent." Stegemann
called Bishop Walter F. Sullivan in Richmond, Virginia,
and Sullivan encouraged Catholic priests in Tidewater to
support Stegemann. He called a Baptist leader, Tommie
Taylor, and United Methodist District Superintendent
Douglas Newman.

"Tommie's a tough little fighter, and Doug is quiet and
effective," Stegemann said. "I had the facts and they had
the feelings." The three of them drew up a list of eighty
pastors, representing 50,000 churchgoers, and presented
the list to the city council. At the packed public hearing on
January 7, the three pastors tried their best to persuade city
leaders that Playboy does not belong among the cable list-
ings in Virginia Beach.

Taylor talked about the ways in which pornography
affects a community and appealed to the civic pride characteristic of the Virginia port cities. He pointed out that early

American settlers had planted the first cross in the New World at Virginia Beach. Stegemann emphasized the connection between violent crime and pornography that the information he gathered seemed to suggest. Newman discussed the council's responsibility to uphold community standards.

Newman's perspective on the issue was somewhat different from Stegemann's and other evangelical and fundamental pastors who signed on in support. He was motivated, he said, by Methodist social principles of women's equality. "We stand very strongly against [pornography] because we are very supportive of the equality and dignity of women."

He and Stegemann worked well together, he said, although there was some tension between mainline representatives and other independent Christians. "The mainline people are a little afraid of the fundamentalists and vice versa, and that's sad because there's room for all of us to do the thing each of us does well," Newman said.

The Three-Time Loser

Stegemann stayed on speaking terms even with his adversary from Cox Cable, Roger Pierce. "We'd see each other in the men's room," Stegemann recalled, "and I'd say to him, 'I wish you'd quit, because it looks like you're gonna lose.'" Both hearings in January 1985 were broadcast by the cable company.

The presentations to the city council produced some heated moments of finger-pointing and shrill exchanges between some pastors and city officials. But Stegemann's conduct seemed flawless. Councilman Robert E. Fentress remembers that Stegemann was "well-spoken, spoke from the heart, kept his composure, and did not get angry. He never came off as a crusader.'' Fentress says it was clear that ''Fritz had developed his information by talking to people all over the country. I knew he was telling the truth.''

Nonetheless, when the rate increase finally came to a vote in the city council chamber, it appeared that the combined efforts of all the pastors added up to nothing. The rate increase passed, and Stegemann trudged to his car, dejected. He wept and prayed, saying, ''God, I don't understand. We worked hard. Everything we stood for is scripturally right; we did nothing that would hurt anyone.'' At this point, Stegemann believes, ''God got mad. He heard his pastors in this city standing together on one issue against this sin, this filth and garbage, and God honored that. God as much as said to me, 'You've done your part. Leave the rest up to me.' ''

Stegemann stayed on friendly terms with everyone involved in the dispute, including the reporters who covered it and dubbed it ''Holy Wars.'' Eventually, it was a reporter who restored momentum to the stalled anti-Playboy Channel campaign. ''We had good relations with the media,'' Stegemann said. ''The reporting was honest. It was not always in our favor, but it was always fair. I had nothing to hide so they could hit me any way they wanted—and they did.''

The Startling Turnaround
One reporter began digging into Cox Cable's financial records and made an astonishing discovery. When the cable company was competing for contracts in the Tidewater area, its officers sold shares to a handful of influential community leaders for $1,000 each. It prospered so phenomenally that it offered to buy back those shares for $450,000

each. When this came to light on top of a 13.6 percent rate increase, Cox's Tidewater subscribers were furious. "The city council was embarrassed and put to shame," Stegemann said.

He jumped at the opportunity to request a reconsideration of the rate hike, and drafted letters to each council member. "I wanted to embrace them, not hurt them—to make them my friends and let them know I was not grinding an axe." A Jewish councilwoman, Meyera Obendorf, had voted in favor of the rate hike but vigorously criticized Cox for keeping its stock buyback hidden. Stegemann told her, "Listen. You and I serve the same God. Do you think it's right to give them a rate increase?" She replied, "I'll help you if you promise not to try to convert me." Stegemann said, "It's a deal." Obendorf made a motion to contradict the earlier vote, and the rate increase was denied. Cox Cable lost an anticipated $4.5 million.

Cox's reputation was on the line, but Playboy was still on the air. Stegemann took his videotape of the Playboy movies back to Paul Sciortino's office and convinced him to watch it. Nicknamed "the streetsweeper" by state penitentiary inmates, Sciortino is a no-nonsense prosecutor who has spent sixteen years ridding movie houses of pornography and cracking down on street crime. What he saw on Stegemann's tape convinced him that the channel may be violating Virginia's obscenity statute after all.

With unanimous endorsement from the city council, Sciortino planned an investigation. He bought ten blank video cassette tapes and began recording the Playboy Channel every evening from 8:00 P.M. to 1:00 A.M. for ten days. He and a team of lawyers viewed all fifty hours of programming. "We knew that most of what they show would not

be found to be objectionable under our obscenity statute,''
Sciortino said. The exception was the ''Hot Spot,'' a movie
shown each night from 11:30 P.M. to 1:00 A.M.

The movies featured sex acts at intervals of every four to
six minutes throughout, including heterosexual, homosexual, and group encounters. Most had no discernible plot,
according to Sciortino, and all of them showed ''female
genitals from all angles.'' He and his lawyers watched
these movies a second time, logging the frequency of sex
acts in each film. They found one out of the ten they
viewed—starring Rock Hudson and Angie Dickinson—that
did not cross over the boundaries fixed by Virginia law,
which says an appeal to prurient interest in sex must be the
dominant theme of a film in its entirety for it to be considered pornographic.

Against the other nine, Sciortino drafted indictments,
and the case went to a grand jury. The grand jury viewed
thirteen hours of films including *Insatiable*, *Nasty Nurses*,
Talk Dirty to Me II, and *Babe*. They returned with seven
indictments, saying two of the films were not pornographic
because one had literary merit and the other showed only
one nude figure at a time.

The grand jury set a trial date, charging Cox Cable with a
Class 1 misdemeanor which carries a maximum penalty of
$7,000. No indictment was entered against the Playboy
Channel itself, which is based in Chicago. In response, Cox
Cable dropped Playboy from its lineup on February 27,
1985. Because of Cox's goodwill gesture, Sciortino said,
''We accepted their olive branch and dropped the charges.
Our goal was the removal of the channel, and the channel
was off the air. We figured we had nothing to gain by gam-
bling and going to trial.''

Principles of Success

Today, there is no trace of an organization left from the efforts of the eighty pastors, and Stegemann believes that is the way it should be. "If it happened again, we would stand together again. We can rally if we know we don't have to spend the rest of our lives together." Stegemann persevered because he sensed the Lord's Spirit at work in the effort to fight Playboy, but he had no natural desire to lead the fight. "I kept looking for a way out of it," he said, because of the harassment he and his wife endured and his conviction that "a pastor shouldn't be out stirring up trouble."

Stegemann received telephone death threats but did not take them seriously. "I'm an old street fighter," he would tell his anonymous callers. "I'm an ex-drunk, so I'm not afraid to fight. If I get killed in the process, I'll only be going home."

The way for a community to launch a sustained effort against pornography, he says, is to recruit lay leadership to organize local chapters of groups like the National Federation for Decency, or Citizens for Decency through Law. "Rather than have one big organization," Stegemann believes, "we ought to have groups of local people where respected, middle-of-the-road businessmen take the lead. Pastors always come off looking like they're trying to push their church."

Above all, Stegemann advocates the power of prayer. "If anyone wants to know how we did it," he says, "we had praying pastors, praying churches—and God was indignant that no one listened to the ministers."

Stegemann is gratified at the way all things worked together, finally, to rid Virginia Beach of the Playboy Channel. He reserves especially high praise for Cox Cable.

"They have become community-oriented, exposing the good works of the community and honoring local people."

Stegemann deliberately framed the issue in terms of broad community values and illustrated his point using down-to-earth crime statistics. He did not present the city council with an argument based on the holiness or sovereignty of God, recognizing that they would be guided by law, not personal religious belief, in reaching a decision.

The manner in which Stegemann conducted himself is a good pattern for other Christians who wish to become active on a public issue. First of all, his personal friendships with city council members and the Commonwealth's attorney gave him access to the circles in which decisions are made. He managed to preserve those relationships with city officials even as he confronted them with an issue some would rather ignore. Many times, citizens who try to pressure local civic leaders overstate their claims or make idle threats about the political futures of those councilmen who ignore the group. (Threats of political reprisal may have to be made, but not before the group is prepared to carry them out.) The keys to effective persuasion are persistence and good, accurate information.

Second, citizen activists must try to stay on good terms with the press. Even before he realized how crucial the media would be in the Virginia Beach campaign, Stegemann maintained relations with reporters despite their frequent jibes about his "fundamentalism."

When reporters cover people of deep religious feeling, they often bring to the assignment a caricature of what a "religious fanatic" is like. This happens for two reasons. First, the press as a whole does not understand the motivations of religious commitment. An individual reporter's own understanding may come largely from biased news stories he himself has read, or unhappy remembrances of his own church background.

Second, church people sometimes are so accustomed to talking in Christian cliches with each other that this language spills over into their conversations with un-churched people. This can very well reinforce the notion in a reporter's mind that they are weird. A Christian might well say to a reporter, "The Lord told me we will win," or "Pornography is the work of Satan." What private impression will that make on a reporter who neither believes in the Lord or in Satan? It will bias him in two ways: first, he will be less inclined to take seriously other information that the Christian provides him, and second, he will be less willing to attend the next press conference or event the Christian activists stage. A pressure group that cannot get media coverage cannot progress very far.

The battle with Playboy on the airwaves was fought and won, but Virginia Beach and the surrounding communities still are not free of other expressions of pornography. Methodist district superintendent Doug Newman believes the next battle line should be drawn in each Christian family's living room rather than in court or at City Council.

"I think Christians have a responsibility to influence community affairs," he says. "However, at some point, we have to face our responsibility to deal with our own people in our own churches and their stewardship of the gospel as it relates to pornography. Playboy is not the only channel putting stuff into our living rooms today that is unfit for children, adults, or anyone else. We do have a way of controlling that—either by limiting use of the television in our own homes or failing to subscribe. That is our major responsibility."

CHAPTER TEN
The Fort Wayne Story

Beth Spring

Fort Wayne is nicknamed "the city of churches" because venerable steepled churches made of stone occupy more than the usual share of city street corners. The last thing the city of churches needs is a handful of pornography shops. But beginning in the early 1970s, that is exactly what the city got.

A pornography entrepreneur based in Durand, Michigan, Harry V. Mohney, gained a foothold in Fort Wayne when he opened an "adult" bookstore near a Catholic high school. A lawyer, Thomas Blee, filed a civil nuisance suit, but an appeals court ruled that Blee did not have sufficient standing as a private citizen.

Blee had opposed pornography solidly—and often alone—for years. The same year he lost in court, 1973, he was heartened by the U.S. Supreme Court's landmark *Miller v. California* decision, which said that a community has the right to set its own standards of morality and enforce them. He sensed Fort Wayne might be ready to do just that when another porn shop, Erotica House, opened for business right next door to the Broadway Christian Church. Erotica House, like two other Fort Wayne porn outlets that opened during the 1970s, was tied to Mohney's organization.

Broadway's pastor, Bob Yawberg, watched in dismay as children on their way to Sunday school walked past lewd window displays. Occasionally, a stray piece of literature from the shop would land on the sidewalk, in easy reach of a grade-schooler. During this period, Yawberg was meeting with ten other pastors from Fort Wayne and the president of the Fort Wayne Bible College at 6:00 A.M. on Fridays for prayer. The group met for five years, praying for the city, for elected officials, and for the city's churches. Gradually, their prayer began focusing on the pornography establishments that had become entrenched in their city.

Finally, Yawberg went to Tom Blee to ask for suggestions. "Let's try picketing that joint and see what happens," Blee suggested. Yawberg was uncertain, so he took the idea back to his congregation. They decided to spend time praying for the conversion of the Erotica House manager. "If that succeeds," Blee recalls thinking, "it will put the conversion of St. Paul in the shade."

After several months of prayer, Broadway's members were becoming convinced the pornography action had to move into another phase. Meanwhile, into the small prayer group came a young Catholic charismatic man, Pat Jehl. Yawberg recalls: "He just kept coming and he wouldn't go away. He kept prodding me and prodding me" to address the pornography problem directly.

Yawberg went back to Tom Blee and contacted other community leaders. Among them were the administrator of a hospital next door to the church, a construction company

owner, a black pastor who was part of the Friday prayer
group, a former police officer, and the manager of a local
Christian radio station. They formed an executive committee of Citizens for Decency through Law (CDL) in April
1982. It was the local branch of a national organization
headquartered in Scottsdale, Arizona. Some of Yawberg's
congregational leaders began assuming some of his counseling and hospital visitation duties so he could spend time
in organizing the antipornography campaign.

Getting Organized

The committee planned a strategy to take to their community. This is an important step, according to Yawberg.
"You don't ask people what they want to do. You put
together a strategy and then you present it. Otherwise, you
get ten different ideas and you never get started."

Each member of the executive committee got in touch
with as many other community leaders as he could reach. A
meeting was convened in June, at the Fort Wayne Chamber
of Commerce, with eighty-three in attendance. Amid rum-
blings of some skepticism around the tables, the CDL committee presented evidence they had gathered. They showed
a film clip of cable television programming. And fresh
from Fort Wayne's own porn shops, magazines and other
items were displayed.

What the community leaders saw that night sent them
into shock. Nearly every businessman and woman in the
room signed a card endorsing CDL's effort. (Many local
organizations have found that people are apathetic only
because they have no idea that hard-core pornography is as
extreme as it is.)

The CDL organizers then approached city pastors and

religious leaders, inviting them to attend one of two break-
fast meetings held in June and July. Yawberg said, "I
prayed for 100 pastors. God gave us 118, from forty-four
denominations. They signed those same cards, allowing
their names to appear in a newspaper ad. Up to that time,
we wouldn't have been able to get five pastors in this city to
agree on the time." Finally, CDL convened Fort Wayne's
neighborhood association leaders, gaining the support of
another fifty-two key citizens.

With opinion leaders in the community solidly behind
the effort, Fort Wayne's CDL team met with Mayor Win-
field C. Moses in mid-July. "Instead of using pressure tactics—making threats and that kind of thing—we sat down
with him and said, 'We have 250 people from the community who are ready to support a campaign against pornography.' " The mayor agreed to lead one, because he had no
use for the porn shops either.

At a briefing on pornography in Cincinnati conducted by
the National Coalition Against Pornography, the mayor
explained why he opposed it. He said it is difficult to attract
new business into a city when it discovers a community tolerates this kind of activity. Moses said, "It is not just a
moral and legal issue. It is in fact a social and economic
disease that has to be battled. Pornography unchecked per-
meates a community in ways that are often only dimly perceived. Adult bookstores and triple-X movie theaters often
facilitate the activities of organized crime: gambling, prostitution, and drugs. Our arrests illustrate that."

Within a week after being gently persuaded by CDL, the
mayor's office issued a press release saying he had instructed
the city attorney to "begin a crackdown on all types of pornography." The threat of the ballot box was not needed

with Moses, but Fort Wayne had a prosecutor who was disinterested in obscenity cases. Fortunately for the antipornography cause, he decided not to run for reelection in 1982. The new prosecutor, Steve Sims, had strong views about the need to enforce the law. When he took office, the groundwork for a sustained, effective assault on pornography in Fort Wayne finally was complete. Citizen support, church support, and the backing of the city's top officials got CDL off to a running start. But the marathon had just begun.

Preparing to Picket

The CDL strategy that was presented to community leaders was designed to produce enough momentum to sustain a lengthy siege of the porn establishments. Throughout the summer of 1982, CDL had not been public about its effort, allowing the mayor's press release to raise awareness and counting on word-of-mouth to spread the message. Each of the business, religious, and neighborhood leaders who had endorsed CDL allowed their names to appear in a half-page newspaper advertisement on August 11, one day after CDL's picketing effort began. The ad was an appeal for mainstream community values, as expressed in current law, to prevail. It asked, "If Not Now . . . When? When will Fort Wayne citizens stand against illegal pornography and street prostitution?"

CDL issued a press release calling on the chief of police to carry out the mayor's order for a crackdown, and they urged the prosecutor to enforce existing laws against obscenity. In addition, they requested prayer at noon each day for Fort Wayne's top officials.

A detailed plan for picketing four sites was drawn up, and a rationale for picketing was explained. The press release noted that the chief of police and prosecutor had asked for a demonstration of public sentiment about how vigorously the laws should be enforced. And picketing would effectively cut into porn-shop business, CDL strategists believed, because "most men fear recognition" when they patronize a porn shop.

The committee set a goal of having 100 pickets at each of the four sites daily, spread over a number of shifts. The four establishments were Cinema Blue Theatre, Rialto Theatre, Fort Wayne Books, Inc., and Erotica House, the shop next to Broadway Christian Church. All but the Rialto Theatre were tied to Harry Mohney's Michigan organization. Because he had faced federal investigation, as well as scrapes with local authorities, CDL believed he was vulnerable. The Rialto Theatre, owned by a local businessman, was suspected of being a center for producing and distributing pornography.

The CDL press release was a good one (see appendix 1 for the text), phrased in a tough, matter-of-fact tone. "Local obscenity laws, like any other laws, should either be enforced or eliminated," it stated. Picketing was intended to "focus community attention on the continued and flagrant violation of local obscenity laws." It made no assessment of pornography, its effects, or its promoters, and studiously avoided overblown language that would make them appear to be a fringe movement, or solely religious. It was a cool-headed appeal for mere enforcement of the law. The nature of the press release ensured that CDL would be taken seriously by newspaper editors. It bought CDL the credibility required for a difficult task.

Fair Media Coverage

As a result of CDL's careful spadework, media support for
a pornography crackdown came even before the press
release was issued and picketing began. After the mayor's
call for a crackdown, the Fort Wayne *News-Sentinel* ran an
editorial urging city officials and prosecutors to go beyond
arresting store managers and clerks and identify the owners
and the corporations running porn shops. "Prostitution and
pornography are serious problems in Fort Wayne," the editorial concluded. "It is time for officials to pay more than
lip service to demands for a crackdown."

When CDL began talking to the press, the ground had
been plowed sufficiently for the message to take root, and
the story received fair, intelligent coverage. A reporter
quoted CDL vice-chairman Jim Schweickart, explaining
that the group "does not intend to impose its moral standards upon the community. . . . We're not asking for new
laws—we're simply saying the time has come to enforce
existing laws." CDL also received a welcome boost from
the Fort Wayne City Council, which in August enacted an
ordinance forbidding any new adult bookstore from opening in the city for three years.

The Reality of the Picket Line

CDL set up an office at Broadway Christian Church, and
for the first year of the picketing, Pat Jehl coordinated the
volunteers, who came from about half of the 118 churches
whose pastors endorsed CDL. Each church assigned its
own coordinator as well, giving him the responsibility of
recruiting picketers to fill the time slots Pat Jehl gave them.
Marching with signs in front of adult bookstores was a dif-

ficult undertaking for Fort Wayne's staid church folks, but once they had been on the line for one or two shifts, they were, for the most part, committed to seeing the task through. They got a firsthand look at what they were opposing, and recognized how picketing was changing the entire debate about pornography in their city.

Lawyer Tom Blee explains: "Like most communities, Fort Wayne had a sort of laissez-faire attitude about pornography. It just wasn't a public issue. Picketing changed that because picketing is news. The media can't ignore you. We had lots of news stories in the paper and editorials pro and con. The radio and television stations editorialized and showed the picketers. It galvanized public opinion. It made the people of Fort Wayne start talking about the problem and made it a political issue." Also, it cut business at the porn shops by about 50 percent while the picketers were marching.

The signs the picketers carried were professionally made, conveying simple, succinct messages that adhered to CDL's stated goal of promoting law enforcement. Most were done in block red or green lettering on white placards covered with weatherproof plastic. They said, "Enforce the Obscenity Laws," "Citizens for a Decent Fort Wayne," "Honk for Decency," "Obscenity is Illegal."

CDL raised money for a first-year budget of $80,000. It received a number of private grants, including $5,000 from the local Catholic diocese, as well as small private contributions. The office produced a newsletter sent to everyone who participated in picketing, giving them news of pornography-related arrests and convictions, profiling people on the picket lines, and serving as a means to encourage volunteers to stick with it.

At first, the idea of going out on the picket line held no appeal at all for Steve McMaster and his wife, Barbara, members of St. Charles Catholic Church in Fort Wayne. "It's one thing to talk about it, and another thing all of a sudden to be out on the street carrying signs. I'll never forget it," he said. A deacon at his church asked Steve to be in charge of scheduling other parishioners to picket, and he agreed. He and Barbara went out on the line one evening at dusk for a three-hour shift in front of Fort Wayne Books, a shop that caters to the city's homosexual community.

"They had 150 people opposing us, and there were only about eight of us there at any one time," McMaster recalls. "I saw guys kissing guys, and all sorts of things that you hear about but can't really believe. Then I saw someone take a little baby into the bookstore. After that it was really easy [to picket]. There was no more fear inside me, just a little anger."

The McMasters are active in a Catholic charismatic prayer fellowship, and it was through prayer that they became convinced they should take a stand. "We were very unsure of ourselves and didn't know if we could do it," Steve said, "but after the first night there were no more questions in our minds about it."

McMaster is a machine operator at a local factory that manufactures axles. He said his picketing activities attracted a lot of interest on the factory floor, a place where pornography tends to run rampant. "You get a lot of razzing," he said. "The silliest question people at work asked me was, 'What do you have against sex?' They don't understand that it's a misuse of sex."

Steve McMaster called between 100 and 125 volunteers in his parish to sign them up for picketing every Saturday.

"There were forty or fifty people I could count on like
clockwork. Another fifty or sixty would picket one month
and not the next." People could choose shifts ranging
between forty-five minutes and three hours. He tried to
schedule eight people for each shift, and never fewer than
four. "It's amazing," he said. "After a person pickets a
couple times, he'd do it by himself if he had to."

Going out on the picket lines, McMaster said, "has given
me that confidence which I'm supposed to have in the
Lord. It is a backbone builder. You take me by myself, and
I couldn't change anything. It was the Lord, the Holy Spirit,
who convicted our hearts. He just used us to bring the issue
forward."

The Opposition Strikes Back

At first, the picketing effort stirred aggressive opposition.
Porn shops blared music at the protesters, and at Cinema
Blue, employees sloshed toilet water on the picketers from
a balcony. One night a beer bottle was lobbed out of a passing car, but a van drove between the car and the protesters,
taking the blow. Anonymous phone calls plagued the CDL
office as well as the Broadway Christian Church reception-
ist, who received a "raspberry" over the phone line every
day at 2:00 P.M. while the picketing continued.

Direct, hostile action against the picketers ceased after
the first two months, because the pornographers saw that
they would only alienate the community further. The porn
shop managers were frustrated, Tom Blee said, because
picketing pits two actual First Amendment rights against
one specious claim to First-Amendment protection. Blee
explains: "Pornographers traditionally wrap themselves in

the First Amendment. They're not entitled to First Amendment protection, but that's their chief line of defense. When people are on the street exercising two First Amendment rights against these people, it puts them in a tight box. The picketers are exercising the right to freely assemble as well as their free-speech rights.''

The people who ran the Erotica House knew about Broadway Christian Church's involvement in the campaign, so on the second week of picketing, it was targeted for a counterprotest. Besides that, bomb threats had been phoned in, and on Sunday morning Yawberg came to church to find police officers patrolling the perimeter of the property. A picket line of pornography defenders blocked the church entrance, so worshipers had to cross the line to get in. One young man marching in protest of the CDL effort was dressed like a nun. He pranced past the church with a sign saying, ''It's NUN of your business.'' The manager of Erotica House came to the service, sat in the front row, and put a pink show token in the offering plate, trying all the while to bait Yawberg into an outburst. Yawberg resisted. ''I never mentioned the issue. I preached the sermon I had planned. I welcomed him along with everyone else.''

Fort Wayne newspapers played the episode on the front page and editorialized about it. That attracted additional community support, and the pornographers retreated from their frontal assault. Instead, they sought to wear down individual picketers. While there were no incidents of physical assault or personal injury throughout the two years of picketing, more subtle means were used. The Rialto Theatre somehow obtained the names and phone numbers of a series of single women picketers and displayed them in huge letters on the marquee (there had been a break-in at CDL headquarters but the perpetraters were never established). The women were, in turn, designated "Picketer of the Month."

In response to this, CDL organizers alerted these women to expect a rash of obscene or anonymous phone calls. Police protection was available, and the CDL office, which maintained phone contact with the police, could be contacted if a woman felt threatened in any way.

Lola Mandra, a great-grandmother at age eighty-two, faced a different sort of harassment one day on the picket line. It was midafternoon when the fragile sparrow of a woman with permed white hair joined the line in front of Erotica House. A male porn shop employee and a young female prostitute began picking on her. "A huge, big boy with a smirk on his face," she said, came from inside the shop and began following close on Lola's heels, stepping on the backs of her shoes.

She remembers, "What he was after was to make me angry. Well, I would never show it. I had white shoes on and I wasn't about to have them all scratched up." One of CDL's picketing captains, with a two-way radio, had walked over to Erotica House to see how the march was progressing. Lola said: "When I marched by that captain, I just reached over and pulled him in behind me. As I did, that big boy pushed him." The picketing captain phoned the police, and three cars responded to the call within minutes. "That big boy was scared. They took him off to one side and talked to him. They made him apologize and he did. He was so sarcastic. Then he went back inside the building."

The same day, a prostitute mocked Lola, marching close

beside her in extremely short shorts and a skimpy top. Again, Lola did not become provoked, but said she felt a great deal of compassion. "It was heartbreaking, it really was. If I had been the mother of that girl, what would I have done? Did the mothers of these girls know what they were doing?" Some of the prostitutes Lola saw at close range looked like high-school girls, still in their teens.

Instead of wearing down Lola's spirit and discouraging her, the mockery had the opposite effect. That day, she stayed on the picket line for three consecutive shifts of three hours each. "I was none the worse for wear the next day, either," she says. "You walk slow, and I'm not in bad shape. It's nothing for me to walk."

How to Picket

Each picketer, regardless of his personal feelings, was required to sign a one-page CDL statement agreeing to adhere to rules of picketing. Written by Tom Blee, they helped ensure that the picketing would be nonviolent and would keep with the goal of the effort: stricter law enforcement.

The rules restricted picketing to the public sidewalk, not the street or porn-shop property. Nothing was to be done to prevent a patron from entering a shop or theater, and picketers could not speak to them or to the press. Entrances could not be blocked. When counterpicketing or harassment occurred, the rules said, "continue to walk in a peaceful manner, but do not respond to any attempts at confrontation." If the opposition became too hot to handle, the procedure was to alert a picketing captain, who would phone the police and ask them to supervise the picketing.

"Remember that you are doing a good thing," the rules concluded. "Your attitude should not be vengeful. Be pleasant to all, and especially those who vilify you." (See appendix 1 for the complete list of picketers' rules.)

Few Fort Wayne picketers fit the stereotypical mold of the sanctimonious do-gooders. Tom Federspeil served CDL as its full-time, salaried picketing coordinator after Pat Jehl left the job. Federspeil provided the marchers with signs each day, and made certain that a volunteer captain from each church had a two-way radio. He visited picketing sites, and gave updates about how the movement was progressing. "Then I would ask one of the picketers to pray. I'm Catholic and it's hard for me to do extemporaneous praying. All these Protestants pray from the heart."

He got to know the life stories of some picketers, and was astonished at the number who had had unfortunate experiences due to pornography. Volunteers from the Salvation Army picketed faithfully, he said, and one day an Army volunteer took Federspeil aside and rolled up his sleeves. He had sixty-four razor blade scars on each arm, and explained to Federspeil: "I wanted to kill myself because I was sick of the fact that I was addicted to pornography. The razor blades didn't kill me, so I jumped off a bridge. A fisherman saw me go and he dragged me out. I decided to turn my life over to God and join the Salvation Army."

Another man told Federspeil his son raped a thirteen-year-old girl after watching an X-rated movie. The son, in his late teens at the time, was convicted and sentenced to twenty years in prison. He became active with a fellowship of Christians in prison, and was released on parole after three years.

At Broadway Christian Church, a new staff member was hired in the midst of the campaign against pornography. Pat Black, a graduate of Fort Wayne Bible College, became Broadway's youth pastor and pianist. When he considered the job offer, he said, "A lot of things [about the church] appealed to me, but the picketing was one of the things that did not appeal to me. I was very hesitant about it. I felt these people didn't need a power play. They didn't need big, condemning signs going around in front of them. They needed the gospel, they needed Jesus."

Black decided to walk a mile in the picketers' shoes, so he signed up for a shift one day. "That was when my thinking about it changed," he said. "To present the good news is nearly impossible in a world where there is no absolute standard of right and wrong," he said. "Picketing was, in fact, a pre-evangelism statement. It is the groundwork that has to be laid before you can even hope to communicate the gospel."

Prosecutions Begin

The new county prosecutor, Steve Sims, took office in January 1983. Sims was well aware of the picketing that had started five months before. He encouraged the picketers to keep it up, telling CDL: "I would like a sign from the community as to how the community defines itself; what the community thinks." Sims already knew what he thought of pornography: "When properly understood," he says, "it is violence. Dehumanizing violence." But, he told CDL, "law enforcement cannot exist in a vacuum. Sitting in an office, there are times when all of us will say, 'Am I old-fashioned? Am I out of step? Is my moral code preposterous?' A prosecutor can't stand alone, and I made that clear.'' The picketing campaign gave Sims the community signal he needed, and he was able to gain forty-two obscenity convictions in eighteen months, while the picketing was in full swing. Sims' victories, in turn, greatly encouraged the picketers.

If the prosecutor took it upon himself to define community standards, that would be censorship, Sims said. ''The community has to define itself,'' and make that definition known to the prosecutor. (The community standard principle was established clearly by the Supreme Court ten years before, in the landmark *Miller v. California* case. See chapter 4 for more on this.) Sims had to know whether his limited time and energy ought to be poured into obtaining convictions of porn-shop owners and managers. With a staff of ten full-time lawyers and ten part-timers, Sims' office already was handling a backbreaking load of criminal and civil cases. When it comes to a major special project like fighting obscenity, Sims said, ''That's why the Lord made Saturdays and Sundays and evenings.''

Stores Begin to Close
The overtime Sims invested began paying off almost immediately with convictions against both bookstores and the theaters targeted by CDL. He worked closely with the vice squad of the Fort Wayne police force, sending undercover cops into the stores dressed as farmers and keeping all the sites under surveillance. Distributing obscene materials is a misdemeanor in Indiana, punishable by a fine. Occasional convictions are scarcely noticed, however, by the corporations that own the stores. ''Profits are so high

that these lower-level convictions become part of the cost of doing business,'' Sims explained. "It's just a nuisance factor, unless a prosecutor is vigorous and is being supported by a good judiciary, good staff lawyers, and community support.''

Indiana's obscenity law is a good one because it is based on the Supreme Court's *Miller v. California* standard, thereby ensuring that it is constitutional. The Indiana law says something is pornographic if "the average person, applying contemporary community standards, finds that the dominant theme of the matter or performance, taken as a whole, appeals to the prurient interest in sex.'' In addition, sexual conduct has to be described or depicted "in a patently offensive way,'' and the material must "lack serious literary, artistic, political, or scientific value.''

Using the state obscenity law enabled Sims to take repeated swats at the porn shops, but it did not allow him to hit hard enough to knock the profit out of them. For that, he employed a state law known as the Racketeer Influenced and Corrupt Organizations Act (RICO). The law allowed authorities, in a civil proceeding, to seize the assets and properties of corporations doing business with profits obtained consistently from illegal activity. Because Sims had racked up dozens of convictions, a pattern of illegal activity (trafficking in pornography) could easily be proven against Mohney's three porn stores in Ft. Wayne: Cinema Blue, Erotica House, and Fort Wayne Books.

The trouble was that RICO had never been employed against someone using the First Amendment as his defense—in this case, free speech. At the trial court, however, a judge upheld Sims' right to slap the three porn shops with the RICO statute. When that happened, police padlocked the stores in March 1983, and Mohney was out of business in Fort Wayne. Sims filed RICO charges against the fourth outlet, the Rialto Theatre. In 1986 these proceedings were still underway, and the theater remained open.

Mohney appealed his RICO conviction. It was reversed. The use of RICO was said to be unconstitutional in fighting a pornography case. The appeals decision went a step higher, to the Indiana Supreme Court, which held oral arguments on March 24, 1986. Meanwhile, an agreement was reached between the prosecutor and Mohney. Two of his establishments would remain closed for good, but Fort Wayne Books was allowed to reopen under stringent control. This was tolerable to Sims because the shop is well off the beaten path in Fort Wayne. Additionally, Fort Wayne Books agreed to stop selling materials depicting human torture or death, sexual interaction between people and animals, or child pornography. "We gave something up," Sims said, "but we certainly gained a lot." Most important, he believes, was demonstrating in court that he was indeed fighting organized crime, not just ordinary citizens who happen to sell dirty books for a living. The closing of two bookstores owned by a major pornography dealer was a triumph for a local prosecutor. Many cities have not yet been able to accomplish as much. (During the picketing campaign, a new pornography outlet opened, and immediately was hit with a misdemeanor charge by Sims' office. It closed quickly rather than risk RICO.)

The Murky World of Paper Corporations
Sims himself did not know just what he was up against until, at the beginning of the process, he visited state police

headquarters in Indianapolis and got a briefing about connections between Fort Wayne's shops and Mohney's Michigan operation. Although Mohney has faced federal
investigation numerous times, he has eluded authorities
with sleight-of-hand management and a bewildering pyra-
mid of holding companies.

Tracing the paper trail to its source proves, in cases such
as these, to be an impossible task. Sims did his best, and
determined that at the top of some 200 holding companies
is a firm called European Investments NV. "It's a Netherlands corporation," he said. "It is stationed off the coast of
Venezuela. And who owns European Investments NV?
After three years I can tell you that I don't know." That
was a sure signal to Sims that he was dealing with well-
concealed, highly sophisticated aspects of organized crime.

This came home to Sims in the courtroom as well, when
the corporations paying the legal bills imported expert legal
counsel from California—a seasoned lawyer who has
defended countless pornographers. Sims, before this particular trial, had never in his life prosecuted a pornography
case. The California lawyer did his best to set up the legal
record so errors were made on technical issues unfamiliar to
the local prosecutor and the judge. "These specialists apply
rules that you don't deal with every day. So you have to sit
down and do forty hours' worth of research to find out how
to do it because you've only done two in your whole life,"
Sims said. "The average prosecutor does not recognize the
magnitude of his fight."

All the effort and the overtime is worth it to Sims, he
said, because "this case carries national implications." If
the Indiana RICO statute is held to be unconstitutional by
the U.S. Supreme Court, then Sims believes "it is critical
that we get a statute that is properly written or written a dif-

ferent way with First Amendment safeguards.'' When organized crime is behind pornography, it is no longer a free-speech issue at all, Sims believes. It is an immediate threat to the physical and emotional well-being of women and children, and a blight on intangible values of community spirit and morale.

Paul McGeady is general counsel for Morality in Media, an anti-pornography organization that, among other things, provides expert legal advice to prosecutors trying to gain porn convictions. McGeady agrees that Indiana's court test of the RICO law is extremely important. If it succeeds, it will bolster a court decision in Florida upholding the use of RICO to clean up pornography. ''It is going to be the ultimate answer to the pornography problem if it is used correctly,'' McGeady said.

Conclusion

Whenever Sims walked or drove past the Fort Wayne picketers, he found more reason to press ahead with his fight. ''It was difficult for me to go by them on the way home, and see people living their convictions, out suffering in the snow. Yet in order to remain effective as a prosecutor, I could not say to them, 'I hear you, and not only do I hear you, but in fact we are quietly putting things in place to stop this.' Nevertheless, I developed a great deal of sympathy and respect for that group.''

The affection was mutual. When Sims won the initial court victory against Mohney's three stores, Bob Yawberg sent a letter to all the picketers and other CDL supporters in Fort Wayne. ''Our prosecutor acted with courage and skill,'' he told them. ''Prayer, persistence, faith, and

patience have paid off.'' Yawberg invited everyone affiliated
with CDL or sympathetic to it to join a march past the
Rialto Theatre in support of Steve Sims.

More than 1,000 Fort Wayne citizens marched four
abreast along the sidewalk that day, marking an end to their
long campaign with a solid statement of community together-
ness. Yawberg recalled the Bible verse that meant the most
to him throughout the long two years: ''And let us not lose
heart in doing good, for in due time we shall reap if we do
not grow weary'' (Gal. 6:9, NASB).

CHAPTER ELEVEN
How a Prosecutor Sees the Issue

Hinson McAuliffe

Larry Flynt was mad. As Georgia's Fulton County prosecutor, my office had brought several cases against *Hustler, Playboy, Penthouse,* and other major pornographic magazines sold in our community. During the eight previous years, my office had become known for being hard on obscenity violators.

Now Flynt, *Hustler's* publisher, was coming to Atlanta determined to do something about us. The phone rang in my home on September 7, 1977, the night before Flynt's arrival. It was a local reporter telling me Flynt had notified the press that he'd leased a local bookstore—not an "adult" bookstore, but a mainline business—and that he planned to sell *Hustler* magazines to the public. He'd actually dared me to do something about it. They wanted to know what my response would be.

"Well, I've never announced our plans to the press before," I said, "and I'm not going to start now."

The next morning I called in my staff lawyer who specialized in obscenity cases and I gave him the news. We realized that all of our investigators would be recognized by the press if they showed up, so we arranged with the police department to send an officer to the store in plain clothes to buy whatever Flynt was selling. We needed evidence before we could do anything.

The store was crawling with newspaper and TV people when the police lieutenant arrived. Flynt had stopped at no expense in making this a publicity stunt. Not only was he selling *Hustler,* but with every purchase he was giving away six additional magazines free—all pornographic and neatly prepackaged in a plastic bag.

When the lieutenant returned, I took the seven magazines to the judge. He inspected them and declared them obscene under Georgia law. And we issued a warrant for Larry Flynt's arrest, charging him with violating Georgia obscenity law on seven counts.

But we weren't going to play Flynt's game. We waited until the press was gone and Flynt had returned to his hotel, then we made the arrest and took him to the Fulton County Jail to be booked under a $25,000 bond.

Six months later, while still awaiting our trial, Flynt was shot and nearly killed while returning from lunch during another trial in a nearby county. Now that he was paralyzed and confined to a wheelchair, we wondered if we should try to prosecute, since juries are known to show sympathy toward invalids. We went ahead and the jury found Flynt guilty on all counts. The judge imposed a $27,500 fine and sentenced him to eleven years' imprisonment—which was suspended because of Flynt's tragic physical condition provided he didn't violate the law of Georgia, nor the United

States, nor any other state during that eleven-year period. Of course Flynt appealed the case to the Georgia Supreme Court and then to the U. S. Supreme Court, but the verdict against him was upheld each time. Since selling *Hustler* in Fulton County would be a violation of the law, to this day you will not find one for sale here.

Cleaning Up Atlanta

This is just one example of how the local prosecutor's office can effectively be used to fight pornography. In 1979, for example, my office prosecuted twenty-nine obscenity cases before the jury and had twenty-eight convictions, with a similar success rate in other years. By January of 1981, the lawyers representing all of the adult bookstores in our county came to my office when their clients were scheduled for trials—more trials than they could handle. The reason for the visit: to make a proposition. They offered to close down all the remaining stores immediately if we would forego the prosecution of the many obscenity cases pending. After much deliberation, we accepted the proposal, provided certain conditions were met, and on January 31, 1981, every adult bookstore in the county bolted its doors. In two months the remaining four adult theaters were also out of business. In December of 1982 I retired at the end of my term, after thirty-three years as a prosecuting attorney, fourteen of them as head of the Fulton County solicitor's office.

Twelve years is a long time to do battle. But it took that long to win. Even so, we might not have had success if it were not for my staff's persistence and dedication, and if it were not for the support we received from citizens' groups.

The Power of the Prosecutor
During the twelve years my office sought to rid Fulton
County of pornography, we found we could best attack the
problem with a fourfold strategy. First, use the state pornography law itself. Second, press local nuisance laws.
Third, push pornographic businesses into involuntary bankruptcy. Fourth, apply consistent, stiff enforcement no matter which approach we took.

1. State obscenity laws. A local prosecutor does not have
to wait for a complaint from the public to press charges
against pornographers. Any person in a law enforcement
position can act if he believes the state obscenity law has
been violated, and most states have workable obscenity
laws. In Atlanta, it was common practice in our office to
send investigators to merchants we believed were dealing in
obscene materials in order to purchase books or magazines
and show them to a judge. If a judge determined that the
material was obscene, a warrant was issued and the dealer
brought to trial. That's basically how it works. Any citizen
concerned about a business selling pornography may alert
the local prosecutor and request that this kind of investigation take place.

2. Nuisance Suits. Pornographic businesses by nature
attract sexual deviants, and it is not uncommon for a number of sexual crimes, like sodomy, prostitution, and public
indecency, to be committed on and around the premises.
Working undercover in Fulton County, our investigators
witnessed many of these crimes and were themselves solic-
ited for acts of sodomy or were on occasion physically
assaulted by customers who did not know they were law

enforcement officers. This of course led to many arrests and convictions.

When, by using this evidence, a local prosecutor can show a judge that a business tends to attract unsavory clientele and to produce a pattern of criminal activity, he can prosecute that business in what is called a nuisance suit. To my recollection, my office never lost any of the nuisance suits we filed against obscenity merchants.

While this kind of suit rarely results in the closing of a pornographic business, it helps in this way: A judge often prescribes that the doors be taken off of the private film-viewing booths, that adequate lighting be installed, and that other renovations be made to eliminate the opportunity for customers to use the premises for perverse activities. When this happens, homosexuals lose interest in the establishment. This hurts the company's profits, making it vulnerable to financial collapse as other costly legal action is filed against it. Most states have adequate nuisance laws.

Sometimes the best way to fight pornographers is to drive them into bankruptcy, which leads us to the third approach a prosecutor can take.

3. *Involuntary Bankruptcy.* Not long after my office began prosecuting pornography merchants and getting a high rate of convictions, we realized that we had a big problem. We were getting the convictions, but the businesses were not going away. The problem was that when we prosecuted these establishments, we could bring a case against the person on the premises—the manager or clerk, the projectionist or ticket seller, and we could also bring a case against the corporation. But most of the time we could not learn the true identity of the owners or stockholders. We were deal-

ing with "paper" corporations, businesses whose owners are carefully concealed. We could put managers in prison but we couldn't find the owners.

At first we didn't understand this and neither did the judges. We didn't want to imprison managers, we wanted to imprison owners. The judges felt the same way, but until we could get to them, fines were usually low, around $300 to $500.

As we arrested the underlings, our standard procedure on the way to jail was to advise them that we really wanted the owners and upper-level managers, and we would encourage them to turn state's evidence. A few did, and this was when we uncovered a remarkable fact. When clerks are hired, they are given four instructions: (1) Under no circumstances must they disclose the identity of a superior or owner, under threat of physical harm. (2) If arrested, they would be out on bond within the hour by prearrangement with a professional bondsman. (3) If put on trial, they would be represented by a company-paid lawyer. (4) If found guilty and fined, the fine would be paid by the company.

As judges learned that this kind of racketeering was going on, fines went up quickly, from $300 or $500, to $3,000 and $5,000 on the average. In one multiple-count case a judge levied a fine of $117,000. In 1979, for example, our county court judges levied fines totaling $605,000. Don't ever let anyone tell you that prosecuting obscenity cases is a waste of the taxpayers' money! Convicted pornographers pay for their own prosecutions, and there is money left over for the county treasury.

But even with the high fines we had a problem—collecting the money. Since we didn't know who the real owners were, we couldn't always collect.

That's when one of my staff lawyers came up with the answer. "Why don't we go into federal bankruptcy court and bring an involuntary petition for bankruptcy against these firms?" he asked. "We press the fact that this corporation owes us money by virtue of the fine levied against it, and we petition for assets of the corporation. In order to avoid bankruptcy, they must establish that they have adequate assets, in which case we collect our fine. If they can't pay, they are forced to go bankrupt and must close their businesses."

This was a brilliant idea. As we pursued these petitions we were also able to take depositions and interrogatories that helped establish who the owners were. This was, of course, the last thing most of the owners wanted the prosecutor to know. We collected one $20,000 fine and were about to collect several others when we were visited by the lawyers for the pornographers, who wanted to make the deal I mentioned earlier: "Drop the bankruptcy proceedings and we'll leave town."

4. *Tough Enforcement.* After all of the pornography businesses closed in our area, one new company did move into Atlanta and open a store despite a rather unusual warning from a lawyer who had previously defended the dealers. He told the new dealer: "If you don't close down, McAuliffe will camp in your parking lot until you do, and he's already bought his tent."

The warning wasn't heeded. The day they opened for business, we sent an investigator to buy some of their material. We showed it to a judge and arrested everyone on the premises—the same day. And we went back and did it again and again about every other day after that, making it clear that we were not going to let them operate. In less than two weeks we made no less than six sets of arrests. By the end of those two weeks that business closed its own doors and left town.

Getting the Job Done

The prosecutor has the power to do all these things. But will he? When I was prosecuting pornographers, I received very little active public support—although what support I did get was treasured and valuable to me. I even got a good deal of opposition, mainly from the media and some political rivals. The latter was settled by the good voters of Fulton County, but the former never seemed to give up.

A prosecutor needs to know that the public is behind him in fighting pornography or he will more than likely not want to stand alone. He may even need public encouragement just to begin a campaign on obscenity for fear that there might be a backlash or that the press might turn on him furiously. Here are four practical steps a concerned citizens' group can take to help fight pornography through the local prosecutor's office:

1. Check the Books. If anybody is going to be effective in fighting pornography, the first thing he must do is determine whether the community is protected by an effective state obscenity law, otherwise a campaign will come to a dead end.

The way to find out is to get a competent lawyer to advise you. The law should comply with the decision in *Miller v. California,* handed down by the U.S. Supreme Court in 1973, and affirmed in other Supreme Court decisions.

If an effective law is not on the books, then the citizens' group needs to influence the state legislature to adopt one. This means lobbying legislators, creating letter-writing campaigns, electing sympathetic legislators, convincing those already in office, etc.

After the 1973 *Miller* decision, some moral-minded people in Georgia went to the Georgia state legislature to bring the state law into conformity, thus making it constitutional. Their first attempt failed. The obscenity merchants had already convinced a few key legislators that this was a gray First Amendment area and that they should not pass a new law. So between the 1974 and 1975 legislatures the "We Care" organization and the PTA and various other organizations went back to the districts of these legislators and they stimulated voters to make their voices heard. When the 1975 legislature met, the obcenity law passed almost without a dissenting vote. We've been to the U.S. Supreme Court many times on obscenity cases from Fulton County and our state law has consistently stood the test of constitutionality—because it comports with the *Miller* decision.

In North Carolina, a citizens' organization determined to fight obscenity discovered that the state had a very cumbersome law, one with no teeth. Before a prosecutor charged anyone for disseminating obscenity in North Carolina, he first had to have a hearing in a civil court to determine whether the material was obscene. If it was, the judge would simply rule it so and tell the merchant he couldn't sell it anymore. Only if a merchant disobeyed the civil court could he be prosecuted criminally.

Since these bookstores are usually owned by paper corporations, what often happened was that the owner would simply take the obscene material out of the store cited and put it into another store he owned. He might own six or seven stores, so by the time the prosecutors could track down each new location and trace the ownership, the material would be outdated or sold. The same was true of films. This is why the prosecutors in North Carolina felt there was no point in spending time and energy fighting pornography.

When the North Carolina citizens' group found this out, they sponsored seminars in several cities to drum up support for a new state law. These seminars led to groups forming in each city, which then agitated for legislation, which was passed. Because these concerned North Carolina citizens had already established contact with so many prosecutors, and because they now have so many citizens aware of the problem, they have been able to launch an effective fight against pornography.

2. *Win Your Prosecutor's Cooperation.* Having a good law is essential, but it is useless if no one cares to enforce it. Some prosecutors believe they have the right to choose which laws they will enforce, and all too often pornography is not one of them. They call this prosecutorial discretion. That is an honorable term, but prosecutors who use it in this fashion use it wrongly. Prosecutorial discretion means that in a particular case, a prosecutor must decide whether he has enough evidence to pursue a charge and get a conviction. If he thinks he knows someone is guilty of a crime but he does not have enough evidence to make his case, he may wait to press charges until such evidence is obtained. That is prosecutorial discretion. It is up to the legislature to decide what laws are to be on the books, and it is up to the prosecutor to enforce all of them. If a prosecutor believes a law should not be enforced, he should seek its repeal by the state legislature, not simply ignore it. As long as it is there,

the prosecutor is obliged to enforce it, whether it pertains to pornography, prostitution, murder, or anything else.

A citizens' group, then, needs first of all to make sure that a workable law exists in their state. Then they must ask their prosecutor: "Will you help us get rid of obscene material from this community?" If he says yes, they should encourage him. If he says no, then in fairness to him they should inform him that since he refuses to do his duty, they will oppose him politically, and will find an opponent for him who promises to enforce the law.

The citizens' group should then pursue these goals and see that a responsible prosecutor is elected.

3. Build Community Support. Remember that the *Miller* decision says obscenity is to be determined by contemporary community standards. This is very important. This may well be the only law on any subject that varies from community to community, depending on local values. If a prosecutor feels that nobody in the community is complaining about obscene materials, he may assume standards are not being violated. The very nature of this law requires that people must make their voices heard.

In court, obscenity merchants will call in all sorts of witnesses and supporters. If a judge looks around the courtroom and sees that the majority of those present seem in support of the pornographer and that few people seem to be there out of concern for decency, this is bound to affect his opinion of community standards.

This is why it is also good for citizens' groups to picket local merchants who deal in pornography—such as the many convenience stores and otherwise "reputable" businesses which carry pornography. When judges, prosecutors, and legislators see this kind of reaction in a community, it builds a case for high community standards. It is not a good idea, however, to picket courthouses. This makes judges defensive and promotes the notion that courts do not render justice. Picketing and protest are best directed at merchants rather than at the legal system. (It is proper, of course, to campaign for or against judges and prosecutors at election time.)

One prosecutor in Jacksonville, Florida, says that when citizens' groups there paraded with placards in front of adult bookstores and movie houses, there was no question that the atmosphere helped his prosecutions, and played a substantial role in finally getting rid of pornographic businesses in that area.

This makes it important to include as many churches, PTA groups, civic clubs, and other community organizations as you can. Some people question whether it is appropriate for protesters to be identified as religious. While you will have to decide for yourself whether this would be a handicap in your community, you should realize that the church has influenced this country's values since the Declaration of Independence. This does not mean citizens should be primarily identified as religious, however. Many secular feminist groups, for instance, who might differ with the church on other issues, such as abortion, may still be sympathetic in the fight against pornography. These people should be included, particularly because they help reflect community standards.

The important thing is that members of the community are involved and that they are organized effectively.

4. Communicate the Right Way with the Right People. Any elected official is very sensitive to communication from the general public. If a politician gets a letter from a constituent about a particular issue, he automatically assumes there are a hundred other people who feel the same way but who didn't take the time to write. If he gets ten letters, he assumes there are thousands who feel this way. And if he gets a hundred letters, he thinks he has a mandate to act. Petitions on the other hand are not nearly as effective. Too often petitions are signed by people who don't know much about the issue at hand. Politicians know this and are not as inclined to give as much weight to a petition as many people would expect.

Moral-minded people, therefore, ought to be writing letters all the time, not just to legislators but to prosecutors, judges, even to the chief of police. It doesn't matter to the politician how good the English is, or how eloquent the argument. What matters to him is that people are concerned and have expressed their concerns. He just wants to see that the letter is original and sincere.

I include the police chief in my list of whom to write because often a prosecutor will need the help of the police. Police chiefs, police commissioners, and public safety directors can all play key roles in successfully fighting pornography. In some places a prosecutor cannot be effective because he cannot get the full cooperation of the police department.

In addition to a good prosecutor and a good police department, a community needs good judges. Besides writing to judges, it is a good idea for a group to request an audience before a judge, or before all the judges of a court, for that matter. Of course a judge is not allowed to speak about a case in progress, but he is free to speak about his general beliefs. This is something citizens are entitled to know and entitled to influence, so citizens should be sure and let the judge know where they stand and why. Since most judges are elected, citizens have the right and responsibility to know where they stand, just as with any other elected official.

Conclusion

A citizens' group can make a tremendous impact in the fight against pornography by helping its local prosecutors. This begins with ensuring that the best laws are in place, and it continues by making sure prosecutors and other community officials are aware of the community's concerns. This means mobilizing community members and civic groups. Since contemporary community standards are the central issue in pornography, there is no one in a better position to help the local prosecutor than members of the community itself.

CHAPTER TWELVE
Video and Cable: Hard-core Porn in the Neighborhood

Randall Murphree

Some of the customers at the Sakitumi Lounge in Indianapolis thought the drinks, by themselves, were just fine. They didn't appreciate the hard-core pornographic video being shown in the bar. They complained, and police arrested Donald Walker, the businessman who rented the movie to the bar owner. In May 1986, a county court jury found Walker guilty of distributing obscene material.

This is a new kind of obscenity case, for Walker doesn't run a dingy adult bookstore with windows painted over and grimy peep-show booths in back. His business is a typical, ''family-oriented'' video store, like many springing up across the suburban landscape. He rents hit movies, Disney cartoons, and hard-core pornography.

The Video Explosion
The explosive growth of the video cassette industry means that suddenly pornography is much easier to obtain. Law

enforcement officers are concerned that they will have a tougher time gaining obscenity convictions against a video store in a suburban shopping center than against a traditional adult bookstore at the edge of town or on skidrow. Many people who would never enter an adult bookstore patronize video stores, including prospective jurors.

The same laws that regulate printed obscenity apply to video cassettes, and so there is no danger constitutionally that legally obscene material will escape the reach of current laws. But the popularity and convenience of videos vastly broadens the market for obscene tapes, so the very size of the problem threatens to overwhelm the resources of local prosecutors. Even as they are making headway against the flow of print pornography, new floodwaters are rising.

Already, the video cassette recorder (VCR) challenges broadcast television, cable television, and theater as the nation's preferred entertainment medium. Nearly 12 million VCRs were sold in 1985, up 40 percent from the previous year. They are now in approximately 28 percent of the country's households.[1] To keep America's VCR's rolling, 50 million cassettes were sold in 1985, up from 10 million just two years earlier. While Hollywood releases only thirty new films a month, some 400 new video cassette titles a month are available.

In 1985 alone, some 1,700 new sexually explicit videos were released, and that trend is likely to continue.[2]

It is not hard to see the effect of the video boom. Nationwide movie theater box office receipts in 1985 were just over $3.5 billion, a 10 percent drop from the previous year. In that same year home video revenues doubled in size, to $3.3 billion. In 1986, home video revenues will probably hit $4 billion.[3]

Nationwide, about 80 percent of the legitimate video stores already offer porn films.[4] A 1985 *Newsweek* poll showed that 40 percent of VCR owners bought or rented X-rated videos that year. Video store dealers in Fort Lauderdale estimate that 20 percent of their stock is X-rated, but up to 40 percent of their total business comes from those tapes. Nationwide the figure is probably lower. A survey by the Video Software Dealers Association in 1984 showed that only 13 percent of the respondents' business was in "adult" titles. Ironically, this *excludes* most of the material which the Attorney General's Commission on Pornography found to be most harmful:

The categories labeled [in the Video Dealers survey as] "action/adventure," "science fiction," and "horror," which together comprise more than half of the market, include many films that include scenes of rape, sexual homicide, and other forms of sexual violence. The harmfulness of these materials is not lessened by the fact that breasts and genitals are covered in some scenes, nor the fact that these films are not given an X rating by the Motion Picture Association of America, nor the fact that the industry does not consider them "adult" materials. Indeed, all of these features increase the availability of these materials to minors. Moreover, the "music video" category, which includes many sexually violent depictions, is specifically marketed to young people.[5]

This is a new industry, distinct from the book and magazine publishing business, but all the familiar "free speech" arguments already are being heard. The Video Software Dealers Association (VSDA) announced in the spring of 1985 that it would adopt a policy to support its members in their "First Amendment concerns." The General Video of America Corporation, one of the largest pornographic publishing companies in the country, has begun offering legal assistance to video dealers hauled in for renting obscene films.[6]

It is clear then that the video cassette industry is an entirely new front in the battle against pornography. Fortunately, convictions like that of Donald Walker in Indianapolis help establish strong precedent. When he was found guilty, other video dealers in Indianapolis began pulling some hard-core videos from their shelves, lest they too be prosecuted.

Elsewhere, however, no headway has been made. In Fairfield, Ohio, a prosecutor filed obscenity charges against a dealer for renting *Taboo*. It is a movie about incest so explicit that the National Coalition Against Pornography uses it to shock people into joining the movement. In the Fairfield trial, the best legal minds for both the prosecution and the defense assisted the local attorneys. The case was tried twice, and both times the juries failed to reach a verdict, allowing the dealer to be freed. The fight to control obscene video cassettes has just begun, and no clear courtroom trend is yet in sight.

The Rise of Cable TV

The cable television industry, now about forty years old, is expanding at a tremendous rate. About 46 percent of American homes with televisions receive one or more of about fifty available cable services. Cable is available to about 70 percent of the 85 million television households in the country.[7] The industry estimates that by the year 2000, more than half of all households will subscribe.

As the cable business developed, it discovered it had to offer something different to compete with broadcast tele-

vision. Thus came a number of new and needed services—
news channels, sports channels, weather channels, etc.
There also came premium movie channels, generally available only at an extra monthly fee. It is on these "pay
cable" channels that the sexually explicit fare is offered.
Most of it comes from unedited R-rated films, and that
means that movies once unavailable at the box office to
children under eighteen are now being piped directly into
living rooms.[8]

Around 1980, the nation's pornography industry began
to recognize cable as an unfulfilled and lucrative opportunity.
A few companies marketing X-rated films and magazines
were soon producing films for erotic cable channels such as
the Pleasure Channel and Midnight Blue. Playboy Enterprises entered the field with its own production, the Playboy Channel.

These are not the only companies involved in pornographic cable television. Some of the others are quite familiar. Until April 1986, the Playboy Channel was distributed
by Rainbow Programming Services, 50 percent of which is
owned by the CBS television network. (After that, Playboy
Enterprises began distributing the service itself.) The Cinemax cable service is owned by Time, Inc.

Cinemax introduced in early 1985 a program called
"Eros America." It deals almost exclusively with sexually
graphic language and pictorials. One program featured a
segment detailing the making of a Japanese porn film. Cinemax also began showing pornographic movies such as
*Naughty Wives, Young Lady Chatterly, Sex Through a Win-
dow,* and *New York Nights.* The last title is a staple on the
Playboy Channel.[9] A subsidiary of the Cox newspaper
chain, Cox Cable, has been trying to introduce the Playboy

Channel in many communities and has been losing some scuffles with the antiporn movement in the process.

Two other prominent cable services are Home Box Office (HBO) and MTV. Home Box Office is a feature movie channel that has begun running soft-core pornography. One of its most popular series late in 1985 was *The Hitchhiker,* featuring violence, bare breasts, and simulated lovemaking. HBO was criticized by Multichannel News, a cable industry publication, in November 1985, for showing the violent film *Fortress* at 10:00 A.M. on the day before Thanksgiving. That movie features a villain named Father Christmas, who wears a Santa Claus mask and gets stabbed repeatedly by schoolchildren, who preserve his heart for their science class.

MTV is a cable service in a class by itself. It is an endless stream of music videos which regularly feed viewers violent sexual content (frequently women in bondage), near- or seminudity, sexual innuendo involving minors (sometimes young children), and vulgar, crude lyrics. The images on MTV are graphic, and fully one quarter of its audience is under age fifteen. A rape in a homosexual bar is featured in one video by the group Frankie Goes to Hollywood. A lesbian encounter appears in a Duran Duran video. The episodes consistently link eroticism and violence, performed not by villains, but teenage idols.

Playboy's Problems

Because cable television has been unable to attract as many commercial advertisers as it needs, it remains largely dependent on individual subscribers, and thus is sometimes vulnerable to community pressures. The plight of the Playboy Channel shows how effective this can be. The Warner-Amex cable company dropped Playboy in Cincinnati in 1983 after Warner was indicted on obscenity charges. Cox Cable withdrew it voluntarily in the face of similar pressures in Oklahoma City and Virginia Beach (see chapter 9). Heritage Cable in Des Moines, and Dimension Cable in North County, California, have also dropped Playboy. In many other communities, strong local reaction has prevented cable companies from offering it in the first place.

Partly for this reason (and partly because some people just get tired of soft-core pornography), Playboy has one of the highest "churn" rates in the industry, meaning that more subscribers have canceled than the company can afford. According to Cox Cable San Diego, the nation's largest cable system, Playboy's churn rate runs about 12 percent a month. In Raleigh, North Carolina, the local cable company dropped the service altogether, citing a 100 percent churn rate.[10] Reports of Playboy's subscribership vary, but the trend is downward. Playboy subscribers dropped from 800,000 in January 1985, to 680,000 by the end of the year.[11] (By contrast, the Disney cable channel had 2.5 million subscribers in 1985.)

In all, 1985 was a tortuous year for Playboy as it sought to improve the performance of its cable business. In March the company turned to more mainstream programming and less porn. By mid-July, however, it had returned to a porn-heavy diet. Playboy Enterprises reported a loss of $1.95 million for the quarter ending September 10, 1985. It attributed the problem primarily to the video division's operating loss of $2.1 million. (It earned $1.27 million during the same period in 1984, including a video division profit of $900,000.[12]) For the last quarter of 1985, Playboy reported a loss of almost $39 million.[13] Much of that loss came from sources other than the video operation, however. (The financial bleeding continued into 1986, according to *Broadcasting* magazine. By the end of the first quarter Playboy reported another $3.2 million loss, mostly the result of its failing Playboy Clubs, which it finally closed, but partially because of the poor performance of the video division. A company spokesman said Playboy Channel subscribers continued to decline.)

The "Unregulation" of Cable

The Communications Act of 1934, passed by Congress, established that the air waves are a national resource belonging to the American people; thus radio and television stations must act in the public interest. Congress authorized the Federal Communications Commission to enforce broadcast standards by license revocations, cease and desist orders, and fines. Technically, cable television is not broadcast, in that it is routed to individual sets via cable. Under current law, regular broadcast television cannot offer either obscene or indecent programming. (The Federal Criminal Code provides a penalty for "whoever utters any obscene, indecent or profane language by means of radio communication." The Supreme Court has ruled this applies to television as well.) Cable (and satellite) services cannot offer obscene programs, but are not bound by the decency standard. The Cable Communications Policy Act of 1984 established the joint responsibility of the FCC and the Justice Department to enforce obscenity standards for cable television, and authorized the FCC to set regulations for enforcing decency standards for cable.

But neither governmental body has acted. The Justice Department has never prosecuted an obscenity case against television. The manual used by Justice Department attorneys directs them to refer such cases to the FCC, which hasn't prosecuted a single case either. This policy rests with FCC Chairman Mark Fowler.

The Gospel According to Fowler

Fowler testified before the Attorney General's Commission on Pornography that he has no intention of enforcing standards already established for cable. He has said elsewhere that "ultimately broadcasters ought to be as free as newspapers or any print medium."[14] (Of course any newspaper that printed pictures or descriptions of the contents of some movies now on cable would risk an obscenity prosecution.) What drives Fowler to this reasoning is his desire to deregulate television, and allow the marketplace alone to govern what should be seen.

In June 1986, a chorus of antipornography organizations, led by Barbara Hattemer of the Florida Coalition for Clean Cable and Brad Curl of the National Christian Association, lobbied against President Reagan's renomination of Fowler for a new term as FCC commissioner. They were unsuccessful. Their feelings were summed up in a statement by Phyllis Schlafly, president of the Eagle Forum: "Deregulation of the airlines has been good because it brought about competitive low fares which enable millions of Americans to ride on a plane for the first time. But try asking those millions of Americans if they want deregulation of safety rules about air travel to follow deregulation of fares. You'll get a thunderous 'no.' Likewise with television and radio.

Price deregulation is welcome, but decency deregulation is unacceptable.''

Conclusion

Cable and video have opened new markets for pornography. Besides that, they have made it convenient and respectable. It is convenient because no one has to patronize a sleazy theater to see raunchy sex. It is respectable because video rental stores carry much more than just pornography. Community pressures have been successful in pushing back the Playboy Channel in some locations, but as long as the FCC refuses to enforce the decency standards for cable television, the gateway into millions of living rooms will remain wide open. It is still too early to know whether local trial courts will be as harsh against obscene videos coming from suburban rental stores as from hardcore pornography outlets, but local prosecutors are very concerned. Very clearly, this is a battle that is only beginning.

Notes

1. Report of the Attorney General's Commission on Pornography, July 1986: 1,387.
2. Ibid., 1,390. (The report also noted that 75 percent of these videos are being made by independent production companies. It identified forty-five of them, thirty-nine of which are in Los Angeles.)
3. "1986 Could Be the Year that Home Video Passes B.O. of Theaters," *Hollywood Reporter*, 2 January 1986.
4. "The Law in Your Living Room," *News/Sun-Sentinel*, Ft. Lauderdale, Florida, 6 October 1985.
5. Attorney General's Report: 1,389.
6. "X-Rated Video Pressures Seen Heating Up," *Billboard*, 27 April 1985.
7. Attorney General's Report: 1,416.

8. Regulations require cable services to offer lock boxes for sale or lease, so subscribers can control access to their televisions. Sometimes people who have not subscribed receive the programs anyway, because of an electronic problem called "bleedthrough." This has prompted many complaints against cable porn.

9. "Cable Programming Services at a Glance," *Broadcasting*, 2 December 1985.

10. "Churn, New Obscenity Law Plague Playboy in North Carolina," *Multichannel News*, 11 November 1985.

11. Ibid.

12. "Playboy Tries Revitalization," *Broadcasting*, 25 November 1985.

13. "Losses Diminish Playboy Sex Appeal," *USA Today*, 6 February 1986.

14. "The Legacy of Mark Fowler," *NFD Journal*, July 1986.

CHAPTER THIRTEEN
"Fight Pornography? I'm No Kook"

If someone wants to clean up his community, what is the first thing he should do? What is the second thing? Is it easy to recruit workers? What does one say to the press?

Chapters 9 and 10 described the local campaigns in Virginia Beach and Fort Wayne. In this chapter, Richard McLawhorn, executive vice president and general counsel of the National Coalition Against Pornography, explains in question-answer format some of the more general principles of recruiting and organizing. Much of what he says reflects what he learned in his own journey from skepticism to commitment.

In 1985 McLawhorn left his job as director of research for the South Carolina State Legislative Council to join NCAP. Before that, he was one of the organizers of CADRE (Citizens Advocating Decency and a Revival of Ethics), an organization that prompted numerous crackdowns against pornography by law enforcement officials in South Carolina.

Most Christian people I know don't want to get involved in this issue because they don't know anything about it. How do I get them interested?

That is a very common reaction. In fact, it was my own reaction. I regard myself as a typical Christian, so let me describe what happened to me a few years ago. My pastor, Lewis Abbott, had asked me to attend a consultation on pornography in Cincinnati. I must say I reacted badly. *Pornography?* I remember thinking. *Come on now, Lewis. I've seen* Playboy *and been to stag movies when I was young. But I don't look at that filth anymore. Why should I be concerned?* And there was another reason. Some of those antipornography people were seen as kooks. *What if I end up being identified with them?* I became involved reluctantly, then, solely as a favor to my pastor. If you wish to recruit volunteers, expect many to be reluctant. And *you* must be persistent.

If you are typical, what actually happened to change you from reluctant participant to dedicated leader?

I spent three years in the military as a single man. I'd seen pornography in Europe. But it wasn't until I was at that antipornography conference in Cincinnati that I saw the worst of what is out there. I had never before seen pictures of women being horribly abused sexually, of people being tortured for the sexual pleasure of others, and especially I had never seen graphic, explicit pictures of children being used for sexual purposes. I still have no words to describe my reaction to seeing a picture of a man lying down, with his erect penis thrust into the vagina of an infant girl, and the baby hanging there, virtually impaled. When I saw that, my mind went blank. I do not remember stumbling back to my room, but I do remember fighting back tears. I remember saying to myself, *I've got to get out of Cincinnati. I have seen evil in its evilest form.*

About a week later, I went to a civic club meeting back home. I had a few minutes before the meeting started, and I wandered across the street to a newsstand. I noticed, speaking as an attorney, a lot of material which was probably legally obscene being sold there. One of the paperback books on sale there was titled *I Took My Bra Off for Daddy.* I cringed. This wasn't even an adult bookstore! This was a public newsstand! These things shocked me. I knew then that *all* of us had a problem. It wasn't just a problem in far-off Cincinnati. It was here, in my community. I started thinking that *somebody* ought to do something.

It was Joseph Cardinal Bernardin who sowed in me the seed of a new concept: pornography was a *Christian* problem. He did this in a speech at the pornography consultation in Cincinnati. He explained it very simply: "The theological foundation for our opposition to obscenity, pornography, and indecency is the dignity of the human person. . . . God makes each person in his own image and likeness. To diminish the human person is to diminish God." I turned to Scripture, and saw that Ezekiel 3:17-21 addresses the issue. The evil of pornography is all around us, and we as Christians must speak out against that wickedness or be held accountable by God. Ephesians 5:11 is also directly on target. We are commanded not only to refrain from participating in works of darkness but to *expose* them.

So it gradually became clear to me, from practical and theological perspectives, what the issue was all about. I thought that if Christians won't stand up, who will? Why don't *they do* something? Then it dawned on me, as it does to so many people when they finally face up to large issues: I was one of the *"they."* At that point my involvement was inevitable. This is the process that convinced me. It is the same process that has convinced many of the most committed workers in the national campaign to rout obscenity.

One of the organizing principles, then, is to expose people to hard-core pornography. Isn't that risky, particularly in a church setting?
There is some risk, but how can you expect people to commit themselves to an issue unless they know clearly what the issue is? One of the video clips I show everywhere I can is from a movie called *Taboo*. It's stocked in many video stores. That means this movie is penetrating neighborhoods across the country. The taboo, about which the title speaks, is incest, and there are actually three movies in the series. The series is about sex between relatives—mother and son, father and daughter, brother and sister.

The movies show explicit sex acts, including anal and oral intercourse. The reason we show clips from this particular series is that a jury in Ohio recently could not decide whether it was obscene. We want people to see what kinds of movies are *not* being found obscene. It is then that they understand the issue. It is then that they get upset, and it is then that they get committed to this fight.

All we actually show is a very brief preview of *Taboo*, which appears on another video before an actual movie starts. It has scenes such as this, in which the young male actor says: "You're the best mother a guy could ever have," and as he says it he's fondling her breasts and ejaculating semen in her face. This is obscenity. This is what Christians have to understand.

I show this clip everywhere I can, because most Christians have never seen anything like this. I try to be sensitive, however, and invite those who don't want to see the clip to leave the room. On one occasion there was a Christian leader who didn't want us to show it to his group. I said, If you don't want to look at it, why don't you close your eyes and just listen to the dialogue? Listen to the announcer talk about the film. He agreed. He heard the mother compliment her son on the size of his penis, and he heard the son talk about his mother's breasts, and he heard the excited announcer repeat the word "incest," over and over. When the clip was finished, that man was ready to lead his own movement against pornography—from the dialogue alone!

If a local antipornography organization seeks its workers from church congregations, won't that be seen as competition with other activities? Most churches need more workers for their programs than they have.
There are many people who just do not want to work in conventional church ministries. They long to use their skills and education in the Lord's work, but the church hasn't thought creatively enough about how to encourage them. These people would never become deacons because they don't want to get into long arguments about paving the parking lot. But they are looking for meaningful ways to

serve. I know because that's where I was.

I don't know how many successful people have told me they would love to be doing something similar to what I am doing, to be committed to Christian work that is extremely important for the advancement of family values and morals. There are many who would welcome this opportunity who are not responding to anything else. I'm convinced of it. If organizers would raise this challenge to church congregations, and teach them actually what hard-core pornography consists of, and point out what Scripture says, they would get a strong, eager response, and they would not draw people away from other work.

Should all Christians who are not actively involved in this issue feel guilty about neglecting it?
Absolutely not. People have many callings. I, for one, am not called to be a pastor. There are many reasons why a lot of people just aren't meant to be fully involved in this campaign. First of all, people who are prone to become addicted to this stuff must stay away. It can be incredibly dangerous and addictive. Just within the last few months I have had conversations with three well-known Christian leaders— giants of the faith today. Each of them told me privately how they have been wounded by pornography. I thought to myself that if pornography could hurt men such as these, what could it do to people who are not nearly so strong in their faith?

In his book *Knowing God*, J. I. Packer comments on Daniel 11:32, and says that "people who know their God shall stand firm and take action." But there are many kinds of action. Some people may feel led to pray. Others can write letters to politicians. Still others can volunteer in the local campaign office. These are all vital tasks, but they do not require exposure to pornography itself.

You became so committed you gave up your position in the state legislature to work full time in this campaign. Have you had doubts since that decision?

Yes, early on some doubts arose. There were people I respect who looked askance at me for getting so involved in this. I also had doubts at first when I saw Christian pastors turn their backs on this issue and not want any part of it. Some pastors do this because they think their reputations in their communities will be harmed. Others feel they are fighting enough battles in their churches already and don't need more challenges. Much of this reaction, however, is simply a result of the right-wing, fanatical image this movement has unfairly had with some of the public. But that is changing, as more and more evidence pours out about the harm pornography causes, and it is changing as store after store stops selling pornography. The tide is turning, and this, of course, is greatly encouraging. This is a battle that will be won. Indeed, it is already being won.

Is a poor image a serious problem for the antipornography movement?

The number one problem facing this movement is image. The news media is very sympathetic to arguments that we are either bookburners or right-wing fanatics, or both. That is the pigeonhole many of them have for us. People who become active should not allow themselves to be boxed into that pigeonhole. They must carefully present themselves to the press and to the public—their words and style must be of a responsible, balanced nature. We are not right-wing fanatics. We are responsible parents and grandparents who are concerned for the safety of women and children. People have to approach this campaign with a style that clearly says: "We are not crazies." How does one accomplish that? Essentially by emphasizing that although this is a moral issue for some, and a religious issue for others, it is a public health and safety issue for everybody. That is the common ground that joins the religiously committed and the nonreligious.

In our local organization in South Carolina, we went after a very broad appeal. We had only two pastors on our steering committee. One was the chairman, Lewis Abbott. The other was the chairman of our pastor's committee. The rest of us were laymen. We were credible and professional, but we were laymen. The average person does not relate to a pastor in the same way he does to a layman. One must understand that for a number of reasons many people in the community will not join this campaign if it is seen only as a fight for biblical principles, because they do not abide by biblical principles. The average person can be made to see it as a public safety issue, however, and that is what must be stressed to him. That is also what must be stressed to the news media.

A second way in which the movement has suffered is by its poorly focused goals. People have not always defined exactly what it is they are trying to eliminate. Some people put network television programs on the same plane with child pornography. They are trying to say that subtle, humanistic influences of network programs undermine moral principles and make inroads on tomorrow's stan-dards. I am also concerned about humanism, but the average person just does not see it. The average person does not even know what the word "humanism" means.

What, then, is a proper focus for an antipornography organization?

At NCAP, our focus is quite narrow. We are out to stop child pornography and hard-core pornography. By "hard-core," I mean the kind of very explicit pornography that, if it were challenged in court, probably would be found obscene, and therefore illegal. There are laws against this kind of material, and there are laws against child pornography. We simply wish to see the laws enforced.

A Gallup poll has shown that 73 percent of adults are against hard-core pornography, and most of them do not even realize what it contains. How many more do you think will oppose it after we have shown them *Taboo?*

Another Gallup Poll said that only about 10 percent of Christians are highly committed. It is probably untrue then that all we need is for the church to wake up. The Gallup Poll indicates that Christian people, as a group, are just not that committed to exercising their faith day by day. Some Christians, of course, are committed to other ministries. But many Christians, sad to say, see nothing wrong with pornography. However, every responsible parent and grandparent is committed to the welfare and safety of their children and grandchildren. So if the issue is framed in that manner, one can get a positive response much more quickly.

If the proper focus is hard-core pornography and child pornography, what about the picketing of 7-Eleven

stores, which has accomplished the removal of *Playboy* and *Penthouse?* These magazines are not considered by the public to be hard-core. Does that mean the picketing has been wrongly focused?

Not at all. All groups who picket to remove any pornography, hard- or soft-core, should be applauded. They are applying economic pressure by peaceably assembling and exercising their right of free expression. That is exactly what the First Amendment protects. They not only have the freedom not to shop in certain stores, but the right to urge others to do the same. The danger is in trying to solve all problems by the use of law. Many issues of *Playboy* may not be legally obscene. Therefore it has a right to be published, and a right to be free of harassment from laws that do not apply. But it has no right to censor the First Amendment rights of those who believe its moral content is dangerous to the public good. People may wish to oppose publications like *Playboy,* and that is clearly their right, but the opposition should be by public demonstration and moral and economic persuasion. If the materials are not obscene, I do not favor the futile use of obscenity laws against them. If people try to apply the obscenity laws to plainly non-obscene material, they will ultimately fail, and become disillusioned. It is very important not to fight for a lost cause. Disillusionment can be fatal to a movement.

How do you think people should view those who actively defend pornography, such as the American Civil Liberties Union?

I think the ACLU deserves the criticism of all morally concerned people. Whenever spokesmen for the ACLU appear in public to defend pornography, they talk about First Amendment rights, but fail to fully discuss the law or mention other rights. You won't hear them say that the Supreme Court has *never* declared obscenity to be protected by the First Amendment. And you never hear the ACLU quote the Supreme Court language that says citizens have a *right* to maintain a decent society.

Now the ACLU cannot have it both ways. If it really wants to stand up for the First Amendment, it must acknowledge that the courts have decided numerous cases involving the First Amendment and have said repeatedly that there are limits beyond which even pornographers must not go. The courts have emphatically said that some material is *unprotected* by the Constitution. On the other hand, the ACLU can say that anything is permissible, even child pornography and movies which promote incest. But if it does this, it cannot claim to be standing up for the First Amendment because this material is plainly unprotected by the First Amendment. They have chosen to do the latter, to claim that the plainly illegal is legal and should be protected. The spokesmen for the ACLU have stuck themselves to the tarbaby of hard-core and child pornography. As long as they do this they make themselves just and fitting targets of criticism by people who are concerned about the safety of the country's women and children, and by all who have even the slightest belief in family values and morals.

Let me make it clear. The ACLU has not chosen to make a distinction between hard-core and child pornography, and milder, soft-core pornography. Not only does the ACLU actively defend hard-core and child pornography, it aggressively asserts that this material should be freely distributed in American society. This position of the ACLU is indefensible, and deserves condemnations by all Americans.

If you could sum up the collective wisdom that NCAP has gathered about basic steps in organizing and operating a local antipornography campaign, how would you do it?
I can sum it up in five words: communication, education, association, organization, and determination. I have talked about many of these elements, but let me review some important points about each of them.

First, communication. Christian leaders must communicate with God, first of all. We must take our fears, anger, confusion and concerns to him. Matthew 7:7-8 promises, "Ask and it will be given to you; seek and you will find; knock and the door will be opened to you (NIV)." Communication with God has preceded *every* successful anti-porn campaign that I know about. Many leaders prayed for months, some for years, before taking action.

Furthermore, one must communicate with people in a well-reasoned, responsible manner. I have already mentioned effective ways of doing this. Do not allow yourself to be deterred by negative reactions. Use those negative reactions to sharpen your own arguments. For example, Dorothy heard me speak on pornography at her church one night and decided to become involved. The first person she approached was Mary, her best friend from another church. Mary's response to Dorothy was: "I wish we could do something, but filth is sold all over the country. It must be legal, isn't it?"

After thinking for a few moments, Dorothy replied:

"Well, drugs like heroin and cocaine are also sold every-where, but that doesn't mean they're OK, does it?" Mary was then open to hearing more about the problem, and Dorothy had another powerful argument in her arsenal.

The second principle is education. It is extremely impor-tant that everyone who gets involved have at least some knowledge in three areas: the content of pornography, its moral implications, and the law. These are the topics that come up time and again, as one seeks to rally workers and answer unfriendly questions. There is excellent information on all three topics throughout this book.

The next principle is association. There are few absolute "don'ts" in my advice to those in the battle against por-nography, and here is one of them: *Don't* begin or continue your activities by yourself. Associate with others. This is a battle against a large multibillion-dollar industry. Pornog-raphers and their defenders spread a great deal of mis-information about their opponents and about pornography. Many in the local and national media are very sympathetic to the pornographers because they shrewdly paint the issue as one of free speech. In short, this is a big battle, and feel-ings of inadequacy, exasperation, discouragement and defeat can result. Christ saw the wisdom of teams. He sent the apostles out in pairs to preach the kingdom.

There are two types of associations that are necessary. The first is personal friendships. People in this campaign need mutual support, love and fellowship. The second is proper corporate association. Seek out people whose skills and philosophies are compatible with and complement your own.

For example, in South Carolina, when our pastor joined the fight, he immediately sought the help of two Christian laymen. One was a certified public accountant, another was a politically-oriented attorney (me). Together we had the necessary skills in financial organization, political knowledge and public speaking to get our campaign moving. You should also establish associations with organizations already at work on the problem, as long as they have a style and appeal suitable to your community.

The next principle is organization. One must establish a formal organization. This step will be much easier if the earlier steps have been taken. Some people don't like the idea of forming another organization, but this step is essential. A battle like this requires the sharing of responsibilities, delegation of authority, and formal procedures for making and implementing decisions. The simplest advice here is to draw on the experience of groups already at work on the problem. An important part of one's organizational strategy must be the gathering of a broad base of thoroughly reputable, upstanding people. This is an important principle: you will be characterized by the people you associate with. In South Carolina, we established our steering committee after weeks of hard work and prayer, as we sought out successful business and professional people. We simply did not want to be tagged from the start as right-wing bookburners. And we were largely successful in avoiding this image because of the work we put into it. Do not build your house on sand. Build a solid organization.

Finally, there must be determination. As Paul said in 1 Corinthians 15:58: "Therefore my dear brothers, stand firm. Let nothing move you. Always give yourselves fully to the work of the Lord, because you know that your labor in the Lord is not in vain" (NIV).

There is nothing ennobling about fighting pornography. Clyde Miller, a pastor active in the Cincinnati antipornography campaign, put it well: "What's glamorous about cleaning up the sewer?" Those of us in this fight are dealing with a subject most polite people don't even discuss. Unfortunately, neither do most Christians. Most of the victories in this battle have followed initial defeats. Prosecutors are reluctant to prosecute, court cases fail, pornographers are hauled into court one day and are back in business the next, the media is apathetic, or worse, hostile. And so it goes.

But more and more victories are being won all the time. Slowly the tide is changing, and with it the critical mass of public opinion. Meanwhile, those of us in the campaign must guard against discouragement, even though it is difficult to be patient in the face of such great evil.

There is a small statue of an eagle that sits on the credenza in my office, and it helps me keep things in perspective. Behind the statue is a framed quotation my mother knitted for me when I graduated from law school. It reads: "But they that wait upon the Lord shall renew their strength. They shall mount up with wings like eagles; they shall run and not be weary; they shall walk and not faint" (Isa. 40:31, TLB).

The following is information about the most active national organizations in the antipornography campaign. Anyone considering local action should first establish contact with a national group, for guidance, and for connections with others who already may be active in the local area.

Citizens for Decency through Law

The oldest and largest non-profit antipornography organization in the U.S, CDL formed in 1957 when its founder, attorney Charles H. Keating, Jr., began the legal battle in Cincinnati. CDL now serves more than 100,000 members in about 100 chapters. CDL attorneys have argued cases before the U.S. Supreme Court and supplied the rationale for the landmark *Miller v. California* decision. It is the only non-profit organization that provides citizen groups with technical legal assistance on obscenity prosecution and control, including attorneys for trials and appeals.

CDL demands and assists law enforcement and warns the public of pornography's harms. CDL's staff includes a speakers bureau of former obscenity prosecutors and a team of attorneys who are authorities on First Amendment and obscenity law. CDL provides consultation services, programs leading to better obscenity law enforcement, and national training seminars for police and prosecutors. It publishes numerous brochures, books, films, slide presentations, and a monthly newsletter, *The National Decency Reporter (NDR)*, which reviews and analyzes current cases.

CDL assists local antipornography groups and chapter status is not required. Funded by private individual and corporate gifts, CDL's mailing list is about 60,000. For more information write:

Citizens for Decency through Law
2331 West Royal Palm Road, Suite 105
Phoenix, Arizona 85021
(602) 995-2600.

Morality in Media

MIM began in 1962 as a New York City community campaign led by three clergymen. Now a national, non-sectarian organization, MIM aims at stopping pornography traffic and indecency in the media. This includes alerting communities about pornography's dangers, and helping them take appropriate action.

MIM operates the Nation Obscenity Law Center (NOLC), a privately-funded, specialized research center providing information on obscenity law for prosecutors, governmental agencies, and attorneys. The NOLC provides a complete cross-referenced and indexed Brief Bank, which is a continuing collection of the oldest (1808) to the newest obscenity cases and briefs. Files include an expert witness bank, abstracts, articles, statutes and ordinances. The NOLC's *Obscenity Law Bulletin* updates attorneys on new developments.

Each year at MIM's annual conference, leaders assess the status of the antipornography battle and develop a "Blueprint for Action" for the upcoming year. MIM also holds regional workshops. It publishes the *Morality in Media Newsletter* (circulation 55,000), numerous pamphlets, an eighteen-page summary of the 1986 Attorney General's Pornography Commission report, the *Handbook on the Prosecution of Obscenity Cases*, and has produced two documentaries. For more information write:

Morality In Media
475 Riverside Drive
New York, New York 10115
(212) 870-3222.

The National Coalition Against Pornography
NCAP is an interdenominational organization of parents and grandparents concerned about the safety of America's women and children. By informing, educating, and coordinating citizen efforts, NCAP mobilizes Christians and all concerned citizens to exercise their First Amendment rights against obscenity, pornography, and indecency. In 1983 leaders from more than seventy denominations and private organizations formed NCAP in Cincinnati, in order to encourage in other communities the same success Cincinnati experienced against pornography. Each year NCAP's National Consultation on Pornography trains community leaders to form task groups, mobilize citizens against pornography, and work for better enforcement of obscenity laws.

NCAP's campaign involves a public relations effort through national and local media, a direct-mail campaign to raise funds and educate, and production of an educational television special aimed at every major media market in the U.S. Funded by foundations and individuals, NCAP has a mailing list of 7,000. For educational materials (pamphlets, books, audio and video tapes), coordination, or consultation, write:

The National Coalition Against Pornography
800 Compton Road, Suite 9248
Cincinnati, Ohio 45231
(513) 521-NCAP.

The National Federation for Decency

NFD fights anti-Christian bias on television, as well as pornography. NFD began in 1977 when its founder, Don Wildmon, and his family could not find a suitable TV show to watch one evening. Today the *NFD Journal* has a circulation of 300,000 and *The Don Wildmon Report* broadcasts on more than 300 radio stations. NFD promotes traditional values and a biblical ethic of decency, with an emphasis on television and other media. NFD also publishes the semi-annual "TV Monitoring Report," which rates sponsors and shows for the amount of sex, violence, and profanity they present. NFD's Coalition for Better Television is an alliance of 2,400 groups working for constructive programing.

Through local chapters and volunteer groups, NFD organizes national letter-writing campaigns, pickets, and boycotts. NFD's primary source of funding is subscribers. For more information write:

The National Federation for Decency
P.O. Drawer 2440
Tupelo, Mississippi 38803
(800) 322-3629.

PART FOUR

What
Washington Says

Two important documents were released during the summer of 1986. They were the report of the Attorney General's Commission on Pornography in July, and the report of the Surgeon General's Workshop on Pornography and Public Health in August. In this section, summaries of the more important sections of both documents appear. Some portions are quoted verbatim, and some are paraphrased for clarity. In addition, Alan Sears, executive director of the Attorney General's Commission, answers a number of questions raised about the commission's work by its critics.

CHAPTER FOURTEEN
The Report of the Attorney General's Commission on Pornography

Introduction

It was a remarkable procession.

From May 1985 to February 1986, the Attorney General's Commission on Pornography convened a series of six public hearings across the country. Addressing the commission were pornographers, prostitutes, nudists, and Baptists. There were child molesters, molested children, detectives, FBI agents, postal inspectors, angry community activists, angrier feminists, sociologists, psychologists, sexologists, the surgeon general, and six U.S. senators.

In nearly every city, law enforcement witnesses and social scientists showed slides and film clips of people doing unimaginable things to other people, demonstrating the varieties of pornography widely available in the United States today. It was, said one observer, like a tour through a sewer in a glass-bottomed boat.

The commission was appointed by Attorney General Edwin Meese in May 1985 at the request of President

Reagan. Officially, its task was to "determine the nature, extent, and impact on society of pornography in the United States, and to make specific recommendations to the Attorney General concerning more effective ways in which the spread of pornography could be contained, consistent with Constitutional guarantees." Because the commission was created by the Reagan administration, it was criticized harshly in the media at nearly every turn for the conservative line it was expected to take on pornography.

Contrary to press expectations, the eleven commissioners were not uniform in their views. They were united, however, in their rejection of major aspects of the last commission to investigate the subject. This was the Presidential Commission on Obscenity and Pornography, which issued its report in 1970. Whereas that commission called pornography "therapeutic" and recommended repeal of obscenity laws, the 1986 commission links pornography with organized crime, sexual violence and degradation, civil injustice, and other societal harms. The commission declared strongly that legal regulation and enforcement against pornography and obscenity should be strengthened and increased.

Because the 1986 commission was appointed by the attorney general, a significant part of its work focused on law and law enforcement. But the commission felt that in order to adequately address the pornography issue, it needed to look also at the context in which pornography exists. Therefore it examined the nature of the industry, and the social, political, scientific, and moral concerns that bear on pornography.

The commission held six public hearings to gain the widest possible perspective from the public. In addition, commission staff members conducted more than 100 personal interviews.

On the basis of this evidence, the commission concluded that pornography containing explicitly sexual violence, degradation, subordination, or humiliation is harmful. Commission members did not agree on the harm caused by depictions of consensual pornography, that is, the type in which there is no violence or degradation. The commission was united in its concern over the impact these materials have on children. It called child pornography "a special horror," since it constitutes actual abuse of the children depicted and is used to seduce other children.

The commission noted that obscenity is unprotected by the First Amendment, but laws making it illegal are under-enforced, particularly federal laws, which could be used effectively to halt the interstate transportation of obscenity. The commission urged that enforcement of existing laws receive higher priority. In all, the commission issued ninety-two recommendations to federal and state policy makers and law enforcement officials. It also urged private citizens to take action, as is their right and duty.

The final report of the commission runs to nearly 2,000 pages. This chapter presents a digest of its more important findings and conclusions. Material quoted directly from the report is in quotation marks. Otherwise, the report is in summary form. In the following pages the term "pornography," when used by the commission, generally means only that the material is sexually explicit and intended primarily for sexual arousal. The commission uses the term "obscenity" to mean material likely to be found legally obscene in a court of law.

Organized Crime

Watchdogs of the pornography industry have long suspected connections between pornography and organized crime. In the past, some have been reluctant to state conclusively that there is a strong tie. The 1970 Commission on Obscenity and Pornography, for instance, concluded that "there is insufficient evidence at present to warrant any conclusion in this regard," despite the fact the FBI furnished it "with documentation of organized crime involvement which for some unknown reason was not included in the . . . commission's final report."

Unlike that earlier commission, the 1986 commission uncovered massive evidence that organized crime is highly involved in the pornography industry. The commission relied heavily on information and intelligence provided by experienced federal, state, and local law enforcement authorities in order to draw its conclusion. This included first-hand knowledge based upon years of investigative experience in the highly complex and covert area of organized crime.

Many of these law enforcement authorities testified before the commission on January 21 and 22, 1986, in New York City at a hearing devoted primarily to organized crime. Of the many investigative reports reviewed by the commission, five major sources were (1) the U.S. Department of Justice, (2) the Office of the Attorney General of California, (3) the Middle Atlantic–Great Lakes Organized Crime Law Enforcement Network (MAGLOCLEN), (4) the Pennsylvania Crime Commission, and (5) the Washington, D.C., Metropolitan Police Department.

Based on this research, the commission concluded:

"Organized crime in its traditional LCN [La Cosa Nostra] forms and in other forms exerts substantial influence and control over the obscenity industry." This does not mean all producers and distributors are members of LCN, but "all major producers and distributors of obscene material are highly organized and carry out illegal activities with a great deal of sophistication." The commission quotes FBI Director William H. Webster's conclusion: "Although La Cosa Nostra does not physically oversee the day-to-day workings of the majority of pornography business in the United States, it is apparent they have 'agreements' with those involved in the pornography business in allowing these people to operate independently by paying off members of organized crime for the privilege of being allowed to operate in certain geographical areas."

Among the many testimonies heard by the commission was this one from a former owner and operator of an adult bookstore, who spent many years in the pornography business. When asked what happens if the mob decides it doesn't want some particular pornography merchandise sold in a particular area, the witness answered:

You don't sell it. Even if they don't even talk to you. You're not going to sell it nowhere. If you go to the store on 14th street and put it in there, they're gonna . . . break your legs when you start going through them. There was a man who went from New York City . . . to Atlanta. Had films to sell. . . . They found him at the airport, with a $5,000 Rolex watch on and about eight grand in his pocket, and four rolls of film in his hands, with his head blown up in the trunk of his car. Nobody robbed him, nobody took a dime off him. They didn't even take the film. . . . Don't come down from New York selling, unless you've been sent down.

The commission reported: "Organized crime elements have found that the large financial gains to be reaped from pornography far outweigh the risks associated with the trade," given that courts and law enforcers devote little serious attention to obscenity violations.

Related Crimes and Activities
"In addition to the myriad of other harms and antisocial effects brought about by obscenity, there is a link between traditional organized crime groups' involvement in obscenity and many other types of criminal activity. Physical violence, injury, prostitution and other forms of sexual abuse are so interlinked in many cases as to be almost inseparable. . . ." Among the crimes the commission found to be associated with the pornography industry were murder, physical violence, damage to property, prostitution, and other sexual abuse, narcotics distribution, money laundering and tax violations, copyright violations, and fraud. Other crimes associated with the mob's pornography connection include child pornography, illegal gambling, and the possession, transfer, and sale of machine guns and silencers. Here are details of some of these crimes, as reported by the commission:

Murder. Michael George Thevis, head of one of the largest pornography operations in the United States during the seventies, and one-time head of 107 corporations, was convicted in 1979 for Racketeer Influenced and Corrupt Organizations Act (RICO) violations including murder, arson, and extortion.

A number of other murders have been linked to pornography disputes, including the disappearance in 1976 of *Deep Throat* distributor Robert DeSalvo, who had provided evidence in the trial of one of the movie's producers, Joseph Peraino. Peraino's son was also found murdered gangland style. Likewise, in July 1985, Patsy Ricciardi, owner of the Admiral Theater in Chicago, was found murdered. Chicago police believe this was a result of his pornography business dealings.

Physical violence and damage to property. "The damage and injuries range from those sustained by performers forced to engage in physically harmful acts which can often result in permanent injury, to damage to property, 'knee-breaking,' and arson."

Veteran FBI agent William E. Kelly told the commission, "Some of the current well-known names in the industry have reported threats against them or physical brutality." A bookstore operator, associated with members of organized crime families, described the "discipline" of the pornography industry against those who disobey rules for pricing, territory, and other matters:

"Bonjay . . . took one of the guys, held him by his arms up against the wall in the alley, and . . . ran [the car] into him, with the front bumper up against the wall and shattered his knees." This same witness reported bombs being thrown into stores that failed to comply with general price agreements or to pay street taxes to organized crime families.

Prostitution and other sexual abuse. "Prostitution is the foundation upon which pornography is built. . . . Pornography cannot exist without prostitution. . . . It is impossible to separate pornography from prostitution. The acts are identical, except in pornography there is a permanent record of the woman's abuse.''

Furthermore, according to Kelly, ''These women, who have been subject to every form of rape, sexual assault, and battery, and whose lives are totally controlled by their pimps, are used and abused by pornographers for the creation of their wares. It is impossible for most sexually explicit books, magazines, or films to be produced without acts of prostitution.''

Narcotics distribution. ''Narcotics are often distributed to performers who appear in pornographic materials to lower their inhibitions and to create a dependency. Profits earned by organized crime from pornography sales have been used to finance drug smuggling.''

This has been documented in the case of *Deep Throat,* the profits of which may have helped finance ''the major drug smuggling base north of the Panama Canal.'' Police also report drug transactions are rampant in areas where adult bookstores operate.

Money laundering and tax violations. ''The nature of pornography business provides inviting opportunities for skimming on every level.'' This is largely due to the cash-only policy of most pornographers.

Bookstores selling pornography also ''have a consistent sales format throughout the United States.'' This consists of two separate operations for accounting purposes: the ''frontroom'' and the ''backroom.'' In the frontroom, sales generally consist of paperback books, magazines, rubber goods, lotions, stimulants, and other materials. ''The frontroom operations' profits are generally used to pay for rent, utilities, materials, and employee wages.''

The backroom usually contains coin-operated peep machines that "produce substantial income that is usually not reported as taxable income.'' A police officer testified that ''the backroom operation usually takes in twice the amount as the frontroom operation.'' A bookstore operator testified that ''such 'skimming' commonly occurs with video cassette rentals and magazines as well as the peep machine coin boxes.''

Retired FBI agent Homer Young testified that when Michael Thevis, once a major pornography distributor in the South, boasted that he owned 90 percent of the viewmatic [peep show] machines in the U.S., Robert DiBernardo, alleged LCN Gambino (and/or de Cavalcante) family member, corrected him: ''Though he may have 'proprietary rights' the machines were owned by 'the family.' ''

''A bookstore operator told the commission . . . 80 percent of the skimming goes on in coin boxes. . . . Because who can tell how many customers come in today, and drop how many quarters, in how many machines?'' He estimated, based on his own machine sales, that a store may make $1,200 to $1,600 a day in quarters.

Fraud. ''Layers of corporations and hidden transactions of all descriptions are used by organized crime families involved in pornography to conceal true ownership and activities.''

Quoting from the *Investigative Report on Organized Crime and Pornography Submitted to the Attorney General of California* (1978), the commission said:

Pornography businesses are often represented on corporate papers by persons with no apparent ties to the company's true owner. Business transactions are commonly conducted with hidden incorporated affiliates which creates an appearance of legitimate competitive business practices. Foreign corporations and banks have been used to circumvent normal business accounting methods. For protection purposes, pornographers frequently form several corporations for one operation. They know that law enforcement authorities, when serving search warrants as a result of possible obscenity violations, are restricted to search only the corporation named. The other corporations remain protected from police inspection.

That these claims are far from exaggerations is made pointedly clear in the case study of Reuben Sturman, the example *par excellence* of the pornography kingpin.

Reuben Sturman's Pornography Empire

"Reuben Sturman, also known as Robert Stern, Roy C. English, Robert Butler, Paul Shuster, and Paul Bekker, of Cleveland, Ohio; Los Angeles, California; and elsewhere, is widely believed to be the largest distributor of pornography in the world. Law enforcement authorities believe that the Sturman empire has financial control of nearly 200 businesses in nineteen states . . . and six foreign countries. Sturman is closely associated with known organized crime members."

Sturman started out more than twenty years ago as a small-time candy, tobacco, and comic book distributor. Managing to avoid any serious legal problems, "he built the business into a mammoth operation encompassing all phases from production to retail sales with a myriad of corporate identities."

Sturman "structured his many companies, from retail stores to video production firms, in a honeycomb of nominees, false names, and dead associates to avoid local obscenity prosecutions. [A 1985 tax case] reveals that the corporate structure has grown hydra-headed over the years, apparently with the more serious intent of avoiding taxes."

The Los Angeles police reported that "580 of the 765 adult video arcade machines there are owned by companies controlled by Sturman." He "typically installs equipment worth $22,000 to $60,000 at no cost to the store owner" in exchange for 50 percent of the income from peep shows.

Although a number of Sturman's corporations and associates have been convicted on obscenity charges and other violations, Sturman has evaded any serious personal consequences for his acts.

"An indictment returned by a federal grand jury in Cleveland in 1985 alleged Sturman conspired to evade millions of dollars in taxes by laundering $7 million through foreign bank accounts and also charges that he destroyed records subpoenaed by the grand jury. One of his co-defendants, Scott Dormen, pleaded guilty to his part in the conspiracy. . . ." As for Sturman, he "professes indignity when legally attacked . . . and fights back savagely. He also covers legal fees and fines of associates and gives bonuses when they face the consequences of arrest."

Sturman's General Video of America (GVA), one of the largest distributors of pornographic videotape cassettes in the U.S., recently released a new publication. *White Paper* notifies video cassette retailers of government action against obscenity. It also announced the creation of a legal defense fund for GVA and others who distribute cassettes, offering a toll-free phone line, on which retailers can call an attorney provided by GVA to advise them on legal matters.

A report was filed with the commission by MAGLO-CLEN, which employed a federally-funded Regional Information Sharing System [RISS], to give the commission a glimpse of Sturman's staggering network of corporations and associates.

According to the RISS report, "These companies stretch from Massachusetts to California, from Michigan to Florida." The seven major states having Sturman-related business, and the number each contains, so far as is known, is as follows: "Ohio, 35; California, 24; Illinois, 15; Pennsylvania, 14; Michigan, 13; Maryland, 11; New Jersey, 10. These states account for sixty-two percent, or almost two-thirds, of all known locations of Sturman businesses."

Outside the U.S., Sturman-related businesses have been found in Ontario, Great Britain, Panama, Liberia, the Netherlands, and Lichtenstein. Several Sturman associates and corporations have bank accounts in Switzerland.

The IRS estimated that for five years (1978-82) Sturman had a personal income of $3,399,734, or an average income of $679,946.80 per year. For the same years, Sturman claimed a total income of only $363,609, approximately 10 percent of the IRS estimate. Having paid only $137,745 in income taxes during that time, the IRS contends that he evaded over $1.6 million in taxes.

"And, this figure could well be just the tip of the iceberg," according to Marilyn Sommers, an expert on analysis of law enforcement intelligence, who presented the MAGLOCLEN report to the commission. "If his personal taxes were underreported, what of his corporate tax liabilities for dozens of businesses? Indeed, it may take a platoon of investigators, analysts, and accountants to find the bottom line in Sturman's business dealings.''

MIPORN

"The most significant federal obscenity investigation and prosecution to date arose in the Southern District of Florida.'' MIPORN (short for Miami Pornography) began as a local police initiative but soon snowballed into a nationwide two-and-a-half year undercover investigation conducted by the FBI in cooperation with the U.S. Department of Justice Organized Crime Strike Force.

MIPORN ''resulted in many indictments for interstate transportation of obscene materials and revealed other criminal activities resulting in indictments and forfeitures including but not limited to racketeering, possession and transfer of machine guns and silencers, child pornography, interstate transportation of stolen property, and copyright violations.''

In October 1977, the FBI established an undercover company in south Florida named Golde Coaste Specialities, Inc., as the basis of the operation. (Note: the ''e'' in Golde and Coaste distinguishes this from other businesses in Florida that use similar names.) Renting an office warehouse, undercover agents used the ''front'' business as a blue jeans store, while in the back they ran a pornography business. Posing as a mail-order operation that distributed hard-core pornographic eight-millimeter films, magazines, and videotape cassettes (when in fact there was no such business), the agents traveled throughout the country and met with pornographers in virtually every major city, including New York, Los Angeles, San Francisco, Las Vegas, Chicago, Pittsburgh, Minneapolis, and Providence. They found that major pornography producers of every medium would meet every six months in various cities. These usually were not conventions with planned agendas. Rather, the meetings took place informally.

The undercover agents received warnings from several pornographers that physical harm, even murder, could result from crossing the wrong people. Others disclosed membership in or connections to the Los Angeles La Cosa Nostra family and the New York Gambino family, and dealings with Reuben Sturman.

The agents encountered dealings in stolen film equipment, the use of prostitution in connection with pornography businesses, and the commerce of films depicting bondage and sadomasochistic themes, child pornography, bestiality, and homosexuality. One pornographer admitted to pirating videotape cassettes of major motion pictures.

MIPORN was a successful sting operation in twenty-eight cities, and, by the end of 1985, produced twenty-eight convictions, with more cases still pending. Special Attorney Marcella Cohen concluded her report to the commission by noting: "The MIPORN investigation has yielded substantial evidence of organized crime involvement in the nationwide distribution of pornographic material, and serves as an example of effective utilization of law enforcement resources to combat the trade in obscenity." In other words, MIPORN proves and shows how dedicated law enforcers *can* fight obscenity effectively, using the current laws and resources available.

Conclusions about Organized Crime and Pornography

The commission noted the difficulty local police have in investigating pornographers. "[A] business in one jurisdiction, in general, is incorporated in another, receives materials from another jurisdiction, and is controlled by individuals in [yet] another. Federal law enforcement involvement is an absolute necessity to attack the real problem of organized crime." Organized crime families need not live in a particular state to "suck the lifeblood out of a community." Their enterprise "tears at the moral fiber of society and through unbridled corruption, it can weaken the government."

Quoting at length from a 1978 FBI analysis, the commission concluded that "organized crime involvement in pornography is indeed significant, and there is an obvious national control directly, and indirectly, by organized crime figures of that industry in the United States. Few pornographers can operate in the United States independently without some involvement in organized crime. Only through a *well-coordinated, all-out national effort* from the investigative and prosecutive forces can we ever hope to stem the tide of pornography. More importantly, the huge profits gathered by organized crime in this area and redirected to other lucrative forms of crime, such as narcotics, and [also the] investment in legitimate business enterprises, are certainly cause for national concern, even if there is community apathy toward pornography."

Civil Rights and Victims

The commission encountered overwhelming evidence that pornography degrades, harms, and "subordinates women and undermines their status and opportunities for equality.'' Not only does it damage women, but men and children and society as well.

The commission heard public testimony from thirty-three witnesses; commission staff investigators interviewed more than 100 persons; and the commission considered numerous letters and written statements, all from people who said they were victimized by pornography.

Women, men and children ''attributed to pornography their having been coerced into pornographic performances, bound and beaten in direct imitation of pornography, and forcibly imprisoned for the purpose of manufacturing pornography.'' Among the commission's many sources of testimony against pornography were the findings of the Indianapolis–Marion County Council. (Minneapolis proposed, and Indianapolis actually enacted, a local civil rights ordinance to protect women from injuries by pornography, but a federal appeals court struck down the Indianapolis law in 1986.) Noting these findings, which matched its own, the commission reported: ''Victims and trained professionals described the harms associated with and attributable to pornography as including rape, battery, sexual harassment, sexual abuse of children, and forced prostitution. Women were coerced into pornographic performances by abduction, threats, drugs, and constant surveillance. Pornography was forced on unwilling viewers, typically children or women, in homes, in employment, and in public places. Some assaults were found to be caused by specific pornography providing instigation as well as instruction and legitimization for the acts. Many experiences of pornography-related humiliation, sexual degradation, enforced servility, and physical and mental abuse were substantiated.''

In spite of the fact that the appeals court ruled the India-napolis law unconstitutional, the commission recommended that legal authorities continue trying to fashion a constitu-tionally sound civil rights law. It said the appeals court accepted the basic premise of the legislation, even if it didn't accept the definition. (In its ruling, the court said: "Depictions of subordination tend to perpetuate subordi-nation. The subordinate status of women in turn leads to affront and lower pay at work, insult and injury at home, battery and rape on the streets.")

In light of the evidence the commission said, "Legisla-tures should conduct hearings and consider recognizing a civil remedy for harms attributable to pornography . . . although controversial, [this] is the only legal tool suggested to the commission which is specifically designed to provide direct relief to the victims of the injuries so exhaustively documented in our hearings thoughout the country."

The Testimony of Andrea Dworkin

Andrea Dworkin is a New York writer and feminist who helped to craft the Indianapolis civil rights ordinance. She testified at the commission's Chicago hearing in July 1985. Her plea probably was the most eloquent testimony the commission heard from anyone. It affected all commis-sioners deeply, and it spurred the commission to look closely at civil rights legislation as a solution to the problem of por-nography. Here, in slightly abridged form, is what she said:

My name is Andrea Dworkin. I am a citizen of the United States, and in this country where I live, every year millions of pictures are being made of women with our legs spread. We are called beaver, we are called pussy, our genitals are tied up, they are pasted, makeup is put on them to make them pop out of a page at a male viewer. Millions and millions of pictures are made of us in postures of submission and sexual access so that our vaginas are exposed for penetration, our anuses are exposed for penetration, our throats are used as if they are genitals for penetration. In this country where I live as a citizen, real rapes are on film and are being sold in the marketplace. And the major motif of pornography as a form of entertainment is that women are raped and violated and humiliated until we discover that we like it and at that point we ask for more.

In this country where I live as a citizen, women are penetrated by animals and objects for public entertainment, women are urinated on and defecated on, women and girls are used interchangeably so that grown women are made up to look like five- or six-year-old children surrounded by toys, presented in mainstream pornographic publications for anal penetration. There are magazines in which adult women are presented with their pubic areas shaved so that they resemble children.

In this country where I live, there is trafficking in pornography that exploits mentally and physically disabled women, women who are maimed; there is amputee pornography, a trade in women who have been maimed in that way, as if that is a sexual fetish for men. In this country where I live, there is a trade in racism as a form of sexual pleasure, so that the plantation is presented as a form of sexual gratification for the black woman slave who asks please to be abused, please to be raped, please to be hurt. Black skin is presented as if it is a female genital, and all the violence and the abuse and the humiliation that is in general directed against female genitals is directed against the black skin of women in pornography.

Asian women in this country where I live are tied from trees and hung from ceilings and hung from doorways as a form of public entertainment. There is a concentration camp pornography in this country where I live, where the concentration camp and the atrocities that occurred there are presented as existing for sexual pleasure of the victim, of the woman, who orgasms to [real abuses, like those which occurred] not very long ago in history.

In the country where I live as a citizen, there is humiliation of women, where every single way of humiliating a human being is taken to be a form of sexual pleasure for the viewer and for the victim; where women are covered in filth, including feces, including mud, including paint, including blood, including semen; where women are tortured for the sexual pleasure of those who watch and those who do the torture, where women are murdered for the sexual pleasure of murdering women, and this material exists because it is fun, because it is entertainment, because it is a form of pleasure, and there are those who say it is a form of freedom.

Certainly it is freedom for those who do it. Certainly it is freedom for those who use it as entertainment, but we are also asked to believe that it is freedom for those to whom it is done.

Then this entertainment is taken, and it is used on other women, women who aren't in the pornography, to force these women into prostitution, to make them imitate the acts in the pornography. The women in the pornography, 56 to 75 percent of them we believe, are victims of incest or child sexual abuse. They are poor women; they are not women who have opportunities in this society. They are frequently runaways who are picked up by pimps and exploited. They are frequently raped, the rapes are filmed, they are kept in prostitution by blackmail. The pornography is used by johns on prostitutes who are expected to replicate the sexual acts in the pornography, no matter how damaging it is.

Pornography is used in rape—to plan it, to execute it, to choreograph it, to engender the excitement to commit the act. Pornography is used in gang rape against women. We see an increase since the release of *Deep Throat* in throat rape—where women show up in emergency rooms because men believe they can penetrate, deep-thrust, to the bottom of a woman's throat. We see increasing use of all elements of pornography in battery, which is the most commonly committed violent crime in this country, including the rape of women by animals, including maiming, including heavy bondage, including outright torture.

We have seen in the last eight years an increase in the use of cameras in rapes. And those rapes are filmed and then they are put on the marketplace and they are protected speech—they are real rapes.

We see pornography in the harassment of women on jobs, especially in nontraditional jobs, in the harassment of women in education, to create terror and compliance in the home, which, as you know, is the most dangerous place for women in this society, where more violence is committed against women than anywhere else. We see pornography used to create harassment of women and children in neighborhoods that are saturated with pornography, where people come from other parts of the city and then prey on the populations of people who live in those neighborhoods, and that increases physical attack and verbal assault.

We see pornography having introduced a profit motive into rape. We see that filmed rapes are protected speech. We see the centrality of pornography in serial murders. There *are* snuff films. We see boys imitating pornography. We see the average age of rapists going down. We are beginning to see gang rapes in elementary schools committed by elementary-school-age boys imitating pornography.

We see sexual assault after death where frequently the pornography is the motive for the murder because the man believes that he will get a particular kind of sexual pleasure having sex with a woman after she is dead.

We see . . . women also suffering the injury of objectification—that is to say we are dehumanized. We are treated as if we are subhuman, and that is a precondition for violence against us.

I live in a country where if you film any act of humiliation or torture, and if the victim is a woman, the film is both entertainment and it is protected speech. Now that tells me something about what it means to be a woman citizen in this country, and the meaning of being second class.

When your rape is entertainment, your worthlessness is absolute. You have reached the nadir of social worthlessness. The civil impact of pornography on women is staggering. It keeps us socially silent, it keeps us socially compliant, it keeps us afraid in neighborhoods; and it creates a vast hopelessness for women, a vast despair. One lives inside a nightmare of sexual abuse that is both actual and potential, and you have the great joy of knowing that your nightmare is someone else's freedom and someone else's fun.

I am . . . asking you to acknowledge the international reality of this—this is a human rights issue—for a very personal reason, which is that my grandparents came here, Jews fleeing from Russia, Jews fleeing from Hungary. Those who did not come to this country were all killed, either in pogroms or by the Nazis. They came here for me. I live here, and I live in a country where women are tortured as a form of entertainment and for profit, and that torture is upheld as a state-protected right. Now that is unbearable.

I am asking you to help the exploited, not the exploiters. You have tremendous opportunity here. I am asking you as individuals to have courage, because I think it's what you will need, to actually be willing yourselves to go and cut that woman down and untie her hands and take the gag out of her mouth, and to do something for her freedom.

Solving the Civil Rights Problem
"The pattern of harm documented before the commission, taken as a whole, supports the conclusion that the pornography industry systematically violates human rights with apparent impunity. The most powerless citizens in society are singled out on the basis of their gender—often aggravated by their age, race, disability, or other vulnerability—for deprivations of liberty, property, labor, bodily and psychic security and integrity, privacy, reputation, and even life.

"So that pornography can be made, victims have been exploited under conditions providing them a lack of choice and have been coerced to perform sex acts against their will. Public figures and private individuals alike are defamed in pornography in increasing frequency. It is also foreseeable, on the basis of our evidence, that unwilling individuals have been forced to consume pornography in order to pressure or induce or humiliate or browbeat them into performing the acts depicted. Individuals have also been deprived of equal access to services, employment or education as a result of acts relating to pornography. Acts of physical aggression more and more appear tied to the targeting of women and children for sexual abuse in these materials.

"Through these means, the pornographers' abuse of individual members of protected groups both victimizes them and notifies all of society that such abuses of them is permitted. This in turn serves to terrorize others in their group and contributes to a general atmosphere of bigotry and contempt for their rights and human dignity, in an impact reminiscent of the Ku Klux Klan. Respect for law is undermined when such flagrant violations go unchecked—even more so when they are celebrated as liberties protected by government.

"We therefore conclude that pornography, when it leads to coerced viewing, contributes to an assault, is defamatory, or is actively trafficked, constitutes a practice of discrimination on the basis of sex. Any legal protections which currently exist for such practices are inconsistent with contemporary notions of individual equality.

"The commission accordingly recommends that the United States Congress should conduct public hearings and adopt legislation affording protection to those individuals whose civil rights have been violated by the production or distribution of pornography. The bill should define pornography realistically and encompass all those materials, and only those materials, which actively deprive citizens of such rights. At a minimum, claims could be provided against trafficking, coercion, forced viewing, defamation, and assault, reaching the industry as necessary to remedy these abuses, consistent with the First and Fourteenth Amendments."

Pornography and Law

Pornography advocates have long argued against regulating it by law. These arguments frequently came up during the commission's proceedings. After careful consideration, the commission concluded that the arguments were unpersuasive.

The arguments against regulation fall into three basic categories: (1) pornography is harmless; (2) regulating pornography is unconstitutional; and (3) government action will not be effective.

The commission said many of the claims of harmlessness are simply erroneous. These claims ignored significant evidence, drew conclusions about all pornography based on right conclusions about its mildest forms, or demanded some extraordinarily high burden of proof which stems from a predisposed bias against regulating pornography.

As to charges that regulation is unconstitutional, the commission noted this claim requires a view of the law strikingly different from that long accepted by the Supreme Court in its rulings on obscenity.

The third category of arguments the commission found most deserving of attention. These arguments essentially ask: "If we had no laws dealing with pornography, would we want them?" Rather than answer this, the commission chose to recast the question: "Given 180 years of pornography regulation in the United States, should we repeal it?" The commission's answer was a resounding "No!" It said: "Although virtually every argument for deregulation presented to us has been in the former tone, it is the latter that represents reality." Although historic positions are always open to reconsideration, nevertheless "there are vast real and symbolic differences between not doing what has not before been done and undoing what is currently in place. To undo makes a statement much stronger than that made by not doing.'' The commission concluded it was not ready to make such a strong statement, especially since it would seem to contradict the evidence. It also concluded that given the long history of the courts and the government in favor of regulation, the burden of proof is on those who would have government make the much stronger statement implied by deregulation.

More Law Enforcement Is Necessary
The commission asserted that pornography-related crimes have received less law enforcement attention than they should have received. Remedying that imbalance by another imbalance—a heavy concentration of law enforcement muscle—is appropriate.

It found that ''images are significant determinants of attitudes, and attitudes are significant determinants of behavior . . . the [pornographic] images are a significant cause [of harm] even when compared with all of the other likely causes of these same harms.'' Therefore, the commission concluded, ''we have little hesitation in making recommendations about increased priority.'' Without a doubt, law enforcement should give increased attention to fighting sexually violent, sexually aggressive, and sexually degrading pornography, using, in most cases, laws which are already on the books.

Existing Laws Are Good Enough
''The laws of the United States and of almost every state make criminal the sale, distribution, or exhibition of mate-

rial defined as obscene'' in accordance with *Miller v. California*. The enormous differences between states and between geographic areas are due not to differences in the laws as written, but to differences in how vigorously these laws are enforced.

Given this position, the commission rejected the idea that obscenity law should be revised to make the display of certain activities automatically obscene or to recommend a definition of obscenity that is broader than *Miller*. First, it has not been shown that current laws are insufficient. Rather, claims to this effect ''have usually been the scapegoat for relatively low prosecutorial initiatives.'' ''The fact that a number of localities had tremendous success when law enforcers were committed to the laws persuades us that the desire to have new or more laws is in fact unjustified.''

Second, a new law would be sure to be challenged in the courts on constitutional grounds and would only stall the fight against obscenity.

The Problems of Law Enforcement

If the laws on the books are sufficient, why the lack of enforcement? The commission found it ''unquestionable'' that ''there is a striking underenforcement, and that this underenforcement consists of undercomplaining, underinvestigation, underprosecution, and undersentencing.'' It said, ''It is clear that the dynamics of this are sufficiently complex that no one remedy for the problem will suffice.''

At the time of the commission's proceedings, cities as large as Miami and Buffalo had but one police officer assigned to enforcement of obscenity laws. Chicago had two. Los Angeles had fewer than ten. New York City takes no action against obscenity violators unless there is a complaint, "and even then prosecution is virtually non-existent." Federal law enforcement is limited almost exclusively to child pornography and to a few major operations against large pornography production and distribution networks linked to organized crime. From January 1, 1978, to February 27, 1986 (eight years), a total of only 100 individuals were indicted for violating federal obscenity laws, and of the 100, 71 were convicted. (Of the remaining cases, only 3 resulted in acquittals. The rest are pending.)

When arrests do take place, judges often undersentence. This has a domino effect on prosecutors and law enforcers, who soon realize obscenity cases are high risk–low reward ventures.

The evidence is almost unanimous that small fines and unsupervised probation are the norm. Why? One reason may be that pornographers often appear in court to be white collar criminals. Therefore, those who sentence them tend not to perceive obscenity violations as serious crimes. The dominos reach the pornographer, who tends to treat the mild sentences as the mere "cost of doing business." The commission urged mandatory minimum sentences for second and further offenses, but admitted that this by itself is not enough.

Whose Job Is It?

Numerous witnesses at the hearings complained that the *real* problem was the lack of federal law enforcement support of local prosecutions. While the commission sympathized with this, it said, "We are dismayed at the unwillingness of the states to assume the bulk of the responsibility for enforcement of the criminal law." Even though the federal government's role should improve, "in our federal system, primary responsibility for law enforcement has always been with the states."

As for federal enforcement, it has been too ready to limit its efforts to child pornography or pornography clearly connected with organized crime. Federal laws call for more than this. The most harmful pornography is distributed throughout the country by means of large and sophisticated distribution networks comprising a massive and complex interstate (and international) operation. Only the skills and resources of federal investigative agencies and the special nature of the federal courts can adequately handle this.

How Much Pornography Should Be Prosecuted?

A community has only so many resources. Which kind of pornography demands first priority in regulation and enforcement?

Special urgency should go into prosecuting obscene material that portrays sexual violence. The evidence is strongest and societal consensus is greatest that this kind of pornography is harmful. Society can hardly take lightly the consequent harms of rape and other sexual violence.

Evidence about nonviolent yet degrading pornography is less strong, but strong enough to conclude that it also harms society. "None of us hesitates to recommend prosecution of those materials that are both degrading and legally obscene. If choices must be made, however, prosecution of these materials might have to receive slightly lower priority than sexually violent materials." This in no way devalues this category.

A division of opinion arose in the commission over the

third category of pornography: legally obscene materials neither violent nor degrading. The commission found no evidence of a causal relationship between this type of pornography and sexual violence, aggression, or discrimination. What of other kinds of harm? The commission's mixed views on the moral influence of pornography reflect those of society itself and thus kept it from agreeing on how much this kind of pornography harms societal mores. But the *Miller* test only requires *community* standards to determine what is legally obscene—not the standards of the nation, nor of the commission. Therefore, the commission agreed that a community may legitimately allocate enough resources to prosecute this kind of pornography as vigorously as it would pornography of the first two categories.

The Role of Private Action

It is a grave mistake to think government channels are the only avenues for citizen concerns. There are times when government action is unwise or unlawful while private action is not. Citizens have every right to condemn a wide variety of material that is protected, and properly so, by the First Amendment. Just because something is legal does not mean it is valuable or beneficial to society, or that citizens cannot fight it. The First Amendment protects and encourages their right to do so. Action by private groups or individuals can even be as effective as government action, and corporations can often do as much as government.

Methods of Protest

Persons concerned about pornography should join or form organizations that will articulate their views. They have a right to protest or picket in places where they will attract attention and where they will have the opportunity to persuade others about their views. This includes the freedom to protest near pornographic outlets. Although this may discourage customers from patronizing these establishments, it is part of the way in which free speech operates and is fully within the traditions of this country, so long as the pickets do not make free access impossible for those want it.

Citizens may organize consumer boycotts against otherwise reputable establishments that deal in pornography. Boycotts are coercive but completely constitutional. Also effective are letter writing campaigns and media events that inform the public of pornography's impact on the community.

Antipornography groups should have three goals:

1. To establish constitutionally sound obscenity laws that meet community needs.

2. To encourage adequate enforcement of these laws.

3. To use private action to curb the flow of pornography and obscenity in that community. Citizens must devote themselves to advocating, establishing, and maintaining appropriate community standards.

The first step is to find out how readily available pornography is, and what kind is sold. Then citizens should determine prosecution policies, law enforcement practices, and judicial attitudes in the community. Are enforcement mechanisms used properly? Is official perception of current community standards accurate? Is legislative change necessary to get better law enforcement, or is there another reason for the lack of prosecution? Is the volume of pornography or offensive material a serious problem in the community?

A successful community action program also needs:

1. Sincere citizen interest in controlling pornography in the community.

2. A police department willing to allocate a reasonable portion of its resources to obscenity enforcement.

3. A prosecutor who, in keeping with his or her oath of office, will aggressively pursue violations of obscenity statutes with due regard for the right to distribute constitutionally protected material.

4. A judiciary that sentences offenders appropriately.

As for specific suggestions, the commission developed what could almost be called a handbook for community activists. It said citizens should:

1. Establish and maintain effective community action organizations.

2. Solicit support from a broad spectrum of civic leaders and organizations.

3. Gather information on pornography in the community.

4. Educate the public about the effect pornography has on the community.

5. Communicate with law enforcement officials and prosecutors about the pornography in their jurisdiction.

6. File complaints, when appropriate, with the Federal Communications Commission about obscene broadcasts.

7. Conduct a "court watch" program.

8. Keep abreast of developments in obscenity- and pornography-related laws. When appropriate, lobby for legislative changes and intitiatives.

9. Support local, state, and federal officials as they try to carry out their duties.

10. Use grassroots organizing efforts to express opposition to pornography.

11. Exercise economic power by patronizing individual businesses and corporations which demonstrate responsible judgment in the types of literature they sell.

12. Monitor the music one's children listen to. Record-

ing artists and producers should use discretion in the fare they offer to children.

13. Additionally, the commission said that publicly funded institutions should prohibit production, trafficking, distribution, or display of pornography on their premises or in association with their institution to the extent constitutionally permissible.

14. It also said that businesses can actively exercise their responsibility as "corporate citizens" by supporting community efforts to control pornography.

The Risks of Excess

Citizens who follow these methods unquestionably exercise their First Amendment rights. But just like the First Amendment rights of some of those who deal in sexually explicit materials, these rights may be exercised harmfully or unwisely.

The commission recognized the problem of excessive zeal, and stated: "We have no solutions to this dilemma. . . . We encourage people to object to the objectionable, but we think it even more important that they tolerate the tolerable."

It said citizen activists should:

1. Recognize that many conflicting views exist over what, if any, regulations on pornography should exist. Even the Supreme Court's definition of obscenity was established only with divided opinion.

2. Be aware of the legal criteria for distinguishing what is obscene from what is merely distasteful to some— although protests directed at nongovernment sources need not be limited to this.

3. Recognize the rights of other individuals and organi-

zations when exercising their own.

4. Guard against extreme or legally unsound positions or actions, such as unfounded attacks on school reading lists, library collections, and general discussions of sex-related topics.

5. Be aware that public officials are duty bound to decide whether material is legal without regard to their personal opinions.

The Importance of Education

So far the suggestions have been largely negative and reactive. Although important, these are only part of the answer. On the positive side, education is the real solution to the problem of pornography. This is not just a matter of textbooks and classroom lectures. It involves facts, values, and morals that must come through images, just as the message of pornographers comes through images. If images can cause certain forms of behavior as the evidence shows, then images ought as well to be able to prevent behavior or cause different behavior. These alternative images and messages might come from family members, or teachers, or religious leaders, or political figures, or the mass media. This is how we learn table manners as well as jaywalking and tax evasion. In this sense the law is limited where society is not. To know what the law can do, we must appreciate what it cannot do. Law may influence belief, but it also operates in the shadow of belief. If we expect the law to do too much, we will discover only too late that few of our problems have been solved. Likewise, protests, boycotts, and the like may prevent negative images and messages from being sent, but this is not enough. They must be accompanied by positive efforts.

Citizens fighting pornography must work at bombarding society with positive, healthy images, just as pornographers have bombarded it with their negative and destructive ones. Images that communicate positive messages are essential— images that say that women deserve respect, sexual violence and degradation are wrong, and sex is private and special. All of these are essential to reversing the tide of sexual depravity and winning the fight against pornography, sexual violence, degradation and discrimination, and the breakdown of sexual morals. In this sense, education is central to successful citizen action against pornography.

Child Pornography

Child pornography is a special horror in that it is not so much pornography as it is the sexual abuse of children. Sometimes children as young as infants are induced to perform before a camera all possible forms of lewd and sado-masochistic sexual activity with adults, other children, and animals. The use of real children creates a special harm unlike those connected with other forms of sexually explicit materials. "Child pornography is child abuse," the commission said. Furthermore, it is child abuse that leaves a permanent record which may haunt the child for the rest of life.

The Perpetrators

Those who sexually exploit children do so for many reasons and come from many backgrounds, but essentially they fit into two categories: situational and preferential molesters. Situational molesters act out of serious sexual or psychological need, "but choose children as victims only when they are readily accessible.'' Preferential molesters actually have a clear sexual preference for children (''pedophiles'' is the term for them) and can only satisfy the demands of that preference through child victims. Both frequently take sexual photographs of children, but preferential child molesters victimize far more children in the long term.

The approaches adopted by various perpetrators vary widely. The most recent research on child sex rings indicates that they range from highly organized, ''syndicated'' operations involving several perpetrators and many children, with production of child pornography for sale or barter, to solo operations in which children are abused and photographed by only one perpetrator for his pleasure. In most cases, the child abuser doesn't sell the photographs he takes. He may use the photographs as a memento, to recreate the experience for himself at a later time, to seduce other children to engage in the same activity, or to blackmail the abused child. But the desire to have collections of a large number of photographs of children seems to be a common, although not universal, characteristic of pedophiles. Many photographs eventually find their way into circulation, even ending up in commercial publications.

Child abusers do a great deal of picture trading. They do it in person, through the mail, and, more recently, by using computer networks.

Besides noncommercial trade, a commercial network of primarily foreign publishers gathers up privately produced photographs and sells these collections in magazine form. While most of these publications are foreign, most recipients and contributors are American. These magazines also contain advertisements for private picture exchanges.

Increased legislative and law enforcement initiatives over the last decade have dealt a serious blow to domestic commercial production of child pornography, resulting in sub-stantial curtailment of the industry. At the very least it has been forced to be even more clandestine and is not nearly as large as the noncommercial trade of homemade, sexually explicit pictures of children.

The strong noncommercial base of child pornography is significant. The commission concluded: "The normal absence of commercial motives, and the strong sexual and/or psychological needs which push both situational and preferential molesters toward sexual abuse of children in pornography, suggest that the *demand* for such material may be somewhat inflexible. While situational abusers may be steered away from children as victims, preferential abusers may not—and they are prone, moreover, to far more frequent abuse. However strong the criminal law, sexual exploitation of children seems likely to remain an irresistible temptation for some."

The Victims

There is no end to the supply of potential victims. They can be children from any class, religion, and family back-ground. Most victims are exploited by someone who knows them because his job brings him into contact with children, or through a neighborhood, community or family rela-tionship.

Many victims are too young to know what has happened to them. Others are powerless to refuse the demand of an authority figure. Some seem to engage in sex voluntarily, usually in order to obtain desperately needed adult affec-tion. Adolescents used in pornography are often runaways, homeless youth, or juvenile prostitutes who may feel with some justice that they have little choice but to participate.

Thus it seems clear that a large class of children and teenagers *vulnerable* to use in pornography will continue to
exist. Even redoubled efforts to teach children to protect
themselves from such involvement will not wholly blunt
the strong social, family, and ecomomic forces creating
that vulnerability.

The pain children suffer from being used in pornography
is often devastating and always significant. Short term
effects include: depression, suicidal thoughts, feelings of
shame, guilt, alienation from family and peers, and massive acute anxiety. In the long term, some may successfully
overcome the event, particularly with psychiatric help, but
many will suffer a repetition of the abuse cycle (the second
time as the abuser), chronic low self-esteem, depression,
anxiety about their sexuality, role confusion, a fragmented
sense of the self, and possible entry into delinquency or
prostitution. All, of course, will suffer the agony of knowing the record of their sexual abuse is in circulation, its
effects on their future lives unknowable and beyond their
control. That may well be their most unhealable wound.

That medical, social service, and legal communities are
in a state of ''conceptual chaos'' about how to help these
victims only makes matters worse for these children. Court
procedures are particularly intimidating for children
because they are asked to describe extremely intimate sexual
details that they know will be received with horror by family and friends. A criminal proceeding, moreover, creates a
double bind for the child: if he is believed, a former
''friend'' will go to jail. If he is not, he must endure the additional guilt from thinking that perhaps he did not tell
enough. Meanwhile, researchers and clinicians attempting
to specialize in the field have faced serious resistance from
their peers. Lawyers and judges, like doctors and mental

health professionals, remain largely ignorant of how to respond to child pornography victims.

Serious Issues in Child Porn

Because child pornography is so inherently different from that of adult obscenity, it should be no surprise that tools designed to deal with adult porn are largely ineffective. Four major factors have guided the development of legal regulations for child pornography.

The first is the problem of the pictures. This permanent record of these inherently nonconsensual acts have a life of their own and follow the child through life. The consequent embarrassment and humiliation are themselves harmful, quite apart from the harm incurred in the taking of the photographs.

Second, there is substantial evidence that photographs are used as tools for molestation of other children. Child molesters show their victims pictures of other children engaged in sexual activity in order to persuade victims that "it must be all right."

Third, these photographs constitute evidence against child molesters. Using them as evidence of the offense, or making them *the offense itself*, makes it unnecessary to put children themselves on the witness stand.

Fourth, the great harm caused by child pornography calls for extraordinary restrictions, restrictions too stringent for regular obscenity cases.

The Escalating Battle

The skyrocketing child pornography industry of the past two decades has repeatedly taxed legislative ingenuity on state and federal levels, frequently requiring more aggressive legislation and law enforcement. After studying the status of pornography in the late 1960s, the 1970 Presidential Commission on Obscenity and Pornography reported "the taboo against pedophilia . . . has remained almost inviolate" even in the hardest of "hard-core" materials. It was not until 1973, shortly after the landmark *Miller v. California* obscenity ruling, that the first child pornography ring—fourteen adults using boys under age thirteen—came to the public's attention. Police and reporters went on to uncover a wide range of child pornography activities. In 1976 the Los Angeles Police Department established a special Sexually Exploited Child Unit to combat child pornography and prostitution. Its founder claimed 30,000 children were victims of sexual exploitation in that city alone. And in 1977 a string of investigative articles in the *Chicago Tribune, Time,* and other major publications helped prompt a full congressional investigation that concluded "child pornography and child prostitution have become highly organized, multimillion dollar industries that operate on a nationwide scale."

With 264 different "kiddie porn" magazine titles sold over the counter in 1977, child pornography had unquestionably become a significant part of the commercial pornography mainstream. This wholly unanticipated by-product of the pornography boom evoked an angry response from Congress and nearly all state legislatures that completely reshaped the child pornography industry.

Congress responded with the Protection of Children from Sexual Exploitation Act of 1977. It prohibited the production of sexually explicit material using children under age sixteen, if the material was commercially sold across state borders. Violations earned stern penalties, and they applied to parents and guardians as well as pornographers. Unfortunately, the 1977 act centered overwhelmingly on commercial traffic. Bartering and giving away child pornography, even through the mail, remained legal. Besides that, the sexually explicit depictions still had to be found legally obscene.

New York and many other states in the early 1980s enacted laws specifically directed at child pornography. These state laws made unlawful any photographic depiction of a *real* child engaged in sexual activity, regardless of whether or not it was legally obscene under the *Miller* test. In 1982 the Supreme Court declared these laws constitutional in its *New York v. Ferber* decision, noting the undeniable "compelling" and "surpassing" interests involved in protecting children against this kind of exploitation.

Ferber limits the category of child pornography to works visually depicting sexual conduct by children below a specified age, and they must be real children, not adults pretending to be children. Nor do graphic illustrations, cartoons, or written descriptions qualify as child pornography. The *Ferber* standards for determining what is prosecutable are not as stringent as the *Miller* standards. These differences stem from the court's radical shift in primary concern—away from pornography's impact on its audience to its effects on the children *who appear in it*. This is why, of all the issues the commission considered, only in the case of child pornography is the *Miller* definition of obscenity wholly irrelevant. Yet the advent of kiddie porn in the years after *Miller* provides vivid illustration of the inadequacy of the concept of "obscenity" for protecting the interests of *performers* in sexually explicit material. (For more about *Ferber*, see chapter 4.) The important thing to note here is that, as a result of *Ferber*, virtually every state, as well as the federal government itself, now prohibits by its criminal law the production, promotion, sale, exhibition, or distribution of photographs of children engaged in any sexual activity, regardless of whether or not the material is legally obscene. *Ferber* energized the fight against child pornography, accelerated enforcement, and substantially curtailed domestic production of commercial child pornography.

The result of the 1977 act was that child pornography became clandestine, so much so that from 1978 to 1984 only one person was convicted under the provisions of the 1977 act. By 1982 the bulk of child pornography was non-commercial. This meant federal enforcement under the 1977 act was seriously impaired by its ''for sale'' requirement. The ''obscene'' stipulation also placed substantial obstacles in the path of prosecutors.

Taking its cue from *Ferber*, Congress in May 1984 approved a broad revision of the 1977 act, wholly eliminating the obscenity restrictions. Furthermore, the Child Protection Act of 1984 no longer required interstate trafficking, receipt, or mailing for purposes of sale in order for material to be found criminal. It raised the age limit to eighteen, and raised the amount of potential fines, while authorizing a set of criminal and civil forfeiture actions against violators. Written descriptions became excluded from the law's reach, and only ''visual depictions'' of real children were criminally actionable.

Accelerated Enforcement

In the first nine months of the 1984 act, the number of people indicted for child pornography offenses matched that of the previous six years. In fact, from 1978 to February 1986, 183 of the 255 indictments under federal child pornography laws were obtained *after* passage of the 1984 act on May 21, 1984.

The 1977 act effectively halted the bulk of the commercial child pornography industry, and the 1984 revisions have enabled federal officials to move against the noncommercial, clandestine portion of the industry. But while the legislative assault on child pornography drastically curtailed its public presence, it has not ended the problem. Sexual exploitation of children has retreated to the shadows, but no evidence suggests children are any safer than before. The characteristics of both perpetrators and victims, combined with the extremely limited state of professional understanding, make it unlikely the problem will go away soon.

Although the commission had much to say about the underenforcement of adult obscenity laws, it could not make as strong a complaint about child pornography laws. While state and federal prosecution of child pornography "needs to be even more vigorous," the scales are tipped in its favor, away from adult obscenity convictions. From January 1, 1978, to February 27, 1986, federal enforcement brought only 100 indictments (resulting in 71 convictions) for federal obscenity violations, while bringing 255 federal child pornography indictments (with 215 convictions) during the same period, even though there are undoubtedly more violations of the federal obscenity laws than there are violations of child pornography laws.

This does not mean child pornography laws and enforcement are without their problems. The commission made almost fifty recommendations aimed at correcting deficiencies. Most of the commission recommendations are technical and are addressed to the law enforcement and judicial communities.

CHAPTER FIFTEEN
Responding to the Critics

Much of the news coverage of the Attorney General's Commission on Pornography centered not so much on what the commission has said, but what its critics have said about it. Generally, there have been three criticisms: (1) the commission was stacked with conservatives who had pre-ordained views; (2) most of the witnesses at commission hearings were known to be against pornography; (3) the scientific research into the effects of pornography, which the commission used for its findings, is inconclusive.

Alan Sears was the executive director of the commission, and before that an assistant U.S. attorney in Louisville, Kentucky. Here, he responds to some of the most frequent criticisms.

Is it true that the commission was overwhelmingly opposed to pornography from the outset?
I believe this commission was made up of people who were fair-minded and capable of laying aside their personal

thoughts about pornography. One of those individuals, Edward Garcia, was a federal judge whose livelihood depends upon him not taking sides but acting as a fair and impartial administrator of justice.

I have never heard any of the critics mention that one of the commissioners, Professor Frederick Schauer, defended obscene materials in court when he was in private practice as a lawyer in Boston in the early 1970s. He argued in defense of a film called *School Girls* when it was taken to court in Memphis, Tennessee. He also defended *Deep Throat* in Burlington, Vermont. The Vermont case resulted in a jury acquittal for his client.

Another member of the commission was Ellen Levine, editor of *Woman's Day* magazine, which is not known to be a right-wing publication. Prior to Mrs. Levine's position there, she was an editor on the staff of *Cosmopolitan*, which is rather liberal in its sexual views. The commission critics have not often pointed that out.

No, I don't believe it is accurate that the commission had its collective mind made up from the start. What stronger evidence can I offer than an article published (in July 1986) by one of our persistent critics, *Penthouse* magazine? Although the article's tone was highly sarcastic and very belittling, the point of the article was that the commission members did not agree on whether consensual, nondegrading kinds of pornography were harmful. This commission was composed of individuals who did not agree on many aspects of the subject.

Given the conservatism of the Reagan administration, why would a person such as Professor Schauer, who

defended hard-core pornography in court, be appointed to a panel such as this?

The Federal Advisory Committee Act, under which the commission was chartered, requires that any such panel be fairly representative of the population at large. A professor such as Schauer, with background in defense work and knowledge of the law on both sides of the issue, clearly qualifies as a fair representative of one segment of the populace.

Critics of the commission have said that the chairman, Henry Hudson, made his reputation as a strong prosecutor of pornography establishments while he was Commonwealth's attorney in Arlington County, Virginia.

Mr. Hudson prosecuted only three or four cases involving obscenity in an average year in Arlington County, Virginia. He has simply enforced the law; he is a prosecutor who took his oath of office seriously. His critics are the ones who have made such a big deal about the absence of pornography outlets in Arlington County.

The New York Times, **on May 19, 1986, reported that two commissioners dissented from the report, implying that its findings are dominated by the views of an anti-pornography majority. How significant are the opinions of these two panel members?**

Two of the women on the commission, Mrs. Levine and Judith Becker, filed personal statements in which they differed with the majority. Their main objection involved the commission's finding of harm in the category of materials defined as degrading, humiliating, or subordinating to women but free of violence. Their second area of concern was with a few law enforcement recommendations. Their opinions in these statements amount to a criticism of 50 or 60 pages of the entire 2,000 pages of the draft report.

This is not, however, a strictly one-sided phenomenon. Other commissioners wrote separate opinions as well, expressing dissatisfaction with some aspects of the report. Dr. James Dobson, for instance, was frustrated about the panel's inability to agree that unillustrated printed matter should be prosecuted. Also, he would have included in the report a strong statement about indecency on cable television. So his concern came from the opposite direction. *The New York Times* apparently chose not to include this fact in its article.

The commission also has been criticized for the procedures it followed. What was it supposed to accomplish, and how was this to be done?
It was not commissioned to do original research, but it was to examine what had been done by others. The commission members were assigned to gather existing information from across the country, bring it together, and produce a report. They were asked to do the job in a year, and they accepted responsibility within that time frame. They held hearings in six cities, where social scientists, law enforcement officials, offenders, clinicians, victims of pornography, and others were among the 200-plus witnesses invited to testify.

Is the scientific research in this field adequate to draw conclusions about whether pornography causes harm?

It was adequate for the commission to draw some very limited conclusions of negative effects in a very limited number of areas. The report takes note of the fact that social scientists have not measured the effects of pornography on two of the largest categories of consumers: the twelve-to seventeen-year-old adolescent, and the heavy consumer—the man who spends virtually all his spare time at adults-only outlets watching heavy doses of film and reading pornographic literature.

Most of the studies involve college students tested in very limited circumstances. Those studies show some very disturbing things, but they are certainly not conclusive. Anyone who looks to social science to provide an absolute answer, from whatever philosophical stripe, is going to be disappointed because the limited data does not give us ultimate conclusions. It merely provides some disturbing evidence pointing in a certain direction.

What would constitute conclusive evidence that pornography is harmful in the way it alters attitudes?
The commission asked that question of Jane Whicher, a representative of the American Civil Liberties Union, who testified at the Chicago hearing in July 1985. She stated on the record that even if scientific proof beyond a reasonable doubt showed a relationship between sexual violence and pornography, the government still would have no reason whatsoever to take action. She based this on the ACLU's interpretation of First Amendment rights protecting free speech.

For people of a less radical viewpoint, the amount of evidence needed might have to be sufficient only to prove a civil case in a trial. But I do not know how, in social science, anyone can draw an exact line. Social science just does not offer hard answers to these kinds of questions.

The commission's report came under fire in the press for another reason. *The New York Times* **reported on page 1 in May 1986 that several social scientists whose research was studied by the commission felt that their findings were misrepresented. Can you explain what happened?**

The report was lambasted in the press based on an erroneous premise. I do not believe this was deliberate on anyone's part, but a number of reporters picked up portions of the report from what critics had said about it. The reporters apparently concluded that the commission had found pornography harmful based upon social science evidence alone. In fact, those conclusions were drawn from a vast variety of evidence, including the testimony of pornography victims, public health experts, and advocates of women's rights. These reporters then contacted social scientists Edward Donnerstein and Murray Strauss and asked them about the commission's conclusions, based on this partial information.

Both Donnerstein and Strauss were rightfully outraged, and Strauss called my office after he had been interviewed by a reporter. I explained to him what had been done and how the commission actually reached its conclusions, and he told me he had no problem with the way the commission made its decisions. Other social scientists, named in the report, read a draft of it and complimented its integrity. I have not seen any news reports that clarified early misconstructions, even though I talked to reporters about it.

Was the witness list arranged to exclude people who would present evidence favoring less control of pornography?

No. On the contrary, many persons were invited to testify from all points of view. At the Chicago hearing on the issue of legal and constitutional matters, more witnesses testified in favor of loosening control of pornography than in favor of tightening control. At the social science hearing in Houston, Texas, the record reveals a very fair representation of persons from all points of view among the witnesses. In October in Los Angeles, a representative of the Adult Film Association was given more time to testify than any other single witness.

At each hearing, there were numerous representatives in the audience from the pornography industry, the pornography defense bar, and other groups involved in the production, distribution, and profit of pornography. With only a few exceptions, these people were not willing to testify before the commission even when they were assured they could be given the same confidentiality as victim witnesses, such as being allowed to testify behind screens and remain anonymous.

There was criticism from the pornography establishment saying that the victims who testified before the commission had no business being there because their accounts were "anecdotal" and not statistically significant. How do you respond to this?

The commission staff interviewed more than 100 persons who said either they or someone close to them had been victimized by pornography. In many cases we were able to verify those reports either through clinical records, criminal records, or third parties. It became very clear to us that there is a significant segment of our society that has suffered negative impact from pornography. Primarily, these people are women, young girls, and boys.

The commission and its staff saw first-hand people whose lives had been permanently damaged through their association with this pernicious industry. We saw too many broken hearts, broken minds, and broken spirits to remain personally unconvinced that something is very wrong in our society. The harm will be compounded if we now neglect to take steps to eliminate the things that lead to such victimization.

Did the commission approach the pornographers themselves to provide witnesses who could testify about the benefits of pornography?
Yes, we certainly did. The commission also invited a number of people who were known to produce sexually explicit material that had been prosecuted and was found to be obscene. The vast majority of those persons immediately declined any opportunity to testify. The president of the Adult Film Association of America was invited. He accepted and then failed to show up at the hearing, and had his lawyer, John Weston of Beverly Hills, testify in his place.

Gloria Leonard, who is affiliated with *High Society* magazine and allegedly affiliated with some of the so-called dial-a-porn telephone services, was invited to testify. She accepted the invitation and then failed to appear. A number of pornography industry representatives were asked to recommend actors and actresses who could present a positive view of the industry. No such actor or actress ever came forward.

During our New York City hearing on pornography and organized crime, we had more people testify about the involvement of organized crime than we had members of organized crime show up to defend themselves. Members of organized crime do not normally volunteer to testify about their activities at government hearings.

The 1970 commission on pornography reported that pornography can be helpful to the consumer. Did you look into that aspect?

The staff worked hard to get people to testify in favor of the material, saying it benefitted their life or marriage. We heard countless witnesses and received many statements from people who claimed pornography is good for our culture, but we could not find one person who was willing to testify, even behind a screen, saying they were the personal beneficiary of pornography. A sincere and substantial effort was made. We talked to clinicians, sex therapists, and many others, but no one was willing to say, "I have benefitted from using pornography."

There have been four lawsuits filed against the commission, at least one of which seeks monetary damages from individual commission members. On what basis were they filed?

These suits are based on a claim that, among other things, the commission caused certain magazines harm because sales went down after a number of retail outlets stopped selling them. The plaintiffs claim that the decision of the retailers was influenced by a letter I sent at the direction of the commission. Here is what happened.

In October 1985, the Rev. Donald Wildmon of the National Federation for Decency testified before the commission at its hearing on production, distribution, and technology. He identified certain retail outlets as distributors of pornographic materials, specifically naming the magazines, the retail outlets, and in some cases their parent companies. The commission members discussed Wildmon's allegations and agreed it was necessary to give these companies an opportunity to respond. The only motivation for this was to be fair to those outlets.

A letter was written and sent, and replies were received from many retailers. Some verified Wildmon's comments, others took issue with him, and some did not answer either way but challenged the commission's authority to ask the questions posed in the letter. One of these replies came from Southland Corporation, owner of the 7-Eleven store chain. Southland's officials said they had conducted an independent review and decided to suspend or drop the sale of certain magazines. After that, *Penthouse* and others filed suit against the commission.

Some in the antipornography movement have criticized the Justice Department for failing to enforce federal laws. What part can the Justice Department play in enforcing obscenity law?
The Supreme Court has said that when a federal obscenity case is brought before it, it will use the standards of the community in which it was tried. Local communities can

do something about pornography. We heard testimony about how the cities of Atlanta and Cincinnati virtually eradicated the sale of legally obscene material from their midst.

But the local community can only stop local distribution. It cannot stop the international and national aspects of production and distribution. That is where the federal government's role comes in. When pornography is involved, the people who manufacture, produce, and distribute this type of material in violation of federal law appear to be the most serious part of the problem. The commission report suggests that United States attorneys should take on a significantly enhanced role in prosecuting obscenity cases.

Could U.S. attorneys be doing more than they are presently doing?

In a number of U.S. attorneys' offices there are a significant number of cases prosecuted which involve fairly small dollar amounts in matters that cannot be prosecuted by state or local courts. Critics of the Justice Department have suggested that some U.S. attorney resources might better be devoted to prosecuting major, organized crime or distributors of obscene, illegal material than prosecuting stolen Treasury checks. It is up to the citizens and the U.S. Department of Justice to determine what the priority should be.

What kinds of pressures could be brought to bear on U.S. attorneys to change their focus?

North Carolina offers an instructive example. It is the U.S. Department of Justice, in conjunction with local law enforcement personnel, that establishes priorities for the U.S. attorneys, by setting up what are known as Law Enforcement Coordinating Committees (LECCs). These committees bring together state, local, and federal officials to determine priorities in that individual district. In North Carolina, the LECC determined that there was great public sentiment for greater law enforcement efforts against obscenity. People serving on the LECC authored an obscenity statute which has led to enhanced efforts to eliminate illegal material from the state.

Is it realistic to expect law enforcement measures to make a dent in illegal obscenity nationwide?
The commission found that there is a very limited universe of people involved in the distribution of obscene material. We found that most of this material is controlled by people who are either connected with members of organized crime or associated with organized crime families. Even when this is not the case, pornographers in most instances have an easily trackable system of operation. Law enforcement officials now know the identities of the vast majority of people involved in nationwide distribution. With an all-out effort, these people could be apprehended, prosecuted and, if found guilty, convicted, and out of business in a matter of eighteen to twenty-four months.

CHAPTER SIXTEEN
The Surgeon General's Report

In conducting its investigation in 1985, the Attorney General's Commission on Pornography asked Surgeon General C. Everett Koop for help in assessing social science research on the effects of pornography. Because of delays in funding the study, Koop's report was unable to be submitted to the commission before its charter expired and work ceased. Therefore the surgeon general submitted the report separately to the attorney general.

Koop convened a meeting of some of the country's most respected authorities in their fields of research (the participants are listed at the end of this chapter). They reached agreement on five consensus statements about what social science can confidently state today regarding pornography and the harm it does to people. They acknowledged that much more research remains to be done before some forms of harm, now strongly suspected, can be proven. The group studiously avoided activism on either side of the issue.

Because the report was written in technical language,

*the portions that appear here have been paraphrased for
clarity. This is not the full report. What follows are the five
summary statements and passages from the elaboration on
each.*

CONSENSUS STATEMENTS

**1. Children and adolescents who participate in the pro-
duction of pornography experience adverse, enduring
effects.**
The use of children in the production of pornography is a
form of sexual exploitation. This kind of exploitation has a
variety of adverse emotional, behavioral, and physical consequences in children, as well as in adults who were
exploited as children. Effects of sexual exploitation appear
to reemerge later in life as a variety of difficulties.

Adult pornography is also used to exploit children.
Adults use it to teach children how to perform sexual acts
and to legitimize their participation by showing pictures of
other children who are "enjoying" the activity.

Since most children and adolescents involved with pornography also engage in prostitution or other sexual activity
with adults, and since many have been neglected or abused
at home, the specific effects of pornography cannot be isolated cleanly. It is one of many influences in the lives of
these youth. There is no reason to believe, however, that
pornography is less traumatizing than other forms of sexual
exploitation of children. There is even some suggestion that
it may produce a unique form of trauma since the child
knows that there is a permanent record of his or her
participation.

2. Prolonged use of pornography increases beliefs that less common sexual practices are more common.

The theme of this conclusion is that repeated exposure to pornography is likely to alter one's belief about how often people actually do what pornography shows them doing. The basis for this conclusion comes mainly from the work of Zillmann and Bryant [see chapter 6 for details of their studies]. While there is only one direct experimental test of this premise, these results match those of other studies of human judgment, which are not related to pornography. The research thus demonstrates that a sound psychological mechanism appears to be operating when individuals are repeatedly exposed to pornography.

3. Pornography that portrays sex as pleasurable for the victim increases the acceptance of the use of coercion in sexual relations.

This statement is based on experimental findings, on the fact that these findings are congruent with theories about how attitudes are formed, and on the results of clinical reports from studies of sex offenders. None of these sources is sufficient by itself to reach a conclusion. Taken together, however, there appears to be a convincingly clear picture.

Tests of subjects' reactions to violent pornography have shown that the portrayal of the victim's enjoyment or repulsion helps shape the viewer's attitude about what he is seeing. Nonrapists have shown higher arousal to pornographic depictions of consenting sex than to rape. Convicted rapists, meanwhile, have shown high and about equal arousal to depictions of consenting sex and depictions of rape. However, rapists have also shown higher arousal to rape depictions that contain greater aggression than to rape depictions with less aggression.

The sexual arousal of nonrapists to rape pornography can be inhibited if they have been exposed previously to depictions that clearly emphasize the victim's suffering and repulsion.

It is common for sex offenders to believe that their victims were either willing, or eventually aroused, by the assault. Many rapists justify their actions this way.

Investigating this justification process further, Scully and Marolla (1984) interviewed 114 convicted, incarcerated rapists and found that a sizable proportion maintained that the victim enjoyed being raped, even in cases where considerable harm to the victim was documented. Obviously, these reports must be interpreted with a great deal of caution. It cannot yet be determined whether the rapist's idea that victims enjoy rape propels him to commit the crime, or whether it comes later as a justification for the crime. These studies are worth noting here only because they show that the theme of victim enjoyment is a consistent factor in the minds of rapists.

It is important to note also, however, that this type of mental justification fits psychological theory. The perceived outcome of any action is a powerful factor in determining whether an individual acts. If rape is constantly portrayed as sexually satisfying for both parties, this could remove inhibitions and produce a powerful conditioned pairing of sexual coercion and sexual arousal. Once this pattern has been established in an individual, it is likely that he will begin to believe that women actually enjoy being victimized sexually.

The effects of violent pornography on the attitudes of

children and adolescents is an open question, because, obviously, experiments cannot ethically be done on children. It is certainly reasonable to speculate, however, that the effects on less mature individuals with less real world experience to counteract the influence of pornography would be equally (or more) powerful than those seen in college students, who most often are subjects for these tests. Attitude formation in childhood is a matter of exploration and "trying on" potential world views. Being exposed to one in which sexual coercion is seen to be enjoyable may well mean that that attitude is adopted in real-life relationships.

4. Acceptance of coercive sexuality appears to be related to sexual aggression.

The association between attitudes and behavior is one of the most difficult to comment upon from social science evidence, but it is obviously important to those who must decide public policy regarding pornography. "It appears that there is evidence that attitudes indicating acceptance of coercive sexuality are, along with a number of other variables, related to sexually aggressive behavior." [Because of the significance of this statement, it is quoted verbatim—ed.] While there is the *possibility* that these attitudes *cause* this behavior, this cannot be said flatly right now. Moreover, it is not clear that exposure to pornography is the most significant factor in the development of these attitudes. One reason we are so cautious is that there are a limited number of ways in which one can examine the relationship of attitudes to behavior.

5. In laboratory studies measuring short-term effects, exposure to violent pornography increases punitive behavior toward women.

An increase in aggressive behavior toward women has been proposed often as one likely effect of exposure to pornography, but there does not seem to be sufficient scientific support for a general statement about this. There is no shortage of hypotheses, however. For example, one hypothesis says that men may become aggressive if they are predisposed to aggression and are then aroused by pornography; another says that violent pornography can change attitudes. Still another says that certain cues from the victim (e.g., saying "no") trigger aggression.

Testing for this in a real-life setting is clearly impossible. It would be unethical to expose persons to pornography and then see how sexually aggressive they become toward innocent people. Laboratory experiments have been done, however. The first experiments found that sexually aggressive films caused more punitive behavior than nonaggressive films. Further investigations indicated that the punitive behavior was a barometer of the outcome of the film (i.e., whether the victim enjoyed it).

In summary, studies have consistently shown that sexually violent films can produce punitive behavior in the laboratory. This fits well with psychological theory about the effects of modeling. Moreover, sexually violent films produce more aggression than do nonsexual—but violent—films.

On one hand, this could be viewed with concern, since these studies show changes from relatively little exposure. After only one sexually violent film, men are more aggressive toward women. On the other hand, there is no evidence that those viewing sexually aggressive films in real life, outside of the laboratory, actually become more aggressive.

In sum, these experiments should heighten concern that aggressive behavior toward women may be increased by sexually violent films, but presently this has only been seen in laboratory settings.

Summary

These statements reflect what the workshop participants believe can be said confidently about the effects of pornography. It has been consistently linked to changes in some perceptions, attitudes, and behavior. These links, however, are circumscribed, few in number, and generally laboratory-based. Pornography does have effects. It is just not yet known how widespread or powerful they are. There is a clear lack of extensive knowledge or unifying theory, and sweeping statements about the effects have not yet been substantiated. Currently, we have only bits of knowledge. Future research is required to make a more comprehensive statement.

While convincing evidence exists about the effects of pornography on attitudes and behavior, it is important to remember that relationships between attitudes and behavior are unclear. They are not necessarily linked in a straight path. For example, it is commonly believed that attitudes cause behavior, but research has consistently shown otherwise. Behavior is just as likely to influence attitudes. As a result, conclusive statements about how attitude changes brought on by pornography influence behavior are just not possible. The absence of clear information does not argue for dismissal of the various hypotheses that have been offered. It only argues that a clear causal link has not yet been demonstrated. Indeed, the coexistence of violent pornography and acts of sexual violence warrants concern and continued investigation.

There is substantiation for the basic concern that sexually violent material has more consistent and more marked effects than nonviolent pornography. Attitudes condoning sexual aggression have been fostered by violent pornography. This has repeatedly brought about behavior and attitudes which are antithetical to society's aspirations.

List of Participants

Gene G. Abel, MD
Professor of Psychiatry
Emory University School of Medicine
Atlanta, Ga.

Albert Bandura, PhD
Professor of Social Science in Psychology
Stanford University
Stanford, Cal.

Ann W. Burgess, RN, DNSc
Professor of Nursing, School of Nursing
University of Pennsylvania
Philadelphia, Pa.

Donn Byrne, PhD
Professor and Chair, Department of Psychology
State University of New York
Albany, N.Y.

Jon Conte, PhD
Assistant Professor, School of Social Service
Administration, University of Chicago
Chicago, Ill.

Jessica Henderson Daniel, PhD
Supervising Staff Psychologist, Judge Baker
Guidance Center, Children's Hospital
Boston, Mass.

William Daniel, Jr., MD
Emeritus Professor of Pediatrics and Chief
of Adolescent Medicine
University of Alabama School of Medicine
Montgomery, Ala.

Robert W. Deisher, MD
Professor of Pediatric and Director of
Adolescent Medicine
University of Washington School of Medicine
Seattle, Wash.

Edward Donnerstein, PhD
Professor, Center for Communications
Research, University of Wisconsin
Madison, Wis.

Bradley Greenberg, PhD
Chair, Department of Telecommunications
Michigan State University
East Lansing, Mich.

Carol Hartman, RN, DNSc
Professor, Boston College School of Nursing
Chestnut Hill, Mass.

Jeffrey J. Haugaard, MA
Research Assistant in Clinical Psychology
University of Virginia
Charlottesville, Va.

Kathryn Kelley, PhD
Associate Professor of Psychology
State University of New York
Albany, N.Y.

C. Everett Koop, MD, DSc
Surgeon General, U.S. Public Health Service
Washington, D.C.

Neil M. Malamuth, PhD
Chair, Communications Studies
University of California
Los Angeles, Cal.

Edward P. Mulvey, PhD
Assistant Professor of Child Psychiatry,
Western Psychiatric Institute and Clinic
University of Pittsburgh
Pittsburgh, Pa.

Carol Nadelson, MD
Professor and Vice Chair, Department of
Psychiatry, Tufts University School of
Medicine, New England Medical Center
Boston, Mass.

Albert Serrano, MD
Professor of Child Psychiatry and Director,
Philadelphia Child Guidance Center
University of Pennsylvania
Philadephia, Pa.

Mimi Halper Silbert, PhD
President and Chief Executive Officer
Delancey Street Foundation
San Francisco, Cal.

Murray A. Straus, PhD
Director, Family Research Laboratory
University of New Hampshire
Durham, N.H.

Joyce N. Thomas, RN, MPH
Director, Division of Child Protection
Children's Hospital National Medical Center
Washington, D.C.

Dolf Zillman, PhD
Professor, Institute for Communications
   Research
Indiana University
Bloomington, Ind.

APPENDIX ONE
Documents from the Fort Wayne Campaign

All persons picketing for decency must read and subscribe to these rules.

In picketing for decency you are exercising two of our most sacred constitutional rights—

THE RIGHT OF FREE SPEECH,
THE RIGHT OF CITIZENS TO *PEACEABLY* ASSEMBLE.

BOTH OF THESE CONSTITUTIONAL RIGHTS MAY BE FREELY EXERCISED, *BUT ONLY IN A NON-VIOLENT MANNER.*

RULES FOR PICKETERS

1. Your picketing must be restricted to the public sidewalk. Do not walk in the street, and do not attempt to enter the establishment. No literature is to be distributed.

2. Do nothing which would interfere with a patron's right to enter the store. Do not harass any persons who enter or leave the store nor attempt to engage them in conversation. Do not block the entrance to the store. Leave space between yourself and your fellow picketers so that any patron may easily enter and leave the premises. Keep moving.

3. Do not engage in dialogue with passing motorists. This could create a traffic hazard. Use signs provided by C.F.D. only.

4. If you are requested to leave by the owner of the premises or someone acting on his behalf, leave the scene immediately without argument or confrontation. Your captain will call on the police to enforce your right to picket. *Do not respond to any attempts to engage you in conversation.*

5. Should you encounter pickets or persons supporting these establishments, continue to walk in a peaceful manner but do not respond to any attempts at confrontation. If attempts are made to confront you by such groups, peacefully leave the scene and your captain will call on the police to supervise the picketing. *You may expect such counter-picketing, at least initially.*

6. Remember that you are doing a *good* thing. Your attitude should not be vengeful. Be pleasant to all, and especially those who vilify you. Also be at the picket site 15 minutes early.

7. You will hear that your picketing is actually helping these establishments by publicizing them. The opposite if true. Their existence is no secret in Fort Wayne. *Do not speak to the news media, make public statements, or mention your local church name. Refer media to picket captain who will give C.F.D. phone number.*

8. God bless you for literally standing up for your beliefs in a decent Fort Wayne.

    Citizens for Decency Through Law,
    Fort Wayne

I have read the Rules for Picketers and agree to abide by them.

I agree to release Citizens for Decency of any and all liability.

APPENDIX

CITIZENS FOR DECENCY
711 W. Wayne
Fort Wayne, Indiana 46804
219-424-3843

NEWS RELEASE

CITIZENS FOR DECENCY THROUGH LAW

AUGUST 10, 1982

FOR IMMEDIATE RELEASE

(FORT WAYNE)-BEGINNING AT ELEVEN OCLOCK THIS MORNING, CITIZENS FOR
DECENCY THROUGH LAW WILL BEGIN SIMULTANEOUS PICKETING AT FOUR ILLEGAL
PORNOGRAPHIC BOOKSTORE/ADULT MOVIE OUTLETS IN FORT WAYNE. SITES TO
BE PICKETED ARE: (1) CINEMA BLUE THEATER AT 2441 BROADWAY (2) RIALTO
THEATER AT 2616 SOUTH CALHOUN (3) EROTICA HOUSE AT 930 BROADWAY, AND
(4) FORT WAYNE BOOKS INC. at 227 WEST PEARL STREET.

THE PURPOSE OF THE PICKETING, WHICH WILL CONTINUE ON AN INDEFINITE
BASIS, WILL BE TO: (1) FOCUS COMMUNITY ATTENTION ON THE CONTINUED
AND FLAGRANT VIOLATION OF LOCAL OBSCENITY LAWS BY THE OWNERS AND
OPERATORS OF THESE ILLEGAL FACILITIES (2) CALL FOR AGGRESSIVE PROSE-
CUTION OF VIOLATORS UNDER EXISTING LAW (3) TO SUPPORT AND ENCOURAGE
THE POLICE CHIEF AND MAYOR OF FORT WAYNE, AND THE ALLEN COUNTY PROSECU
TOR'S OFFICE IN WAGING A CONSISTENT AND EFFECTIVE CAMPAIGN OF ARREST
AND PROSECUTION OF VIOLATORS.

CITIZENS FOR DECENCY THROUGH LAW OPERATES UPON THE BASIS THAT (1) THE
UNITED STATES SUPREME COURT HAS RULED THAT OBSCENE MATERIAL IS NOT
ENTITLED TO FIRST AMENDMENT PROTECTION (2) THE UNITED STATES SUPREME
COURT HAS UPHELD THE CONSTITUTIONALITY OF INDIANA'S OBSCENITY STATUTE
(3) LOCAL OBSCENITY STANDARDS HAVE BEEN ESTABLISHED THROUGH RECENT
NUMEROUS ARRESTS AND CONVICTIONS OF THOSE SELLING OBSCENE MATERIAL
(4) LOCAL OBSCENITY LAWS, LIKE ANY OTHER LAWS, SHOULD EITHER BE
ENFORCED, OR ELIMINATED.

CITIZENS FOR DECENCY THROUGH LAW IS A BROAD-BASED LOCAL ORGANIZATION
COMPOSED OF OVER 250 COMMUNITY LEADERS REPRESENTING THE BUSINESS, PRO-
FESSIONAL, RELIGIOUS, AND CIVIC COMMUNITY. THOSE ON THE ADVISORY
BOARD REPRESENT A CROSS-SECTION OF BUSINESS AND INDUSTRIAL CONCERNS,
AS WELL AS NUMEROUS NEIGHBORHOOD ASSOCIATIONS AND OVER 40 RELIGIOUS
DENOMINATIONS. CITIZENS FOR DECENCY THROUGH LAW IS COMMITTED TO
PUBLICLY SUPPORTING EXISTING LEGISLATION DESIGNED TO PROTECT INDIVIDU-
ALS, FAMILIES, AND COMMUNITIES FROM THE EFFECTS OF PORNOGRAPHY. CITI-
ZENS FOR DECENCY THROUGH LAW IS ALSO COMMITTED TO PUBLICLY OPPOSE THOS
WHO CONTINUE TO FLAGRANTLY VIOLATE OUR LAWS AND COMMUNITY STANDARDS.

FOR FURTHER INFORMATION, CONTACT THE CITIZENS FOR DECENCY THROUGH LAW
OFFICE AT 711 WEST WAYNE, PHONE 424-3843. ALL MEDIA INFORMATION WILL
BE DISSEMINATED THROUGH OUR MAIN OFFICE.

7/7/82

APPENDIX TWO
Pornographic Rock Lyrics

Although the Attorney General's Commission on Pornography did not deal directly with pornographic lyrics in rock music, it did hear testimony from reporter Kandy Stroud at its Washington, D.C., hearing on June 19, 1985. Her review of the contents of many current rock songs was shocking to those unfamiliar with these lyrics. Here are portions of her testimony:

The average teenager in this country listens to rock music between four and six hours daily. That works out to an average of 10,560 hours of music between the seventh and twelfth grades alone. When you realize that a child receives only 11,000 hours of classroom instruction by the time he's graduated from high school, after twelve years of education, you can see the concentrated influence of music in a very short time span. Anything we're exposed to that much touches us deeply and is going to have power in our lives. And if the average parent spends only fourteen minutes a week in conversation with a child, it becomes apparent which influence holds greater sway over the formation of a child's value system.

Rock music has assumed the role of teacher. And today its lessons and messages are often pornographic, obscene or violent. The song "Eat Me Alive," from the double platinum album *Defenders of the Faith* by Judas Priest, deals with a girl being forced to have oral sex at gunpoint rape. In "Ten Seconds to Love," Motley Crue sings about making love to a woman on an elevator between floors. "Reach down real low and slide it in," he instructs her. After ten seconds of intercourse, the woman gets off at the next stop and the couple never meet again.

Concern heightens when we recognize that teenagers are not the only listening audience. Larger and larger numbers of elementary school children are becoming consumers of rock music. And the younger the listener, the more unsettled the listener is in terms of identity and values. Here are some of the role models that are teaching children today. And in their lyrics the themes of masturbation, homosexuality, incest, bondage, savagery, and rape are being presented as acceptable, even desirable forms of behavior.

But the only control parents have over rock, it seems, is the command, "Turn it down." Parents are not tuning in to the problem. The attitude is, if it's music, it must be safe. Ninety-nine percent of the parents I interviewed for a *Newsweek* column I wrote on pornographic rock admitted they were unaware of the words. They were uninformed that today's rock is drastically different from the music they listened to in the fifties, sixties, or seventies.

But there has been a quantum leap from Elvis Presley's "I Want You, I Need, I Love You" to Prince singing, "If you've got no place to go, I'll take you to the movie show,

sit you in the back and I'll jack you off." When the Stones
sang "Let's Spend the Night Together" twenty years ago,
it had to be edited before it could be performed on the Ed
Sullivan Show. Now every radio station in America plays
songs like Animotion's current hit, "Obsession," whose
refrain, "What do you want me to do to make you sleep
with me?" is repeated over and over again in the course of
the song. And MTV plays videos like Duran Duran's
"Rio" which features lesbian scenes of nude women wres-
tling or Van Halen's "Hot for Teacher" in which teacher
dances suggestively on a desktop in front of elementary
school children.

The late Jimi Hendrix made a statement that every parent
should know and be concerned about. He said this:

You can hypnotize people with music and when they get at their
weakest point, you can preach into their subconscious minds
what you want to say.

The basic philosophy of sex in today's rock is summed
up perfectly in Tina Turner's smash hit, "What's Love Got
to Do with It?" "It's only physical," she sings. "You
must try to ignore that it means much more than that. . . .
What's love but a second hand emotion?" The theme is, if
it feels good, go for it. . . . Madonna, the idol of hundreds
of thousands of young girls, appears on stage in sheer
underwear and peddles sledgehammer sexuality. The fact
she is covered with crucifixes has nothing to do with her
behavior. Madonna simply says a crucifix is sexy because it
has a naked man on it. The twelve-, thirteen-, and even
seven-year-old girls who attend her concerts imitate her
right down to the lingerie, crucifix earrings, and Boy Toy
belt buckle. In concert and videos when this female role

model writhes passionately on a bed singing, "Like a virgin touched for the very first time . . . it feels so good inside," her sexual message is not lost on her audience. As one girl told *People* magazine, "Madonna's able to do something our parents would never let us get away with— the whole slut image."

The words of Sheena Easton's major hit, "Sugar Walls" written for her by Prince, leave very little to the imagination when combined with moans, sighs, and orgasmic squeals. Played sometimes as many as ten or twelve times a day on radio stations across America, the lyrics have to do with vaginal arousal:

The blood races to your private spots
Lets me know there's a fire
Can't fight passion when passion is hot
Temperatures rise inside my sugar walls.

She goes on to whisper erotically:

I can tell you want me
Your body's on fire
Come inside.

In concert some rock stars reinforce the sexual theme of their music, holding up bumper stickers like these that read, "I Love Pussy," for their teenage audience. Prince, Cindy Lauper, and Joan Jett sing the pleasures of autoerotic sex. "Hurry up and come over," Jett sings. "I'm tired of masturbating." Jett calls herself a role model and performs on stage in attire reserved for strip shows. Vanity, a protégé of Prince who also performs in scanty attire, sings songs like "Wet Dream," and "Drive Me Wild." In "Nasty Girl," a single from her album, *Vanity Six,* and also a popular video, she sings, ''I can't take it. I want seven inches or more tonight.'' Her album *Wild Animal* contains the song, ''Strap on Robbie Baby,'' which has to do with a male penis or vibrator.

Homosexuality is another theme which has found a comfortable niche in contemporary rock. [An] album by the English group Frankie Goes to Hollywood, who sing about gay love, is the fourth best-selling album in British history. Its smash single . . . ''Relax When You Want to Come,'' is devoted to sexual arousal and climax. The video of ''Relax,'' also banned in Britain, depicts a gang rape in a gay bar in which the victim is urinated upon. There are no restrictions on either the video or record in this country. They are available to children of any age. The group's new album, ''Welcome to the Pleasuredome,'' features a Picassoesque rendering of animals engaging in oral sex. Their singer, Holly Johnson, told me he suggested that the orifaces be covered with fig leaves because he felt cunnilingus was going a bit too far for a record cover. And yet the animals' activity is barely disguised. Open the album and the centerfold features animals crawling onto and into the ''pleasuredome,'' which is nothing other than the glans of a penis.

Prince, one of the biggest names in rock history, has always been at the vanguard of pornographic rock. His past albums have contained songs about incest, bisexuality, masturbation, and oral sex, all in graphic detail. In concert, he masturbates the neck of his guitar until liquid spurts from it in mock ejaculation. His videos often show him lowering himself onto a prostrate woman. . . .

The material I have dealt with, Mr. Chairman, is only

the tip of the iceberg. I have restricted my presentation to mainstream rock music, the kind played on radio and MTV and purchased by millions of children. But violent and sadomasochistic rock is a burgeoning problem. Obviously, the barriers of decency have fallen considerably. Even people with the rudimentary moral standards would be shocked and shaken by the rock messages being shouted to our children. But there is no handle on the situation. Children of any age can purchase any of the songs you have just heard or heard about. And the pornographic messages are reaching young children and early adolescents at a crucial age when they are developing lifelong value systems. Adult minds can be discerning, but children are often unable to reject what they see and hear.